THE KARMA BUS

Dear Gillian

Enjoy the book

[signature] x

greenhill

greenhill

https://greenhillpublishing.com.au/

Gunn, Leigh (author)
The Karma Bus
ISBN 978-1-923589-04-9 (paperback)
FICTION

Typesetting Calluna Regular 10/15
Cover and book design: Green Hill Publishing
Cover image: Adobe Stock

THE KARMA BUS

AN INDUSTRIAL ACCIDENT. A MURDER.
WHAT IS THE PRICE OF TRUTH?

LEIGH GUNN

1

LIAM O'DONOGHUE WAS RUNNING late. He wanted to be gone by two o'clock, but it was already closer to three and he still had to finish his notes. Chemical plants didn't run themselves and he had to finish the instructions for the last few weeks of this year's pre-emergent T campaign – a key product in the company's herbicide range. Normally he could leave it to the other engineers or the shift supervisor, but recent changes had left his plant understaffed and inexperienced. He was virtually left on his own.

As he entered the production office block, he bumped into the new plant operator – David Johnson (Johnno) – who was looking for extra batch sheets and the work instructions. Johnno's eyes widened, surprised to see Liam. "I thought you'd left already, so I came over to look for the work notes."

"I'm still here, but not for much longer. I'm running a bit late," replied Liam. "Once I finish with these notes, I'll be on my way. Can you wait a minute?" Liam sat down at his desk, at the back of the open-planned workspace, and started typing on his laptop.

The shift supervisors had a large desk area and three chairs at the front of the production office. Four supervisors worked the 24-hour coverage for the entire site on a rotating 12-hour roster. The rest of the open area was comprised of another four stations in a grid layout. The first desk beyond the supervisor station was vacant, awaiting a replacement for the synthesis plant supervisor; opposite was Sam Kernahan's desk, the day supervisor who looked after almost all other jobs. Sam was retiring in six months which was likely why he'd survived the last round of cuts. Liam's desk was in the back left corner, with the remaining spot a utility space used mainly by the day permit writer, Mario, but shared with contractors or engineering students.

"Sure," said Johnno. "Cracking day, isn't it?"

"I love this time of the year. It's the best time in Melbourne." Liam had come to learn that March and early April retained the linger of summer, crisp and warm. It was without the sometimes searing heat of the summer days where the Celsius could rise above 40, before cooling down to pleasant evenings that seemed to forestall the impending chill of Melbourne's winter.

"You're eager for a Thursday night. Where did you say you were going?" Johnno asked, taking the only visitor chair at Liam's desk. "I thought you'd be in that meeting up the front with all the permit writers."

"I'm going back to Adelaide for my sister's twenty-first birthday this weekend." A smile lifted on Liam's face as he typed the last of his notes. "What's that meeting about? I wasn't told. Not that it matters, I'm out of here." Liam went to the front of the office block to collect his printouts from the communal photocopier/printer opposite the shift supervisor's station. He left one copy on the supervisor's desk then returned and gave a copy to Johnno for him to take to the plant control room, keeping the other copy for his files. "Johnno, I know you're new, but your supervisor Frank has run the plant for many years and should be able to guide you. After all the technical material is consumed, probably early next week, we can use the rework from the last season, but it's important to follow the notes closely. Stick to the instructions and if you're not sure, don't guess. Stop and ask for help. Understood?"

"Sure," Johnno replied, his answer to almost everything.

Liam had his doubts, but trusted Frank to keep Johnno on the straight and narrow. Johnno was young and keen, but overconfident and always in a hurry to 'do' rather than to 'think'. He wouldn't have been Liam's first pick for his plant, but he had no say in staffing – that was the production manager's responsibility, and Jim Statler knew all; just ask him.

Just as Liam was closing his laptop and packing his bag, Statler burst in, heading to his office at the back behind Liam's desk, passing Johnno who was on his way out. "O'Donoghue, you should be up the front for the meeting in the training room."

Johnno looked back and gave Liam a thumbs up and a cheeky grin.

"Sorry, Jim, I didn't know about it." Liam shrugged. "And besides, we agreed I could go early today."

"Cancel that and get yourself up to the meeting. Barry Billings is going over the update to the permit system and needs all permit writers in attendance, and that includes you."

"But a few weeks back you agreed that I could take two weeks off to go back to Adelaide. You agreed," Liam pleaded with Statler. "I only agreed to come in today for a few hours to set up the last of the T-plant campaign and to organise the

MOC for my handover, otherwise I would've already been halfway to Adelaide."

"That was last week, but things have changed." Statler threw his hands in the air in a 'what if' gesture. "I've come from the weekly meeting today and the boss wants everyone on deck at this meeting. No exceptions were his instructions. My hands are tied, but you can still go on leave after the meeting."

Liam glared at Statler. "This is bullshit, it's not fair. You guys are changing the rules as you please."

Statler didn't flinch, just shrugged his shoulders. "Rant as much as you like, just get yourself up to that meeting."

"What about the permit writers that are already away, or the blokes that are on night shift? There must be another session later for them. I could attend then," Liam said. "I want to get to Horsham by dinner time and I should be leaving now!"

"Yeah, well sorry about that. As I said, the boss wants you all there and his parting comment was: 'They all need to get on board, get on the bus, or check out and find somewhere else to work.' No exceptions." Statler smirked as he relayed the instructions.

Liam couldn't believe what he was hearing. "Some flexibility can't hurt. Besides, I helped Billings with his notes and already know his plans for the new permit system. Didn't you explain that I was already on leave?"

"I'm deadly serious. No wriggle room. If you are on site, then you are required to attend. We are bringing others in from home. Stop whining and get your sorry arse to the meeting, or else start packing your bags. It starts at 4:30pm and you don't want to be late!"

There was no credit for all his extra work, and Liam suspected Statler hadn't fought for his cause, nor did he care. The plant operators called Statler 'the Muppet Man' behind his back. He still had no clue what it all meant. It was a take on the grumpy old men in the Muppets, one of which was called Statler. Operators loved making up names for the management, and besides, our Statler had become the new production manager twelve months ago after the 'clean out'. The popular belief was that he only got the role because he was the best 'yes' man at the interviews. He fitted the mould of a head kicker with a history of strongarm tactics in warehousing management; nothing remotely associated with chemical plant operations, process safety or hazardous chemicals. The boys considered him a puppet for the top brass; a first-class muppet in their eyes.

Liam snatched up his bag and was about to storm out, thinking he might just skip the meeting and be damned with the lot – call their bluff and tell them they could jam their job where the sun didn't shine.

This place has been falling apart, ever since the new management took over, Liam thought to himself. *It surely isn't worth the stress.*

Liam picked up his phone and made a mental check that he had both of his phones: his work phone that they grumbled about him having, and his own phone he used for personal use. He thought about his sister Zoe and all her sacrifices, and his new friend Sarah who might be becoming a steady thing. He took a moment, calmed his thoughts, and just walked out without giving the Muppet Man any more consideration.

I'll just go to this damn meeting, check out from all these hassles and take two weeks off, calm down and see how everything sits when I get back. Stuff you in the meantime, Jim Muppet Statler.

The production office was buried in the depths of the facility and stood alongside two similar blocks: one housing the maintenance and engineering staff and the other the site laboratory and plant chemists. These plant offices skirted the side of the chemical plant area and was wedged between the plant and two large warehouses. Liam walked along the dividing roadway back the three hundred meters towards the front gate and the front administration complex. He stopped at the gatehouse to catch up with the security guard, Paul Wilson.

Liam knocked and opened the security office to find Wilson was sitting glued to a bank of eight screens. Liam laughed. "What are you looking at, mate? See anything interesting?"

Willo swung around, catching Liam smiling at him. "Nah, all quiet. Boring as batshit, although I saw you walking up the road." He pointed at one of his TV screens. "I thought you would have been well gone by now. I suspected you'd done a runner and had welched on our bet."

"Never, mate. I'm no welcher. I have a six pack in the car, VB just as you like. I thought Port would start the season better and your boys would be struggling after all your off-field dramas. But it's still early days, and I'll get my comeback when we play you in Adelaide later in the year. Do you want to go double or nothing?"

Willo pointed at his AFL ladder on the noticeboard, with his beloved Melbourne Demons in the top four after four rounds and Port Adelaide winless. Their bet of a six pack of beer was a standing arrangement between Liam and Paul.

"Sure, why not. It's a pleasure doing business with you and may it always continue." Paul's Demons had won five straight matches against Port Adelaide, so the fun of their bet was starting to wear thin for Liam.

"See you later, Willo. Just ducking into a Barry Billings permit meeting for a few minutes."

"Good luck, you could be there for hours. Once Billings gets talking, you know how that goes."

"Yeah, yeah, I know. I'm going to stay in the back, I won't ask questions and then I'll shoot out as soon as he's finished." Liam laughed and waved as he headed for the administration building. He went to the change rooms, changed out of his hi-vis clothes, gathered his bags, and made ready for a quick getaway.

He looked at his watch. It was just a couple minutes after four so he had time for a few calls. He extracted his private phone from the internal phone pocket of his new work satchel – a lovely leather satchel that was the envy of his colleagues; his graduation present from Zoe. He already had the number for the Golden Grain Motel in Horsham in his contacts from staying there three or four times a year, travelling back and forth between Melbourne and Adelaide. It was a nine-hour drive at best and could be done in a single trip with a few stretch breaks, but Liam had the habit of always stopping halfway, taking time for a steak at the Victoria Hotel next door to the Golden Grain Motel – the best steaks he had ever eaten.

The owner-manager, Ben Bettess, was ex-Navy having left the services ten years ago, in search for a simpler life. Liam had struck up a good friendship with the man and liked his style.

Bettess answered the call on the second ring. "Golden Grain Motel, how can I help you?"

"Hi Ben, it's Liam here. I'm booked in this afternoon, if you remember?"

"Certainly, Liam. Your room is all ready for you, the same as usual. Number 11 on the corner. Come up to the office after you arrive and we can catch up. Cora will want to see you. Have a cuppa and some of her tea cake. We're looking forward to seeing you."

"Sounds good, but that's why I'm calling. I've been held up at the plant in Melbourne and won't get away until a bit later. I won't get to Horsham until much later now, probably closer to eleven. Sorry to be a nuisance."

"No problems, mate. Don't sweat it. I'll leave your key in the lock box up near the office. You know where it is, and I'll text you the code in a minute."

"Thanks, Ben, you're the best. Maybe we can have that cuppa in the morning?"

"Good one. I'll tell Cora. She'll be angry if she misses you, and you can even see little Tina before she goes off to school. Will you want breakfast in the morning? I can take your order now if you like."

"No thanks, mate. I'll just have a quick cuppa with you then get on the road. I want to get to Hahndorf by lunch time to catch up with my sister and an old school mate."

"Cheers, all good. We can have a chat tomorrow."

Liam looked at his watch, now fifteen minutes until the meeting. He should call Sarah and let her know his change of plans but decided to leave that until he was in the car. He had enough time to quickly pop in and see Sandy, his mentor, before the meeting to vent his frustrations about Statler.

—

Sandra Hudson, best known as Sandy to her friends, had been at Agro Alliance for eight years and was a well experienced chemical engineer with a petro-chemical background. She was hired to help bring the site's process safety systems into shape. The site was now listed on Victoria's Major Hazard Facility (MHF) list and was required to demonstrate compliance with the key Process Safety Management (PSM) conventions. Sandy had written the last round of the Safety Case documents for Work Safe. Documents that were required for a licence to operate as a MHF, and she had the task of implementing PSM into practice.

Her role was challenging enough but made even more difficult due to the limited awareness of PSM across the plant at all levels. As a strong-willed woman and with meticulous attention to detail, she was making some good progress. That was until the Board changed out the management team. The new Board hadn't heard of MHF, PSM and had little experience with chemical operations, which was both a travesty and a problem. The new focus was on cost savings, volume production and increasing margins.

Two years ago, the Board recruited Paul De Zaale as the new CEO, and he swept through a raft of changes. He had carved success into some South American business and was seen as the Board's man. Although De Zaale had chemical plant experience, his only safety focus was 'no accidents', which when translated meant that no one was to be injured or reported to be injured. Good and bad, it was an intent built on sound principles, but it was based on fear that drove the reality underground.

Sandy was struggling with this new safety overlay, and her work had become even more difficult particularly after Barry Billings replaced the previous Safety Manager. For the last two years, Sandy had worked under Billings, her Jekyll and Hyde supervisor. Billings was all smiles and head nodding when talking to management but forgot everything when executing his style of management with his staff and others. His demands and expectations continued to increase and there was no support or understanding of work conflicts.

Sandy felt that she was on an emotional rollercoaster and at her wit's end. She sat in her office contemplating her future when Liam knocked at the door.

"How're you going, Sandy? Got a minute?" Liam slumped into her visitor's chair and exhaled a deep breath. "Statler and Billings are lunatics. They're being jerks, bullying everyone. I don't know if working here is worth it."

Sandy tried to stay positive, putting her own reservations aside. "What's got you all riled up? Aren't you about to go on leave back in Adelaide?"

Liam explained about the permit update meeting, the change of his departure plans and the inflexibility from the bosses. "They like jerking everyone around. I reckon they actually are pushing us for a reaction."

Sandy looked equally exasperated. "I'm not sure they're smart enough for that. My worry is that we're heading towards some major accident. Don't start me on their collective lack of process safety systems."

"Statler told me that the message is 'get on their bus or pack your bags'. I'm not sure I like their bus."

2

AGRO ALLIANCE WAS ESTABLISHED in 1982 when three wealthy farmers convinced a local farming co-operative to join with them to invest in the purchase of the old Monsanto site in the western suburbs of Melbourne. Monsanto was divesting their Australian operations and the farmers saw a chance to diversify and vertically integrate. The early days were a struggle, but they gradually grabbed a foothold supplying a limited range of agricultural chemicals for the farming industry. The business was built on Australian-made loyalty and being a supplier that was always at the ready for the farmer.

The founding farmers gave employment to family and friends and built a culture of support and togetherness. All was good as long as there were profits and for several decades the business flourished. In time, an additional formulation plant was added in Queensland and later a head office was established in the business district of inner Melbourne, along St Kilda Road. De Zaale was in the St Kilda Road offices along with the marketing, sales, accounting, and human resources teams.

The fourteen-year drought at the turn of the century came along and farmers were being progressively squeezed between rising costs and the pressure of supermarkets to reduce prices. Small farms were gobbled up and amalgamated into large corporate farms. Costs for the inputs of seed, fertiliser, fuel, and chemicals became an increasing burden for the modern farmer. Cheaper imported materials offered savings and the previous farmer loyalty for Australian-made was being fully tested.

The founding farmers of Agro Alliance were retiring, and by the mid 2010s had sold out their shares to corporate raiders. The old family associations broke down and a stock exchange board mentality took over. After the exiting CEO retired, the Board looked for an aggressive leader to sharpen their business. They headhunted across the world and found Paul De Zaale. They liked his background of reducing costs in South America and convinced him to come to Melbourne in 2021.

De Zaale didn't waste time and quickly appointed an old acquaintance from South America, Antonio Brazzos, as his manufacturing manager, who relocated near De Zaale in Melbourne's affluent Toorak area. De Zaale and Brazzos both maintained offices in St Kilda Road and at the West Footscray plant.

Every Thursday at 11:00am sharp, Brazzos held a weekly meeting at the plant with his site leaders, all of whom had been appointed in the last eighteen months. The De Zaale/Brazzos team had implemented a round of redundancies across the site. They worked on the theory that it was easier to train new staff than change existing or older staff. Their mantra was that if you had been there for more than ten years (or maybe five) you were part of the problem. The staff at large weren't aware of *'the problem'* but found themselves in the crossfire.

The meeting was held in the site conference room next to Brazzos's office. He insisted on punctuality from his people, a practice he sparingly adopted himself. This day, however, Brazzos dressed in a smart Italian suit and silk tie, and was early. He had a lunch appointment in town that took priority, so a short and sharp meeting was the order of the day.

The HR manager, Michelle Buchanan from St Kilda Road, had arrived with Brazzos and would be his taxi back to Melbourne, and his date at the lunch. She was making coffee for Brazzos as the others were arriving, overdressed for a barista in her power suit and pump heels. Stuart Jennison, the maintenance manager, entered and sat at the far end of the conference room table which could seat ten. Others arrived and took their seats. Barry Billings (Health and Safety), Keith Dwyer (Technical support and Laboratory) and Suzi Murray (Brazzos's PA and minute taker) were in position as the meeting was due to commence, but Jim Statler (Production) was still in absentia.

Brazzos looked at his watch and checked the room, all the Footscray managers in their hi-vis gear. "Is Statler here today?" he asked.

Jennison nodded. "Yes, I saw him earlier in the plant." He knew that it wasn't worthwhile to be late. Statler was not well liked by his colleagues, so Jennison just sat quietly, waiting. Statler was certainly going to get his right whack.

Five minutes passed in silence. There was never small talk with Brazzos, so most of his direct reports had found it easier just to remain quiet. Brazzos was a small, stocky man with a near bald head and a permanent frown on his face.

His thick neck made him look like a bulldog and thus suited to his workplace nickname of 'Bullyboy'. The plant workers used Bullyboy amongst themselves but called Brazzos 'Tony M' to his face, code for his physical likeness to the Australian drug kingpin Tony Mokbel.

Statler finally rushed in. "I'm sorry I'm a bit late, there was an issue in the plant." His face was flushed and he was short of breath, having run most of the way.

Brazzos glared at Statler with a look that could have cut him in two. "It would want to be good. Five minutes is not a little bit late," he demanded. "We are all busy people and can't be just sitting around waiting for you. Organise yourself better in future. I'm warning you, don't be late again!"

"Yes, sir. I won't let it happen again."

"So, what was so important?"

"Well, the forklift operator that was complaining of a bad back last week reckons it was from the seat on his forklift. It looked okay to me, so I challenged him that it was a personal injury. He plays football locally and who knows how he got his sore back. I've put him on light duties doing paperwork in the office but he's still complaining today and insists on putting in a Workcover claim."

Brazzos's eyes narrowed and his glare pierced Statler. "This is news to me. When did this supposed injury happen?"

"He reported it to the warehouse supervisor yesterday, but reckons it occurred last week."

"That's bullshit. I told you before, and I am telling you all again, I don't like surprises. This forklift driver sounds like a troublemaker. We should just cut him before it goes any further."

Michelle Buchanan felt compelled to comment and leant

forward so that the attention was drawn to him. "From a HR perspective, it is a bit tricky to just cut him amidst a potential Workcover claim. We should reassign him to an alternative job, challenge the claim and then in a few weeks we could look to make him redundant."

Brazzos pondered this, but liked what Buchanan was saying. She had balls and he was impressed. Besides, the forthcoming lunch may come with extra benefits. Her reputation was as an industrial firefighter who hosed down people trouble. She was sometimes called MFB a reference to the old Melbourne Fire Brigade. The plant staff call her 'Michelle Fucking Buchanan'.

Statler squirmed in his seat. "We don't really have alternative work as we already have Phil Buckley on light duties, recovering after a car accident."

"I like Michelle's thinking," Brazzos interjected, "and this Buckley guy is also not our problem. We are not a charity. Jim, I want you to follow Michelle's advice and I want both out by the end of next week."

Statler hesitated but then added, "Buckley has been with us for almost twenty years, and it may be a problem to just sack him. He suffered an acquired brain injury in the accident and needs time to recover."

Brazzos was on his feet, strutting up and down at the front of the room. "Listen! We are not a charity case. Didn't you hear me? I don't care how it's done, just get it done, otherwise I will find someone who can. Make him redundant if you feel all gushy. I don't want you to just bring me problems – I want solutions. Am I making myself understood?"

"Yes, Tony," Statler responded without conviction and shrank back into his seat.

On his bandwagon, Brazzos lectured the group further. "You might remember that pack-off operator that tripped on a trolley jack and broke his wrist the week I started here. Yeah, remember that." His eyes scoured the room, challenging everyone. "Well, the former safety manager came up with the same bullshit: *it was an accident, he's a good bloke, a system error, blah, blah, blah.* I told him straight – no accidents, make an example of the man and give him his marching orders. Then all I got was *but, but, but, blah, blah, blah,* all dribble. Remember that? Both the operator and the former safety manager left within a month. Redundancies, realignment, sacked, whatever – that is just detail. We must have compliance, no idiots, no second chances! Sometimes I think the problem is we have too many old-timers working here stuck in their way! Get on board or get out!"

The room was deadly silent. Best not to interrupt the volcano, let his lava flow out and keep your head down.

"Enough of that, let's keep going. I need to make it snappy, just the big issues or important items. I need to leave at noon on the dot for another important meeting." Everyone nodded while Buchanan was smiling to herself internally.

"Just a couple of things from me, Tony," Billings said, and waited to secure Tony's nod of approval before continuing. "We have Work Safe coming next week for an annual inspection and a review of our MHF licence." He paused, then added, "All should be in order as Hudson will take care of it. We will be getting all the permit writers in for refresher training and introducing a new risk assessment strategy of 'Take-5' and 'Safety Risk Assessments'. Work Safe have previously made comment about our permit system and this should satisfy them."

"What the fuck is it for Work Safe to tell us what to do? We have a great safety record and this MHF licence baloney is just a fundraising exercise by Government agencies. Tread lightly, Barry, and don't over commit. We need to steer the ship and make efficiency improvements and not add complexity just because some pen pushers in the city think that their shit don't stink."

Billings was already a Brazzos convert and wanted to look good in his boss's eyes. "I fully agree, but we have a legal problem. We must resubmit a Safety Case to have our MHF licence renewed. Hudson is working on it, and I told her to just dust off the last one and cross check what's relevant. She thinks we need to rechallenge the basis and repeat workshops to review hazard analysis and introduce the Work Safe's concept of LOPA."

Brazzos was growing irritated, his voice raising as he yelled, "What the hell is LOPA? You guys talk too much jargon. It's just gibberish to me. I remind you, we run the operation not third-party government hacks."

Billings was quick to side with the boss. "I understand, I will check this LOPA stuff and get Hudson to fast track it. Besides, I need her to refocus on the 5S programme you introduced after that broken wrist accident."

"Yes, all good. Get that licence report or whatever you call it wrapped up, and I want to see the current results of the 5S programme at next week's meeting. Thanks Barry. What have you got, Stuart?"

Stuart wasn't fully listening but quickly reset at the sound of his name, took a breath, and made his report. "Not a lot from me. We have scheduled safety inspections on the T-plant due next week, but the production campaign is extending longer, and we will have to defer them for a few weeks, maybe a month."

"Thanks. I assume that won't be a problem. Marketing and sales are on my case. The pre-emergent demand is strong, and they can sell as much as we can make."

"Should be fine," replied Stuart. "Our PSM protocols require us to raise an MOC for the deferral of the safety checks. We'll work with Sandy to get it sorted."

"PSM protocols, MOC, just more jargon. Whatever! Don't waste time on paperwork, just get it done. What is MOC anyway?" Brazzos was ready to challenge the team but corrected himself. "Forget it, another time. Jim, how's the campaign going, will we get everything finished?"

Jim, still worried from the earlier berating, cleared his throat, and nervously answered, "Everything's good. We will use up all the available technical material and then rework some old remnants from the last campaign. I expect to have everything finished by next week as scheduled. Our only issue is that the plant superintendent is away for two weeks, but he has left instructions for the shifts to follow."

"Who is the superintendent? It's imperative we get the campaign completed on time. Cancel their leave if necessary!"

Statler felt a squeeze. "That won't be necessary, we should have it covered."

"All right, but you can change 'should' and replace it with 'will'." Brazzos smiled at his own wit.

"Jim, if Liam O'Donoghue is still here, make sure he gets to the permit writer training before he leaves," Barry Billings said.

"I assume he's that superintendent," Brazzos added. "If he isn't here, get him back and he can start his holidays tomorrow or not at all."

Statler nodded and thought to himself, *Shit, I think Liam was going after lunch. I better hightail it and cut him off before he gets away.*

"Anything else?" boomed Brazzos. "If not, let's call it a wrap and revisit all this next week." He closed his diary and got up, signalled to Buchanan, and made his exit.

3

THE TRAINING ROOM WAS a large multi-function room at the back of the canteen in the front administration complex, just behind the staff changerooms. The two-storey building held a few offices on the top floor for IT support, purchasing staff, the safety group, and spare offices for visiting marketing personnel. There was also a senior management section with offices for De Zaale and Brazzos with an executive conference room in between.

Barry Billings was laying out papers in the training room, which was set up with desks in a large U pattern facing the front. Two speaking podiums were positioned on either side at the front stage, with whiteboards at the ready and a full dropdown screen in the centre stage, which received vision from an overhead projector stationed in the roof.

As Liam entered, he noticed several permit writers already in position occupying the rear wing of the U-shaped desk configuration. He was forced to take a position along the side but chose the closest available spot to the doorway. The room filled quickly, and Liam noted that several night shift staff had indeed come in early, and almost all the maintenance staff were now in attendance. He was quite impressed at the attendance and suspected the threats he'd received had also been served out universally.

Billings projected a PowerPoint presentation on the big screen and cleared his throat. "We are all here today to go over our new risk assessment strategy. The previous work permit system is being upgraded and we will replace it with a detailed risk assessment process." He stopped to gauge the reaction of the room, receiving blank expressions from everyone.

"There's no need to remind you all that Work Safe have been critical of our previous permit system and this revamp should address all their concerns. We will still have the one person and one lock strategy and insist on the lock out and lock box programme from last year. Primarily, we will now require a full pre-work planning discussion to be documented on a SWMS form."

The overhead flipped to a slide outlining SWMS as Safe Work Method Statement and Billings continued highlighting the need for a discussion between the permit writer and the trades person or the person doing the task. It must be held and this form completed, answering all the elements.

Dean Rodgers, a mechanical fitter who had worked on site for twenty-five years, spoke up. "You mean the permit acceptor, and isn't that what we already do on the existing 'permit to work form' anyway?"

"Thanks, Dean," Billings responded. "Okay, permit acceptor, if you will. The SWMS is more structured and is a comprehensive risk assessment."

"Does the SWMS have start and stop times and checks?" Dean added.

"No, once the SWMS is completed, you attach it to the

permit form and use that form to record times and the signatures for the sign-on and sign-off provisions for all the workers."

The room produced a simultaneous groan until Leon the electrician entered the discussion. "Seems like a lot of extra paperwork for the same outcome. This will slow things down even more than they are now."

As heads nodded around the room, Billings felt like he was losing his argument. *If only these dipsticks would just stick to the plan and stop living in the past. This is going to be like herding cats.*

"No, it shouldn't," Billings resumed. "Believe me, it works in other industries and aligns with Work Safe's requirements. We'll roll this out next week and my staff will be in the plant helping to iron out any issues."

"I still think it's overkill," said Leon, who was emerging as the group spokesman. "So, we have all this pre-work meeting and then still fill in a permit, even for simple things like changing a washer in a leaky water tap."

"Leon, listen to me. This is the new system, and if you don't like it, you can pack your bags," Billings repeated his message with increased emphasis and volume. "Your water tap example can be conducted with a simple Take-5 review, which we will cover next."

Liam sat quietly, internally shaking his head. He had heard of the Billings two-tier system, built on his warehousing background. He thought that the SWMS approach added value, especially for high-risk work, high pressures, or potential exposure to dangerous chemicals. It made good sense and, as Billings tried to explain, was well used throughout industry. But Billings's impatience and his lack of thought in how to integrate his new approach into the existing permit system was a recipe for confusion. Let alone this new Take-5 simple permit that had confusion already built in.

This could become long and tedious, especially when he gets started on his plan to make everyone a permit issuer, Liam thought.

Billings and the group continued in an exchange of 'what ifs' while Liam drifted away to his thoughts about Sandy. Why wasn't Sandy here at the briefing to hear the issues, especially if she was supposed to be coaching everyone next week?

When he'd popped into her office, she was distracted and to Liam's senses, she was upset. Sandy said that everything was building up and that she was struggling with the Safety Case and the extra work that Billings was demanding. It sounded as if it was all coming to a head. She brushed him aside when he asked if he could help in any way. She had changed subjects and talked about the MOC coordinator role. Because Liam was on leave for two weeks, his role needed to be handed over to another coordinator. Sandy said that Brazzos had told Billings to give it to Ernesto Gonzales, the new production clerk. When Billings had told her this suggestion, she was completely stumped.

Ernesto appeared to be a nice young man, just twenty-four years old and newly arrived in the country from Columbia; of course, a nephew of Brazzos. He didn't have any process plant experience but was a wizard with a computer and would learn the systems quickly. Sandy was aghast that there was no proposed handover with Liam, nor any pre-training with anyone. Billings just told her to give

Ernesto the MOC procedure and be on call to assist with any questions. There was much more that Sandy wanted to say, but Liam had no say in the decision and had to cut it short to attend the permit training. He left Sandy still in a daze, promising to call her for a longer debrief in the morning while driving from Horsham to Adelaide. Sandy smiled and saw him off, saying that something would work out, to not worry about it and to have a good catch-up with Zoe.

Liam, still oblivious to the permit debate going on around him, pricked his ears up when he heard Billings tell the group that if the permits needed an MOC approval they were to check in with Ernesto.

So, it was real and it had apparently been fully endorsed by the hierarchy. He hoped they'd thought this through. Work Safe would be expecting supportive plans and details in an MOC coordinator handover document, none of which he had seen to date.

He shook his head, thinking to himself, *Another recipe for a disaster!*

4

BRAZZOS AND BUCHANAN DROVE back into the Melbourne CBD along Footscray Road, coming into the city grid from the top northern end. Michelle was driving her sporty BMW 2-series coupe, her pride and joy. Antonio felt cramped but happy to be close enough to inhale her scent, like fresh flowers, and close enough to caress her thigh. Michelle always insisted on calling him Antonio. In her mind, it sounded sexy and turned her on. They'd been down this track before, and this afternoon promised to be another happy dalliance.

Brazzos interrupted her daydreaming. "Where're we going again, babe? Remind me what this meeting is about?"

"This will be a treat, and maybe we can have a celebration later," Michelle responded. "We are meeting with representatives of a superannuation investment service. Remember last month De Zaale asked us to look at divesting the company superannuation trust and all the administrative obligations."

"Yeah, yeah, we have to meet a whole bunch of financial obligations, risk management, policy stuff, extra shit that isn't core business. Paul wants us to shut it all up and get it outsourced."

"That's right, but our employees have the right to choose. So, the plan is to check out some major players and make a recommendation to move our portfolio in total across to our chosen suitor. Everyone will have an option to opt-out and follow their own plan, but the majority will probably just roll-over. Our funds under management amount to around $200 million dollars and hence several fund managers are extremely interested. The employees are no worse off and we divest ourselves of the effort to manage everything, saving over $250,000. It's a no-brainer."

"How do we choose which is the best option?" Antonio asked.

Michele smiled as she winked at him. "That's the best part. We have three main suitors. At the end of the day, I think we'll select the one that gives us the best presentation, translated to mean the best fine dining experience. So today it's number one on my list. We're meeting with people from Westpac, who will be promoting their BT wealth solutions. They may take some beating as we're going to Vue de Monde."

Michelle jogged her BMW left and right along the CBD grid, down William Street, then turned into Flinders Lane and found parking underneath the Rialto, just short of the Kings Way intersection. They pulled up twenty minutes ahead of schedule. Michelle unbuckled her seat belt and swung around to front Antonio. "Before we go up, I just want a quick chat about today's meeting back at Footscray."

"What about the meeting?" said Antonio with a slight aggrieved tone. *I'm the boss and know what I'm doing. Tread carefully, little lady.*

Sensing the undertone, Michelle quickly retorted, "Nothing wrong. In Australia we must be careful when we terminate employees. We can easily let them go for doing the wrong thing or being ineffective, but even then, it may need documented prior warnings. For a long-term employee like that Phil Buckley bloke, we can't just sack him because he's injured. We can redeploy him or make him redundant, but ..."

"That was what you were saying, I agreed. What's the problem?"

"If we go that way, we're semi obliged not to replace him. Which means if a forklift operator is made redundant, we can't just hire another to replace them, because we have claimed that their job is not needed."

"I'm confused. Why were you recommending it?"

"Just to say that we must be careful how we word everything. The redundancy comes with a tax-free outplacement payout accepted by the Australian Tax Office, the government in effect. It costs us a few dollars, and the more years of service for an employee, the more they are entitled to as a payout. But the ATO would frown on the tax deduction in the payout if we were to just immediately rehire."

"All right, so what then?" he asked.

"Well, we can say that we are restructuring and looking for upskilled multi-function operators, even if in fact we just re-employ a forklift operator or subcontract the position. We could claim we are scaling back the role and looking at a variable workforce. Ultimately it's a story we use to justify the redundancy and avoid unfair dismissal claims."

"Sounds messy, but whatever. I'll leave you to deal with the details and the words."

"Yes, but we need to be mindful how often and what reasoning we use, if we continue to want to exit people as 'redundant'."

"Enough. Too much detail," Brazzos scoffed. "You Aussies carry on a lot, like all this safety process baloney. Let's review this again later, and you can give me all the ins and outs back at your place. Time to eat!" He opened the door, got out and stretched while checking out Buchanan.

They met the Westpac representatives at the front of the Rialto building, spot on at 1:30pm and took the elevator up to the fifty-fifth floor. Clive Wright and his colleague Makhala Russell had booked the table weeks ago after Buchanan had contacted them. Their presentation was relatively simple, and they had relevant information with colour graphs to impress, although it was akin to death by PowerPoint. They were far from naïve; this pitch was more about impressing the clients. They understood the assignment and Vue de Monde was their first trump card. The views over Melbourne and across the Yarra River were stunning. A tick to the Westpac team, hang the expense. The second trump card was having the owner greet the party and welcome them into his restaurant. He gave them an overview of the restaurant and a brief history. Once they were settled, the head chef came out to introduce himself as well. All pre-arranged, and all at a cost.

The group took in the view and made small talk. They compared life in Melbourne against Brazzos's homeland in Columbia. Buchanan expertly managed the discussions throwing in a few technical issues about the company's superannuation requirements. After the chef's introductions and partaking in several glasses of the finest wines, they sat down to a three-course meal.

Clive Wright ordered some after dinner liqueurs and toasted his guests, hoping the $2,000 lunch would win the contract. A hard copy of the proposal sat in Buchanan's briefcase, and they all gussied over how lovely the lunch was. *Many thanks, much appreciated. Talk soon.*

Back in the car, Brazzos loosened his tie and was slurring his words. Buchanan had stopped drinking after two wines, not that anyone had noticed. She needed to have her wits about her.

"Nice meal, don't you think?" said Michelle.

"Very nice, they're my favourite thus far. Where are we going next?"

Enjoying the control, she paused a little then said, "The National Bank people with their Plum superannuation contacts are taking us to The Flower Drum, Melbourne's exclusive Chinese restaurant, next week on Friday. Then the Black Rock group aren't booked in yet, but I'm thinking about the Crown Casino, either Japanese at Nobu or steak at Rockpool. Do you have a preference?"

"Feed the man meat."

They drove back to her apartment on St Kilda Road, a few blocks down from the Agro Alliance head office. She had entertained Antonio several times before and was happy with the progress she had made. She didn't mind a bit of sex; Antonio was good looking and her ticket to the top. The fact that he was married didn't deter her, just a minor inconvenience was all.

Michelle smiled at Antonio as she parked in her underground car park. "Shall we resume our earlier discussion about redundancies? I'll give you some more about those ins and outs?"

5

BILLINGS FINALLY STOPPED TALKING at 6:00pm, after an hour and a half of circular lecturing. Everyone was crystal clear about the consequences of noncompliance, but most were still left confused about the technical details. Liam bolted as soon as Billings said, "Thanks for coming," and he was in his car heading out of the car park within minutes. If traffic on the Western Ring Road was good, he could get onto the Western Highway and still be in Horsham before 11:00pm. It was after the peak of the afternoon traffic, but you could never be sure with Melbourne's over-crowded road system. He would normally fill up at the petrol station on the ring-road and grab some McDonald's, but his priority was to get out of the suburbs and re-assess around Ballarat, about an hour and a half into his 300km drive to Horsham.

Liam settled back with the traffic flowing steadily and decided to call Sarah. His car, a white Mazda 6, was paired to his private phone so he just had to hit the phone icon on the steering wheel and call up Sarah's number.

Sarah picked up immediately. "Hello Loddy, nice to hear from you. I thought you would've called me on the way to Horsham. How are you?"

"I'm fine but my day has been a total shamble. I'm just leaving work now, at least four hours later than I wanted. Where do I start ..."

"Sounds like a shit day. Give me a kiss and start from the beginning."

It was just like Sarah to put a smile on his face. He sensed that he was instantly relaxing. A kiss into the phone and then he rambled on about his boss the Muppet Man, Billings and his circular lecture and the stresses that seemed to be impacting his friend Sandy. Sarah added just the right amount of empathy as they slowly unpacked everything.

Without noticing, Liam was suddenly in Ballarat. He looked at his fuel gauge and made some mental mathematics, then reset his refuelling strategy to Ararat, a further hour down the track.

For the next hour, they changed subjects and prattled on about everything and anything. They covered Sarah's nursing and the upcoming stint of several night shifts, the status of tennis for her and her brother Ryan who were both key players at the Wattle Tennis Club in Bentleigh, Liam's tardy start to the football season, their social calendar, what the boys (Liam's flat mates) were up to, the plans with Zoe, and on and on.

"Two weeks is too long, Liam. You're going to have to make it up to me when you get back," Sarah chided.

"You were away for two weeks in Bali, and I was devasted and lonely. I wish I could turn around."

"Very funny. We weren't officially dating then, so this is different."

Liam had met Sarah at his football club last year, a new face as a friend of a girlfriend of one of his teammates. It had taken months for Liam to build up the courage to ask her out and he still pinched himself that she had agreed. Their relationship was still in the early stages.

"Touche, sweetheart. Look, I'm coming into Ararat and I need to get fuel. I'll call you in the morning on my way to Adelaide."

"Not in the morning – I'm on morning shift tomorrow, the last one before a break on the weekend, then the night tour of hell."

"Okay then, in the afternoon. Sleep well, I'm thinking of you."

Liam passed the Ampol Foodary as he came into Ararat, but it appeared to be closed. It was only 9:30pm so surely something would be open. He was close to empty and would have to stay overnight in Ararat otherwise. He hated running his fuel tank this low – a compulsive habit he had developed. His Mazda rarely ran below quarter full, a deliberate strategy he'd exercised ever since running out of fuel in his early driving days. He followed the by-pass around the town centre, recalling that there were at least another couple more stations on the road out of town. He saw the Shell station come up immediately as he turned the corner: Shell Ready Express Ararat. There were no cars at the bowsers, but it looked open. He pulled up to the bowser in front of the main door and was pleased to see an attendant inside.

The tank took 45 litres; the most he'd added in ages. He couldn't remember when he was last so low, but his diary would tell him.

After paying and getting a chocolate milk for the road, he got back in his car and took out his diary from the glovebox. Opening the latest page, marked by the diary tab, he entered the fuel price, the quantity, and the mileage from his dashboard. He got out his phone and with the calculator function computed the fuel efficiency since his last refill. Not until all this was complete could he move on – a quirky habit, a compulsive obsession, one he'd had since buying the Mazda. Initially he did it to check the fuel efficiency, but it grew to an important part of the routine as much as securing the fuel cap. He flicked back through his diary records and wasn't surprised that this was the largest refill in his records.

Wow, that was close, he thought. *Should have refilled in Ballarat per my plan. Sarah's fault.*

Back on the road and with an hour to go, he was feeling good with his worries about work now pushed aside. He would give Sandy a call tomorrow, knowing full well that it might bring it all up again. Maybe he wasn't going to last with the new broom at Agro Alliance. It used to be a wonderful place when he'd started. Everyone was happy and they worked for each other. He recalled the former production manager Eddie Gundy telling him on his first day that the company culture wasn't words on a website nor posters on the wall – it was how the people felt on a Sunday night!

He didn't want to dwell on work anymore and spoil what was a happy two hours chatting with Sarah. He dialled up his Dire Straits playlist and turned up the volume, happy as he sang along all the way into Horsham.

—

Liam got into the motel just on 11:00pm and retrieved his key from the lock box. Ben had left him a note on the bed in his room, his regular spot at the end of the front row and on the bend. There was a welcome note and a cold beer in the bar fridge welcoming the late traveller. *Cheers,* thought Liam, a nod to a good host.

He slept well and was up early, packed, and ready for the road. He locked the door and was stretching on the veranda when he noticed Ben on his morning rounds. It was a crisp, fresh morning, typical for many inland towns. Despite the drop in temperature overnight, Liam knew it was still certain to be another warm day under the Wimmera sun.

"Morning, Ben! Thanks for the nightcap."

"You're welcome, my friend." Ben winked as he shook Liam's hand. "We have to look after our regulars. How did you sleep? Come and walk with me on my rounds. Then Cora will have that cuppa ready. She's made you one of her teacakes."

"Slept like a baby, even the shunting of the railway out back didn't disturb me. The sounds remind me that I'm in the bush." They walked off and Liam noticed Ben's footwear. "Nice shoes you have. The latest, I assume. You always surprise me. What are these?"

Smiling even more than normal, Ben put a foot up on the nearest windowsill to display his latest acquisition. Proper running shoes with padded bases that were like clouds with an orange and yellow flash; a fire. "These, my friend, are Nike's Alphafly 3 Premium, just released and around $380 a pair."

Liam jovially punched him on the shoulder. "You are certifiably crazy. You don't even run, but they do look wicked."

They talked about the weather and football before ending back at the front office; a small room with a counter, a stand with local brochures, a couple of chairs and an Australian landscape painting on the wall. Ben threw some keys behind the counter and waved to Liam. "Come through, they'll be waiting for us."

Liam followed Ben past the counter through the stained glass panelled double doors, into the residence and onwards into the small kitchen. Tina was dressed for school, sitting at the table having some cereal for breakfast.

Cora got up from her spot and hugged Liam hard. "Great to see you, Li. Come have some tea. I know you like Irish Breakfast, so we have it for you. Come. You sit and eat teacake. I made it yesterday." Cora beamed, talking at top speed. She always called him 'Li', for reasons unknown, and despite several past attempts to correct her.

Ben chipped in, "I told Cora you were going to be late yesterday, and she wasn't happy." Cora nodded in the background. "Now you're going again so quickly, so sit and tell us all the news."

"Not a lot to tell," Liam answered. "Work and all that is pretty much the same. It is getting busy, a bit crazy. But main thing is I'm going back to Adelaide for my sister's birthday."

"Very nice, good boy," exclaimed Cora. "We have present for Zoe." She left the room and went into their formal lounge, returning with a small parcel already gift-wrapped.

"You guys, you're too kind. This is not necessary." Liam smiled and hesitantly accepted the gift.

"No, no, she good girl. Stay with us last year when you dad was sick. She family like you." Cora beamed.

Liam recalled that Zoe and their father were coming over to visit Liam a year ago and stopped for a night in Horsham at the Golden Grain, per Liam's instructions. Dad had a bit of a turn and was poorly. He had to be admitted into the Wimmera Base Hospital in Horsham for several days. The motel was booked out at the time, so Ben and Cora put Zoe up in their spare room until Dad was well enough to travel. Zoe took him back to Adelaide and unfortunately a few months later, he'd passed away.

Liam blushed. "Cora – and you, Ben – you were so nice to Zoe, and we both appreciate what you did. But this is not necessary."

"Liam, stop, we want to. You like family. I tell Ben we look after family. We want Zoe to be happy twenty-one." Cora smiled and waved her finger at Liam. "Take it. Now come sit, have cake."

Liam's departure was delayed half an hour with small talk and getting the update from Tina about her school. She had grown so much since he first met them. On Liam's first motel visit, she was just four and going to kindergarten. Now a chatty big girl at primary school.

Ben checked with Liam as he got up to attend a bell from the front desk. "Are you all booked for a return?"

"Yes, most certainly. Two weeks from tomorrow, Saturday night."

Cora hustled Tina with her bags. "Tina must catch bus now. Say goodbye to Uncle Li."

"I must be going myself," Liam said, standing. "Thanks for the tea, the cake, and the present." He held up the present, making his way to the front. "See you in a couple of weeks. Zoe is working at a winery in the Adelaide Hills, so I'll bring you back one of their wines and we can have a proper catch-up. I might even arrange for a late checkout on the Sunday and use your heated pool."

Cora hugged him again, Tina smiled and waved, then Liam shook Ben's hand and went back to his car.

Nice family, simple ways but always happy, Liam thought as he headed off. *No stress. That's the life. Be your own boss and just be good people.*

Liam left Horsham just as the town was waking up, his music playing as he passed the Dimboola turnoff. He had stopped at the Dimboola Motel on his first ever trip to Melbourne eight years ago, thinking it was half-way. It was nice enough, but it was a few kilometres off the main highway and just a bit inconvenient. He then stopped in Horsham the next time and found both the Golden Grain Motor Inn and the steaks at the Victoria Hotel.

He was happy that the traffic was light, and that he was on schedule to be in Hahndorf by 1:00pm for lunch with his friend Chris Jackson. Zoe worked nearby and would hopefully catch up later with them in the afternoon. Hahndorf was more than four hours away, but there would still be time for a quick stop at the Bordertown Bakery – a tradition that Liam had maintained on every journey. It was a famous stop for everyone on the Western Highway, with tourists enjoying the ambience out the back, the old Bordertown lock-up, and the fine food.

He waited until after his Bordertown stop to call Sandy and catch her mid-morning. She answered almost straight away. "Good morning, are you on the road? "

"Yes, making good time. Had a break to stretch my legs at the Bordertown Bakery, you know the one I keep telling you about."

"I promise I'll stop there whenever I do that road trip. However, I normally prefer to fly to Adelaide."

"At least once you should give yourself a treat and drive. I'll map it out for you," he said laughing and mentally questioning whether she would ever do it. "It's strange, Sandy, but once I crossed the border, I felt a weird feeling of connection. I get it every time I get back into South Australia. I don't miss Adelaide or South Australia, but in some strange way it feels like home, or as I said, I get this feeling of connection. I don't know how to explain it, just a feeling."

"Interesting. I always have a similar experience when I go back home up near Shepparton," Sandy said. "I feel something similar whenever we go that way. It's the countryside, the hills, the vibe, I don't know. But I do get this strange feeling – connection is a good word. I know."

Liam knew she'd understand. "Sorry I couldn't talk much yesterday. I had to run to get to that permit meeting. It was a bit of a waste of time if you ask me, it went around in circles and I'm afraid some of the boys were left a bit confused."

Liam heard a big sigh down the line. "Well, that's life with our Mr Billings. He does my head in as well." She was quiet for a moment, before adding, "Don't get me started."

"Have you time now? How can I help?"

"There's nothing you can do, it's my problem. I just ..." Her voice began to falter.

"Take your time, Sandy. Let's talk about the switch for the MOC coordinator. Is it true you're assigning it to Ernesto?"

"Ha, you're mad. I have nothing to do with it. It's all the brainwave of Brazzos, and surprise, surprise, Ernesto is his nephew! Forget the technicalities, Ernesto can learn on the job. Then Billings wants me to coach him, and this morning he wants me to spend more time deploying permit updates and managing the 5S programme."

"What about the Safety Case? How's that going to get finished?"

"Billings thinks I can just revamp the last Safety Case and update with any minor changes. He has no idea about revisiting the risk assessments. He doesn't even know what a HAZOP is, let alone what the LOPA requirements are, nor does he care that Work Safe are asking for this detail. It's a mess ... no, no, no ... it's a total disaster."

"What are you going to do?"

"What can I do? I was employed for the Safety Case and now I don't know. I'm going to speak with Brazzos later today and see if I can work for him directly or get some help."

"Have you spoken to Billings about this? Won't he get mad?"

"I did have a discussion last week, and he said I should just stop whining and get on with it. He tells Brazzos everything is good, then tells me to jump and forget my stuff, focus on his needs. I think he's a madman."

"Maybe that's why they hired him. A hardnosed bully, a bit like my Statler."

"I don't know, but I can't keep going on like this. Work Safe are not going to be happy. We haven't had a management review meeting in months and the MOC situation has totally broken down."

"How do you mean? I was the MOC coordinator and I thought we tracked all the changes."

"Yes, we do, but only for those that were raised. You ran the system well and got the signoffs as required. But many changes are not being run through the MOC system. Those that are raised with Brazzos are just authorised on the fly without documentation."

"Say that again. Give me an example, please," he asked.

"I don't know all the issues because Billings has me focused on his stuff, and I bet that Statler and even Jennison just operate under self-authority or the nod from Brazzos. It stems back to when they appointed Billings and Statler in the first place. There was no MOC raised for either appointment, nor was there any plan to induct them into the governance of pross safety. It's so frustrating."

"I can hear it in your voice. Have your meeting with Brazzos and then reset."

"Maybe, Liam. I don't know, we'll see." Sandy paused. "Enough of all that now. You have a great couple of weeks. Forget about this place and enjoy the catch-up with your sister."

When they hung up, Liam's body slumped, felt flat and defeated. The Agro Alliance world was imploding all around him, and he was powerless to do anything. It sounded like Sandy was struggling, and she was the last hold-out for the structures of process safety. PSM needed leadership and nurturing. Maybe she was the last hold-out for himself as well.

He drove on, passing over the Murray River with just forty minutes to Hahndorf. He liked the PSM structures because they aligned with his passion for detail and order. Design the process, complete risk assessments, build extra layers of protection, develop procedures and maintenance methods, train the staff, operate the plant, assess the critical controls, and manage all changes. It needed leadership across all aspects. Sandy's Safety Case was supposed to illustrate how the elements were functional and outlined the leadership controls and the governance process.

At university, he was only barely exposed to hazard analysis, a failing he often reflected upon. The course focus was on general chemical engineering providing a base for a wide range of possible career paths. Industry had to fill the void with specifics of process safety. Starting his career at Agro Alliance, he thought the process design had considered all the risks and consequently incorporated the required safety design features to eliminate failure. If only it was as simple as having a relief valve set to protect a vessel from over pressuring. He was naive and never thought about what would happen if one of the design safety features failed. This was the basis of the Hazard and Operability Studies (HAZOP).

Sandy Hudson had taught him that superior design had multiple layers of control. Add a pressure controller to shut down the source of pressure before requiring the relief valve to work, add a second independent pressure switch and others if required. The world of chemical processes was littered with catastrophes where releases killed multiple people and threatened communities. The history of Bhopal, Buncefield and even Australia's Esso Longford explosion were horrific. Communities no longer tolerated the loss of containment of flammable and toxic materials. Regulations now identified Major Hazard Facilities (MHF) and they required chemical operators to design rigour into the plant to reduce the risk to as low as reasonably practical. Sandy had explained that each layer of protection could be assigned a risk reduction value and that Work Safe and the community were expecting that a hazard facility site should be safer than the risk of driving a car to work.

The amount of work that he did with Sandy and others

in the last Safety Case was phenomenal, but now if there was no monthly or regular review, no MOC governance, where would it end? Sandy had previously told him that Work Safe were requiring a complete review of the risk assessments. All the HAZOPs would need to be re-validated and cross-checked against any changes. Then they were expected to conduct a complete LOPA programme to ensure the safety design had enough controls to reduce the risk to less than one in a million. This would need a lot of technical support and a lot of focus on detail.

It was a grim situation, and Liam couldn't see how it was to be achieved unless De Zaale and Brazzos took it seriously. In his mind, the likes of Billings and the Muppet Man lacked the experience and capability. He was beginning to wonder if he should look for other opportunities when he returned.

6

PAUL DE ZAALE CAME to the West Footscray plant on an impromptu basis, a plan to keep his people on their toes. This Friday, he needed to catch up with Brazzos and maybe take a short plant tour to check on progress. He had a spare office adjoining Brazzos on the other side of their executive conference room, and he had Suzi to run errands if required. On arrival, the reception ladies had standing instructions to buzz him through the security doors without him having to fish around for his pass, which he never bothered to carry. It was a stark contrast to when he was being recruited and when he first started. Back then, he had brought flowers for the reception ladies and was all smiles and laughter, all a bit too friendly. The reception ladies knew it was phony and just for show – and true to their suspicions, the flowers quickly evaporated to be replaced with grunts and finger pointing after he secured the job.

Today, he had arranged for Brazzos to take him on a tour but insisted on going around in Brazzos's car. He didn't want to make small talk with the operators or staff. He wasn't there to be their friends. They had their jobs and stopping to talk with them was inefficient.

De Zaale didn't know the workforce despised him, and they had no time for him. If ever he met any plant staff, they generally called him Pablo, which prompted nervous smiles all around. He was always Pablo to the plant staff, not as the friendly Spanish variation of Paul, but rather for their universal disrespect for the man, a walking example of the infamous Pablo Escobar. They thought that De Zaale treated them poorly, pawns in his bigger plans, same as the Columbian drug lord.

In the car as they drove around the plant, De Zaale asked Brazzos, "Is everything under control, Antonio?"

"Of course, boss. We've cut out the old soft underbelly. Now we have people that listen, we are getting results."

"Very good, looks clean. How's the safety record?"

"Excellent, no accidents for two months now. I think the messages are getting through!"

"Good." De Zaale smiled. "I knew you were the man. Keep it up! Let's get back to the offices and go through a couple of things."

They ended the token tour, in a quickfire ten-minute circuit of the plant and quickly returned back to De Zaale's office. There was a leather couch on the side with adjoining pot plants, and impressionist paintings hanging on the wall. The De Zaale desk was a large mahogany unit with a completely clean top, and the chair was a super plush hi-back leather unit fit for a President. De Zaale waved his hand to usher Brazzos to the couch, where Suzi had placed pastries, slices, and biscuits, along with freshly brewed coffee, a stainless mug with milk and a china bowl with sugar lumps.

"Help yourself to coffee, Antonio. I'll get us a starter," De Zaale said, opening the cabinet at the little bar and sink on the opposite side of the room. He withdrew a bottle of Buchanan Special Reserve scotch whiskey. When he opened the top, he took a long whiff of the aroma. "Nice, you'll like this one, same as we used to have in Bogota."

He poured a couple of fingers into two fine crystal tumblers and moved across to the couch.

"Salud, mi amigo," he said, offering a glass to his manufacturing manager. Agro Alliance was supposed to be an alcohol-free facility, but De Zaale and Brazzos had given themselves exemptions for their offices.

"Very smooth, Buchanan 18. Excellent choice." They clinked glasses, Brazzos adding, "A tu salud, Paul."

"Also very apt I think, Buchanan whiskey. I hear you have been collaborating with our Michelle."

Brazzos's face reddened but he quickly answered, "All in the aim of good progress. She's helping with a couple of troublemakers in the warehouse. Nothing you need to worry about. We will have it all sorted in a few weeks." His hardened face relaxed into a smile, pleased with his own response.

"What about these lunches in the city?" De Zaale asked.

"Nothing unusual there, Paul. I'm working with her to select a superannuation fund to divest our Agro Alliance trustee. You may recall you suggested we get out of the superannuation administration business. We should save over $250,000 a year and the best part is that we appear to be giving the employees their choice and their own control."

"Yes, I have heard. But a word of advice, my friend," De Zaale handed over the whiskey bottle for Brazzos to refill their glasses, "make sure you don't go mixing up work with pleasure! I don't care what you do outside work, but don't get it too messy inside the business. Do you understand me?"

"Certainly. Absolutely, Paul. All above board."

"Okay let's move on. But she is a ball breaker and her initials MFB, make sure they stand for Michelle Fucking Buchanan and not Michelle Fucking Brazzos. Yeah!"

Brazzos didn't answer, just nodded as his best form of defence: *Don't dig the grave any deeper.* He might have to be a bit more discreet now because how did De Zaale know? Or maybe he was just guessing. *Note to self, be careful.* He topped their glasses up and handed the bottle back to De Zaale, who placed it on the coffee table and picked up a pastry.

Changing subjects, De Zaale asked, "How's your nephew Ernesto working out?"

"Pretty good, I think. He's a smart boy and a wizard with the computer. He's been coordinating all the production reports, but we're now getting him to also act as the MOC coordinator."

"MOC, that reminds me, let's talk about that later. What about my cousins, the Rodrigeuz brothers? Are they any help?"

"Good boys." De Zaale nodded thoughtfully. "We haven't got them as official signed-up employees, but we do use them as contractors for odd jobs. They said they prefer it like that – is that all right?"

"Sure, okay by me. Provided they're happy. My aunt told me to look after them when they left Bogota. What sort of 'odd jobs' have you got them doing?"

"Anything that pops up. Last week they covered shortages on the fill-out line, we've had them help in office renovations and shifting furniture. But recently they said they were needed elsewhere, so now they just call me and let me know when they're available, and I try to get them some work."

"Do that. How do you pay them?" Brazzos asked.

"They have their own company: Calica for Hire. They give us an invoice and we pay them direct straight to a nominated bank account, all kosher."

"Whatever, as long as they're happy. Let's change subjects again. Tell me, Antonio, how are our production programmes going, especially the pre-emergent campaign? You know the marketing boys are hot on this pre-emergent stuff. They can sell everything that we make."

"I know, I had that feedback yesterday. All production runs are good and the pre-emergent is on schedule. We only have a limited supply of technical material and will have it finished next week."

"Any chance of getting some more technical?"

De Zaale shrugged. "We've tried, but nothing in time. It all comes from abroad – Israel, I think. We do have some old rework material from the last campaign that we can recover and consume at the end. That should be good for another 10,000 litres of product."

"Okay, add that rework and maximise the volume. Apparently, it's like 'gold', so keep it cranking. Full speed ahead."

"Certainly, top priority, Paul. Next month I'll get Suzi to grab us a bottle of Aguardiente to celebrate."

"Good idea, some old-fashioned Columbian 'Firewater'. I haven't had any of that for so long. Let's do it!"

De Zaale stood and walked across to his desk and extracted some papers from his briefcase. Coming back to the couch, he passed a letter to Brazzos. "The other issue on my agenda today is this letter from Work Safe. I'll let you read it, then we need to discuss."

Brazzos was noticeably quiet and frowned as he made out the contents. It was from the CEO of Work Safe and was directed to De Zaale as the CEO of Agro Alliance. The letter outlined the legal expectations for Agro Alliance's upcoming Safety Case, and with a few bullet points that included improvement in the site's Management of Change governance and revision of the use of risk assessments to include LOPA methodology.

De Zaale waited until Brazzos finished reading. "Can you translate this for me, either in English or Spanish? What is all this mumbo jumbo PSM, MOC, HAZOP, LOPA etc.?"

"It's just safety speak, meaning risk assessments and making sure we don't change things in the plant without checking that it doesn't introduce further hazards. That's what Billings has told me. I hadn't heard much of any of this previously."

De Zaale scratched his chin. "Sounds like a lot of paperwork. Who is doing this for us?"

"The safety team under Billings has it under control. Largely, it's checking the last submitted Safety Case, and cross checking that nothing significantly has changed, which it hasn't."

"But this letter talks about revisiting the risk assessments and applying LOPA, whatever that is."

"Billings has Sandra Hudson as a specialist in this area, she wrote the last Safety Case and is across the preparation for this one. He also has the Work Safe inspector visiting next week to discuss everything."

"I'm not sure about this, Antonio. I sense problems, and you know I don't like problems!"

"Again, I think it's all covered. Coincidently, this Hudson

lady has asked to see me this afternoon. Let me get her input, and I'll get back to you."

Suzi knocked on the office door and waited to be invited to enter. "Sorry, Pablo," she said with a smile. "I was going to clear the dishes, but I'll come back later." She left and closed the door behind her.

Brazzos smiled at his boss. "They all love you, Paul – or should I call you Pablo as well?"

De Zaale didn't answer, opting instead to shoot him a withering glare. "Let me know what this Hudson says!"

7

LIAM ARRIVED AT HAHNDORF earlier than expected and parked in the side street behind The German Arms. He had arranged to meet CJ inside at around 1:00pm, so he had time for a stroll down the iconic main street. The town was established in the 1830s as a settlement of German immigrants and had retained a rustic Germanic feel, good traditional food options, arts and crafts and a range of eclectic shops. He had time enough for a quick stroll to check out the options, scanning for a gift for Sarah.

Chris Jackson arrived at The German Arms and lucked out to book a table out on the balcony, but waited for Liam inside at the bar nursing a pint of HB lager. He was lucky with the table, catching it as other guests were getting up to vacate. Chris now lived in Sydney and hadn't seen Liam for almost two years – not since his mother's funeral. They went to school together and became best friends while their families lived in Glenelg. Even after taking separate paths through university, they remained close and still talked regularly.

Liam returned from his stroll and entered through the front door, venturing down the internal steps to the back bar where he saw CJ standing next to a life size figurine of a German waiter in traditional dress. “Looking for a job, mate?”

CJ beamed and embraced Liam with a bear hug, before stepping back to check him out. “Great to see you, buddy. What can I get you?”

Liam noticed CJ’s pint on the bar. “Same, anything, it’s all good.”

Liam waited while CJ ordered another pint, looking around the old place with happy memories. It was like a regular Hofbräuhaus with wooden beams and the large wooden heater in the middle – a very cosy place in winter. Although Liam was in Melbourne and CJ in Sydney, this was their meeting place whenever they were both in town. CJ’s parents had moved up into the Adelaide Hills five years ago to run a bed and breakfast, a ‘tree change of sorts’ late in life.

“Come,” ordered CJ as he gestured for Liam to follow. “I lucked out and got us a table on the balcony. Is Zoe going to join us?”

“She’s working today but she said she might try and come over in the afternoon.”

Settled down at their balcony seats, they clinked glasses and toasted to each other’s health. They sat in silence for a few minutes, watching the world go by while enjoying the view and their beer.

Liam broke the silence. “It’s been too long. How’s life in the harbour city?”

CJ smiled. “It’s good that we could both be back at the same time …” Then pausing for another sip of his beer, he raised his glass in another toast to his friend. “Sydney is very good, very busy, lots to do, exciting. Where do I start?”

"How's work? Are you still in the same flat? How's Kelly—"

"Whoa Liam, all good, all in time. We have all afternoon. Let's order first?"

They picked up their menus and checked out the German specialties. CJ was happy to be home and needed to slow his mate down. Sydney life in a high-profile accounting firm was exciting at first but now it was too time consuming and demanding. He was trying to get a relocation back to Adelaide to be a bit closer to his parents, but his longtime girlfriend was fully devoted to her Sydney lifestyle. It was a tricky situation, and he needed some deeper reflection with Liam, not a quick-fire question and answer session.

Liam took the menu to the bar and placed their orders, then returned with two fresh pints of the same HB lager. "Here you go, chief. Are you staying with your parents?"

CJ laughed. "Yes, I am but they would probably want me to pay for accommodation in the back. They have a very nice little bed and breakfast up off the main street passed the Old Mill Hotel. I prefer to bunk on a sofa bed in their spare room."

"How are they? I haven't seen them in years."

"I think they're good. I feel a bit guilty that I haven't been home for a couple of years. The tree change came out of the blue. I don't know, but part of my plan is to check it all out." CJ paused in reflection, before adding, "Mate, sorry about your dad. I couldn't get away to get back for his funeral. That was a bit sudden, wasn't it?"

Liam sighed. "Don't worry about it, we understand. He went downhill quickly after Mum died, but Zoe has been magnificent in my absence."

The mood had taken a sombre and reflective turn. They

sat with their beers for a few more minutes before unpacking their family issues. CJ slowly worked through his Sydney dilemma, Liam doing a power of listening with his own similar thoughts bouncing around in his head.

Lunch arrived and they both welcomed a break. Liam joked and offered, “Maybe we can go into business together. Maybe find some venture back here in Adelaide?”

Over lunch, Liam gave CJ the rundown of the new management at Agro Alliance and his disgruntlement with the way it was trending. He felt guilty leaving Zoe with the family issues but was still tied to Melbourne with his new relationship with Sarah.

They switched tack after lunch, both happy that their problems were out in the open. Solutions yet to be found and maybe still a way off. Discussion switched to Zoe and her birthday. Liam had been told that she didn’t want anything special; she was happy enough for her brother to be home. They would spend some time together, catch a Port Adelaide game, go out for dinner, visit their uncle and aunt in Victor Harbour, and talk through the sale of their dad’s house.

The afternoon meandered on, filled with memories, catch-up chat and periodically delving back into their woes. The world problems would have to wait for another day. Time had flown and they were both on their fifth pint when Zoe arrived, still in her uniform from the local winery; Shaw and Smith. Both men rose and gave her a kiss and a hug. Zoe, all smiles.

“Good to see you boys together. Nice to see you, CJ, it’s been a while.” Zoe thought he was a good-looking man but she had never been attracted to him, always treated him as a brother rather than a prospect.

Liam pulled over another chair. "Can I get you something, Zoe? A wine maybe?"

"No, not a wine, as much as I like it, it's my job nowadays. Maybe just a pint of HB if you don't mind. How many have you guys had already?"

"Will a ball-park figure suffice?" said CJ, smiling while Liam went back to the bar.

Zoe smiled back and waved her finger at CJ. "You boys better not be driving."

"No, definitely not. I might ask you for a lift to my folk's place if that's okay, and Liam should leave his car here."

"Good, I'm off now, so I'll give you a lift when we're finished, then I'll take Liam home. I'm coming back tomorrow morning anyway, so I'll bring him back up to fetch his car then."

"How's your work going? Doing weekends as well, I see," CJ asked.

"It's good, I like it. I'm learning heaps about wines and marketing. It's not the university plan I started, but it pays my way and that's good for now."

"Last time I saw you, I thought you were at uni. What happened to that plan?"

She didn't answer straight away, looking out over the balcony watching the pedestrian traffic. She turned back to CJ, clearing her throat. "A bit of a long story, that one. The short version is that I deferred when Dad was sick. I might ..."

She left it hanging unfinished as Liam returned with the drinks, announcing, "I also got us some nibbles." He returned carrying the 'Arms Sausage Platter'. "I hope you like bratwurst, sauerkraut, pickles and pretzels."

"Zoe was telling me that she's on a gap year," CJ said, continuing on their conversation.

Liam looked at his sister cautiously. “Yes, Dad was extremely sick, and Zoe was the only one available to help. You know, with me stuck in Melbourne and all.”

“It’s just what you do,” Zoe interjected. “Deal with the cards you are dealt.”

“Of course,” noted Liam, “but I tell you, CJ. She’s a living legend, and she did it all with such grace.” The boys raised their glasses with a nod and a toast to Zoe.

Zoe and Liam filled in the rest of the story. When their mum had been diagnosed with breast cancer, Zoe was still in high school and Liam had started chemical engineering studies at the University of Adelaide – the first in the O’Donoghue lineage to go to university. Their mum didn’t want Liam to compromise his career and swindled a way for Liam to transfer to Monash University in Melbourne. Career opportunities were greater, time to spread his wings, etc. She knew her health was declining and would soon need a lot of care. She didn’t want her children to be distracted from their own career paths and she had arranged with her husband to take the lead. Pushing Liam over to Melbourne was all part of her plan, and Zoe to University. Zoe finished high school with top five percentile marks in the state and followed her brother to Adelaide University, sciences instead of engineering.

It was a tough first year for Zoe, watching her mother deteriorate only partly shielded by her dad’s support. He had retired from his sales manager job and looked after Mum full time. Liam graduated in Melbourne, but Mum was too sick to travel and a year later she died. She insisted Liam follow his career and that Zoe continue her studies. Zoe was looking at trying to do medical science research to potentially join the fight against cancer.

Then Dad seemed lost without Mum. He couldn't stay in Glenelg and needed something to keep him busy. He used Mum's life insurance and sold up the family home in Glenelg and bought an old tenant house in North Adelaide. "Fantastic location, excellent prospects," he kept saying. Close to uni for Zoe. His plan was to renovate it as a project and make a huge profit to share with his children. Then he started getting forgetful, more than normal and Zoe was always saving him, checking on him. She took him to several doctors who reassured her that there was nothing significant to worry about. Short-term memory loss was normal, simply a part of getting old, they'd said. But then his eyesight started to deteriorate, and he started to struggle judging distances or reaching for objects.

Zoe explained, "It was when I finally took him to an optometrist and then from there to an ophthalmologist, we learnt that it might be something significant. We went to another specialist and found that Dad in fact had an exceedingly rare condition ..."

Liam picked up after Zoe's pause: "He in fact had Creutzfeldt-Jakob Disease, and that was that. There is no treatment. It affects the brain and although it is extremely rare, it's sporadic in people between fifty-five and seventy. The doctors don't know a lot about it and thus far they only focus on the treatment of pain management, antidepressants, etcetera ..."

"So," Zoe added, "within two years of Mum passing, we had to deal with Dad dying late last year."

CJ wanted to hug Zoe, but stayed in his seat. "So much, so quick, so young. I'm sorry, guys."

Zoe and Liam spoke at the same time. "We don't—"

Laughing that they were about to say the same thing, a message they had shared privately many times – *We don't dwell on it, just another step in life's journey.*

8

SANDY HUDSON PAUSED, MENTALLY gathering herself and running through her discussion points. She took a deep breath to gather her courage then entered Brazzos's office. Suzi was stationed at an internal reception area and Brazzos had his office behind another door.

"Excuse me, Suzi, I have a meeting with Mr Brazzos." Sandy looked around the room and saw a vacant waiting chair on the other wall. "Is he available?"

"Yes, and he's expecting you, Sandy. Let me check with him." Suzi picked up the phone and had a short conversation, then smiled at Sandy and waved her to the door.

It was the first time Sandy had been in these offices, and she both admired and squirmed at the opulent finish, a stark contrast to the rest of the building of cubicles and modular framed rooms. As she walked into the room, Brazzos got to his feet and came around his desk to welcome her offering his hand. "Come in, Sandra. I do believe I've met you."

"Yes, sir," replied Sandy. "When you did the induction tour of the offices, in a group meeting with Barry Billings and his team."

"Call me Tony. I remember now. Come and sit." He waved her to the plush visitor's chair. "How can I help you?"

"I'm not sure where to begin." She took her seat and waited for Brazzos to return to his chair. "I'm having a problem with the Safety Case and getting support and the priority that I need. It's a big job, much bigger than people realise and, well—"

"Okay, I don't have long, maybe thirty or forty minutes. How about you start with a summary of this Safety Case. Why do we need it?"

Sandy was a bit staggered, thinking, *Surely, he's supposed to know all this, or Billings should have kept him informed!*

"All right," she responded. "Every business is required to operate safely and there are standard workplace regulations."

"Yes, of course," nodded Brazzos. "But not all workplaces prepare a Safety Case."

"That's correct. A Safety Case is mainly triggered when a workplace has inventories of flammable materials or highly toxic chemicals more than a set criteria, although other factors may also be included."

"Mmm." Brazzos didn't care about all this Safety Case legality but pretended to stay interested. "Are you telling me we exceed the criteria?"

"Yes, we do. We exceed it by a large margin." Sandy did an internal stocktake; *Simple basics that you should already know.* "Unfortunately, it's the nature of our business, as would also apply to the petroleum refineries and several chemical plants. Victoria has about forty MHF sites that have to comply with these stringent legal requirements."

"What's the Safety Case?"

"It's the key requirement that Work Safe use to decide whether a business will have a licence to operate as an MHF. It's a document that details the high-level risks and the control measures that are adopted in the design and the operational strategies that are used to mitigate all these risks."

"Very interesting. What if we reduce the inventories below the criteria, are we still an MHF? What does MHF stand for again?"

Taking a breath and trying to stay calm, Sandy answered, "MHF is an acronym for Major Hazard Facility. If we reduce inventories, we can remove the main triggers, but the law also allows the regulator, Work Safe, to deem a business, such as ours." She paused to think ... "It could be done, but we couldn't synthesise and formulate the products we have today."

"Okay, so we need a Safety Case. We already have one and that had demonstrated all the requirements. Why do we need another one? Isn't this all just bureaucracy running wild?"

"The regulations require we check it periodically and, in our case, every three years, and then we resubmit it."

"Billings told me that as well. So, we dust it off, check it over and resubmit." Brazzos was starting to think this safety exercise was just another paper exercise and recalled De Zaale's description of government hacks.

"I wish it was all that easy," said Sandy. "The checks need to validate the initial design against the physical reality, and then against any changes. That takes time, cross functional teams, and attention to detail."

"How many people and how long?"

"Actually, that's why I wanted to meet you. My boss, Barry Billings ..." Sandy deliberately used his full name to avoid being too friendly with just his first name, or too brash with just a surname. "... Well, he thinks I can do it by myself and then as a part-time exercise. He wants me to focus on other things like permit training and 5S programmes."

"5S is pretty important, Sandra."

"I agree, very important and it can add a lot of value in many areas, especially in our high manual handling work areas. Sort, Set in Order, Shine, Standardise and Sustain. I like the programme, and we need it here. But I can't do both. Work Safe are expecting us to extend the validation with a LOPA assessment."

"Ah, yes. I've heard of this LOPA. Tell me more," Brazzos said, looking down at his watch.

"That stands for 'Layers of Protection Analysis', which requires us to check that we have adequate independent controls to reduce risk to as low as is reasonably practical. It's a technical process that builds on HAZOPs and the existing design details."

Brazzos sat back, thinking, *This girl knows her stuff, but this is all too technical.* "I'm not sure we have enough time today to cover all the detail. How is it measured, what is reasonably practical, etc?"

"I know," replied Sandy. "MHFs require management and staff to be fully trained in all this and often send people for specific process safety training. The change in our leadership itself should have had an MOC raised, but that hasn't happened. I'm here today asking for help."

"MOC, another acronym."

"That stands for management of change. Once the plant design and operating parameters are set, we have what we call the 'Basis of Safety'. Then any change needs to be reviewed against this base."

"Are you saying we can't make changes?"

"No, not at all. MOC is about checking that it won't affect the Basis of Safety. Anything that is like for like changes and plant repairs are totally within the scope of safe operation. For other changes, we just need to ensure the controls, risk reduction measures, are not compromised."

"What about people? You just said that when we change managers, we also have to do an MOC." Brazzos was getting a bit annoyed with the sense of over control of these MOCs.

Sandy took a deep breath, trying to stay patient. "The issue with personnel changes is to make sure that the responsibility for process safety is carried forward. If the new person is responsible for any safety elements, then they need to be competent or need support and training."

"Have you taken this to Billings?"

"Yes, sir, a few times. But ..." *Here goes* ... "He doesn't understand process safety and I'm afraid that the existing systems are falling apart. We aren't resourced to get this done – the Safety Case, I mean. Frankly, we need more than just me. LOPA will take months with a dedicated team. Also, he tells me to pull my head in and refocus. I feel like I'm going around and around in circles getting nowhere."

"Mmm, I hear your concerns. I'm not sure how to solve it, we all have multiple competing demands. Let me give it more thought over the weekend and I'll chat with Barry on Monday."

"Thank you," Sandy said, getting to her feet. "But please, understand I'm not trying to go around my boss. I have raised this with him, and I'm just concerned we won't get it done. Also, it's important that we all understand that a breakdown in our process safety systems could lead to a major accident."

She left the office relieved at having put her position, but suspected she was fighting a losing battle. *Let's see what Monday brings.*

As Sandy opened the office door to leave, Suzi took the opportunity of the opened door to enter. "Excuse me, Tony, Jim Statler wants you to call him. There's some problem in the plant." Then, making eye contact with Sandy, added, "Ernesto has been trying to catch you as well, Sandy."

Brazzos, seeing that it was 4:30pm on his watch, grumbled under his breath before picking up his phone. Sandy heard part of the conversation "... It's late on a Friday afternoon, and I'm about to go home ... I don't care ..." The rest of the conversation was unintelligible as Sandy walked out of the outer office, but heard the near shouting, "Whatever, get it done ... We are not stopping production."

Moments later, Brazzos pushed passed Sandy, hard hat in hand, making his way to the plant.

9

LUNCH CONTINUED WELL INTO the afternoon at the German Arms, ending with a few more rounds of drinks and some more food, spicy popcorn chicken, garlic bread and more pretzels. Zoe had agreed to drive the boys home and had switched to water. She reiterated her plan for Liam to leave his car overnight and said she would arrange a lift back in the morning and collect the car herself.

The catch up was ambling along as they enjoyed the view from the balcony, until Liam's work phone rang in his bag, startling everyone. Liam reacted and fished the phone from his bag. "Wow, work. Friday afternoon, I'm on leave and interstate and they still call me. What now?" He saw that the call was from Jim Statler and half pretended to hurl it over the balcony. "I better check out what they want."

CJ took the opportunity to head off and find the toilet, while Zoe stepped aside to arrange tomorrow's lift with a colleague.

Liam answered the call. "Hello Jim, something up? It's 4:00pm and I'm in Adelaide."

"Bit of an issue here, Liam. Looks like the shaft on the

agitator for reactor 2 in your plant is broken," Statler said, sounding a bit harassed.

"Okay, we used to have a spare in the maintenance store. Mario can check with them and arrange it to be swapped out, might take a couple of hours though."

"Yeah maybe ... Mario has already checked, and they don't think it's there anymore."

"What does that mean? Get him to check with a fitter, Deano or Adrian or someone. If Bussy was still at Agro Alliance, he'd know for sure."

"I'll ask, but they're already talking about the universal spare. Mario reckons we'll need an MOC. What do you think?"

Liam had to stop himself from laughing. "You know the rules. Like for like is all good, otherwise you need to raise an MOC."

"Don't be a smart arse. We need to get it sorted and get the plant running again."

"I wasn't being a smart arse, Jim," Liam said, annoyed that Statler was challenging him. "I was just reminding you, that's all. I'm not sure why the big rush. Get the engineers to check over the universal spare and raise an MOC. Do a hazard review on Monday and get the MOC authorised."

"I'm not sure we can wait. We need all the production finished ASAP."

Liam could feel Statler's impatience over the phone. "Really, are you sure? If you ask some of the old guys, like Frank and Mario, they used to say that the unwritten rule was that any of this product not in a can by the start of April was always returned. It was a common story every season."

But Statler wasn't listening. "This year is different. De Zaale has the word. We need to get the plant back running pronto."

"All right, but I can't really help. Get them to check the universal spare and raise the MOC and get it fast tracked. Get your boy Ernesto on the job."

Liam hung up, shaking his head in disbelief. He had to take a few calming breaths as he put his phone back into his bag, just as CJ returned from the bathroom.

Zoe looked at the boys. "Are you guys ready to go? Is everything okay back at your funny farm in Melbourne, Liam?"

"Yes, let's hit the road," replied Liam. "They have a maintenance problem, and they were just checking with me, not that I can do anything from here."

Ten minutes later and with Zoe driving, they arrived at the bed and breakfast of CJ's parents. CJ opened the rear door and lent forward, tapping Zoe on the shoulder. "Thanks for the lift, Zoe. Great to see you both again. Let's catch up again in the next few weeks."

Liam leaned over the back of his chair and shook CJ's hand. "Good idea. Don't forget about the footy on Sunday."

From the driver's seat, Zoe responded, "See you on Sunday. I have tickets." Liam and Zoe burst into a line from the Power song, CJ joined in and when they finished, Zoe added, "I've also arranged a wine tasting session at work next week, with a share plate of nibbles. You could get your parents to come, if you'd like. We haven't seen them for ages."

CJ's eyes darted, nervous about how his parents would respond, but simply answered, "That could work, let me check with the folks."

"No sweat, CJ – it would be later in the week. I'm thinking of having a mini-informal function, just a catch-up with Liam and a couple of friends. A very low-key birthday thing. I'll get you a date and time, and you can check if you or your parents are available."

"Thanks, Zoe," CJ said as he shut the door and walked towards his parents' house.

Zoe and Liam drove off, heading back towards Adelaide when Liam's work phone buzzed again. This time, Ernesto Gonzales was calling. He raised his phone as an indication to Zoe. "Something must be really up!"

Zoe smiled back. "Even on leave. You must be indispensable."

"Ha, ha. I bet he wants my help with a formal management of change request for that maintenance issue."

Liam had barely picked up before Ernesto got to the point. "Hello Liam, I think you heard that the T-plant agitator shaft broke. They want me to raise an MOC. Can you help me?"

"Buddy, that's why you're the MOC coordinator. I can't really do much from interstate. Not sure how I can help."

"To be honest, Liam, I don't know where to start ..."

Liam nodded his head in acknowledgement then shook it in frustration. "Straight into the deep end. If the spare is the same as the broken one, then you won't need an MOC. Check that first."

"What do you mean by the same? And what if it's not?" Ernesto felt out of his depth, caught in a trap not of his own making. His uncle had talked him up as a smart boy, but now he felt like a kid on his first day of school.

"Ernesto. Look, I'm on holidays. Maybe try Sandy Hudson. Otherwise put the problem back to Jim Statler and Barry

Billings, they should be managing this stuff. Sorry man, I've got to go." Liam hung up and shook his head in disbelief as he smiled at his sister.

"Problems?" asked Zoe.

Before he could answer, his phone rang again, this time Mario the permit writer. Liam answered, "Hello Mario. Busy Friday night, I hear."

"Mate," Mario laughed, "you should be here. It's a circus and Statler is going to explode."

"Well, the basics of process safety, 1-0-1 if you like, is trained leadership in all elements. The karma bus might be about to back up over Pablo and our Muppet Man."

"It's all right for you 700 kilometres away, but I'm stuck here, Mario in the middle."

"Okay, what do you want?"

"The agitator shaft is buggered, and no one knows where the spare is. I told them Bussy would know. Now they reckon the universal spare will work, but it's not an exact same as the broken one. It will fit and it will mix, but it ain't the same."

"As far as you're concerned, the permit writing is about doing the job safely. Get the old one out safely, no one gets hurt and put the new one in safely. Locks, keys, tags; the full LOTO. The permit form asks about MOC, but that's just a check for the system to stop and question, like what you're doing now."

"Yes, got that. I'm at the stage I reckon they need an MOC."

"Perfect, don't prepare the work until the MOC is ready, get them to give you an MOC number. If they can't do that, then someone – Statler or Brazzos – should sign off the permit. They should tell you that either they've made a risk assessment and it's okay to proceed or that an MOC is not needed."

"Wow, can you see that happening?"

"I don't know, Mario, it should happen that way. It's not your job to assess the risks of any change. Push that back up the line while you focus on making the job safe."

"Okay chief, thanks." Mario signed off.

Zoe looked at her brother. "Sounds like stress city over there."

"You're not wrong, and they're trampling all over proper process," Liam said, still at a loss at how quickly the place was unravelling.

"I overheard you mention something about a karma bus. Are you still banging on about that bloody karma bus thing?"

"Too right. I certainly believe in that. If you act all high and mighty, and if you have no consideration for people or their feelings, well then ... someday it will come back to bite you. Sure will, that karma bus will back right up. Then you don't want to be crying foul, because you'll be getting what you deserve."

"The world order, according to Liam and his karma bus," quoted Zoe.

For the rest of the drive down from the hills, Liam gave Zoe a quick summary of process safety and the errors flooding across Agro Alliance. The changes made when De Zaale took over saw a large drain on plant experience and there was no structure to re-establish a knowledge base. The new crew were learning on the run. De Zaale's focus was on cost control and efficiency. His safety focus was on physical order, trip hazards, handrails, and the obvious items to avoid loss time injuries. This was driven into his managers, and they went to extremes to avoid reporting accidents, even near misses. Collectively, they had no idea about process safety or high risk.

Zoe was happy to arrive at the house, and to pull the plug on Liam's lecture. "Well, here we are, bro."

—

They unpacked Liam into the larger of the two spare rooms and walked through the house, looking at the renovations. Zoe put the kettle on. "I'm going to have a cuppa, do you want one?"

"Yes, thanks, that would be great," replied Liam. "You know, I haven't seen this place. I stayed at a motel when I came back for Dad's funeral."

"It was Dad's dream after Mum died. He sold up and moved over here, supposedly so that I was closer to the university, but I think he saw it as a project."

"I know, looks all right. What are we going to do with the place?" Liam motioned to the dining table. "Make the cuppas, sis. Let's sit and chat."

Zoe fiddled with cups and raided the pantry for a few biscuits. She handed Liam his tea and sat on the opposite side. "Funny that thing with CJ. You know when we started saying the same thing at the same time ... *We don't dwell on it, just another step in life's journey.*"

Liam noted the change in subject and answered, "That's right ... we don't dwell on it."

Zoe smiled. "We don't dwell on it. But we need to break the trend of dying young in this family."

"It starts with us then, or should I say, it's left with us?

Are you worried that they both died in their sixties and that Grandma also died early with breast cancer?"

"Yes and no..." Zoe thought on this for a moment. "It's a concern, even Dad's dementia or CJD thing. Forewarned is forearmed. We can do regular checks, stay healthy, and monitor how we're going."

Liam nodded, silently reflecting. He sipped his tea and sat back.

"Don't get all gloomy on me now. What's your plans for the weekend, bro?"

Liam took another sip. "Nothing much: look around here while you go to work tomorrow, maybe walk into town and check the shops. Do you want to go to the pub for dinner?"

"Yes, but just us and just next door here at The Lion. Next weekend we must visit Aunty Julie and Uncle Joe in Victor Harbour, maybe on the Saturday. We're going to the footy this Sunday, Port's playing Freo ..." Zoe paused, thinking. "CJ will come, won't he? I'll get the tickets sorted tomorrow."

Liam smiled at his sister. "Do you fancy CJ? Don't forget he has a steady girlfriend back in Sydney."

Zoe got up and punched her brother in the arm. "Don't be an idiot. He's just a mate, a big brother type. I thought the three of us would enjoy a day at the football." Then, refilling her tea, she turned the questions back on Liam. "Now tell me all about Sarah."

10

JOHNNO WAS FLICKING THROUGH a magazine in the plant control room when his supervisor Frank came in on his last rounds, collecting the production data for his shift report. He looked over Johnno's shoulder and noted that the three o'clock readings still hadn't been recorded. Taking the magazine out of Johnno's hands, he challenged him. "No time for goofing off, mate. Where are your last readings?"

"Sorry, Frank, I was out on the plant and I completely forgot."

"That's bullshit, Johnno. It's 3:30pm. Get off your backside and take them now. You stretch my patience at times, and I'm not joking." Frank looked over the screen displays and flicked around to the alarm screen. "What about this, low amps on the reactor 2 mixer?"

"I don't know, boss. Must have come up while I was on my rounds," Johnno, now struggling to explain his oversight, avoided eye contact with Frank and made to exit the control room.

"More bullshit, mate, total crap. Someone acknowledged the alarm and I'm guessing that was you. Look, it was 2:39pm when that alarm came up. Get out there and check it out." Frank followed him out into the plant and up onto the second floor where the mixer motor was located. They found the motor running, but the shaft underneath was stationary.

Frank was angry and was considering issuing Johnno a formal reprimand. Now he had to sort out this mess as well, and just ahead of shift change. He glared at Johnno and instructed him to get Mario and a fitter up here. "You have a broken shaft and should have been on top of that an hour ago."

Frank then called Statler to tell him the bad news. Jim was sitting at his desk, packing up ready to leave, when he took Frank's call. "What's up, Frank?"

"Bad news, boss. The agitator on T-plant's reactor 2 has a broken shaft, and we'll have to pull it down. I will be down in your office in a minute."

Statler wasn't plant savvy and didn't really know what this meant. "How long will that take? Why are you telling me all this?"

Frank walked into the production block, threw some papers on his desk, and saw Statler coming out of his office. "Just keeping you in the loop, Jim, and we may be down for days if we haven't a spare. Mario is on his way, and he'll check it out with the maintenance boys."

Statler just glared, angry about the delay. "This is not good, not good, not good." He nervously paced up and down in front of the supervisor's desk. "Why are you talking days? We must finish this campaign in a few days. We can't have delays – get it fixed."

Frank sat down at his desk, unperturbed by Statler's rantings. "I'm sorry, Jim, it is what it is. The shaft is broken, and we can't continue. We can't repair it in house anymore and I suspect we don't have a spare. Besides, I don't know what all the rush is about – in past seasons any pre-emergent product that wasn't packed off by April never sold."

"I don't care about the past. Brazzos and De Zaale are backing a marketing push to make more, make more now. There must be something we can do. Why can't we repair it in house?"

With his head in the shift log, Frank responded, "Maybe you should talk with maintenance, call Jennison, and get him involved. They lost a lot of expertise when we outsourced to that consultancy mob."

The old engineering and maintenance regime had contingencies. The boss back then, Alexander Scotland, ran a good operation. He had everything well organised. Critical spares were identified and readily available. Scotland valued his people and ensured the maintenance crew had skills to address any issue. When Scotland left in the round of redundancies, everything changed. De Zaale let the skills walk out, and had contract maintenance fill the gaps. De Zaale justified everything as cost reduction and efficiency improvement. Unfortunately, while that was the De Zaale spiel in St Kilda Road, the reality on the Footscray shop floor was the exact opposite. Costs were soaring, contract labour at a premium, and the maintenance process seemed to have more people getting less done.

"Yes, good idea." Statler returned to his office to make the call, as Mario came into to talk to Frank.

Frank looked up and said directly to Mario, "What's the verdict, Mario?"

Mario sat down opposite the supervisor and sighed. "Maintenance are still checking, but I'm almost positive we don't have a spare. We'll just have to wait and see."

Mario and Frank both knew that the only spare was used a few years back in another part of the plant, and after the restructuring, maintenance went lean on spare parts. If John Buss were still here, he would know for sure. Bussy was the storeman across everything who always had parts on order and knew where all the nuts and bolts were. He knew what was possible and had contacts for trades, contractors and all the suppliers. He had pulled off many a Friday night miracle in the past. But alas, Bussy was another victim of the De Zaale restructuring. When the store's management was sent to the purchasing department in the front offices, miracles were also a thing of the past.

Statler came back from his office and confronted Mario. "Jennison tells me we may have a universal mixer shaft which could do the job. He's checking and will get back to us in a few minutes. In the meantime, let's get ready."

Frank intervened, "I'm going off shift soon, so I will hand over to Jake. Mario, you might want to stay back to help the afternoon shift fitters if you can."

Statler looked at Mario. "You can write the permit and coordinate the changeout."

Mario, cornered but ever appreciative of extra overtime, agreed. "Yes, all right, I will. I need to make a few calls as I was supposed to be going out tonight. Maybe I can get away later and still attend my function. Will you organise the MOC?"

"What, why do we need an MOC?" Jim asked. "Aren't we replacing a mixer with another mixer. We don't have time for paperwork."

Mario shrugged. "It's not up to me. If it's not the exact same, we'll need an MOC. I just write the permit and you guys arrange the change management stuff. You should get

Ernesto to start the ball rolling. He's the new MOC coordinator." Mario looked over at Frank, who was sitting quietly watching the commotion, internally laughing, while Mario was deliberately pushing Statler's buttons.

Statler went back into this office, yelling back at Mario, "You get Ernesto before he leaves, I'm checking this with Jennison, then I'll call Brazzos."

Frank and Mario exchanged looks again and Frank picked up his phone, dialled Ernesto and handed it to Mario. "You can tell him the good news."

Twenty minutes later, the production office was a buzz. Ernesto had arrived and was in discussions with Statler, while Jennison was discussing the spare unit with Mario, Frank, and Jake. Statler apparently hadn't spoken with Brazzos as he was in some meeting. Ernesto was stressing, needing help from Sandy, who wasn't answering, and Mario was still insisting on an MOC.

Statler called Brazzos again, left an urgent message with Suzi, then looked over at Mario, "How long will an MOC take?"

Mario threw his hands up. "Hard to say, Jim. It's up to you guys. You need to do the risk assessment and it all depends on the extent of the changes. It takes what it takes. Shortcuts will lead to mistakes and mistakes may lead to accidents."

"What changes?" countered Statler. "Don't give me this 'ring-a-rosie' bullshit. It's just a mixer, it still turns and it will still mix the contents."

"I know, but it's not the same mixer. It's a different model, different agitator blades, might even be shorter. I'll write the permit to do the job safely, but I need an MOC number to justify the change, or at least a plant owner to co-sign the permit that an MOC is not required or that the risk assessment has been done separately. Process Safety First, mate."

Dean the fitter, who had been quietly sitting at another desk waiting for his instructions, added his two cents. "For what it's worth, Mario, the shaft is not set for the T-plant vessel. We may need to make a bush to align the universal shaft with the vessel mounts. Also, it has a mechanical seal not an oil seal like the one in there now."

Statler's phone rang while he was considering this latest problem and pondering the extra delays. It was Brazzos, so he retreated to his office and shut the door. "Tony, we have a problem on T-plant. The agitator shaft has broken, and we are down. It looks like we don't have a spare and we are scrambling for a makeshift replacement."

"We can't stop," Brazzos responded abruptly. "It's late on a Friday afternoon, and I'm about to go home. You need to get it back running. I don't care what it takes but make it snappy."

Statler was getting agitated and he felt sweaty. "The boys reckon that the mixer is different, and we need a risk assessment. Can you come down and look at it, pull some weight? We have it set up on the second floor in the T-plant."

"Whatever, get it done. We are not stopping production. I'll be there in a minute, but make sure everyone is ready to go."

Brazzos arrived and looked decidedly unhappy. He had a short conversation with Statler and Jennison on the stairway, then walked to the new agitator shaft, gave it a cursory inspection. "What's all the fuss about? You guys should be able to sort this out."

Jake, who had taken over from Frank as the shift supervisor, explained the technicalities of the different mixer and also explained to Brazzos of the need for a minor adjustment of a bush to make the unit fit. Brazzos stared blankly, then with frustration made his point. "It's just a big mixing stirrer, it'll still mix the contents, am I right?"

Jake shrugged. "I guess so. I haven't measured it exactly, but it looks like it'll reach the fluid level and it should work."

Brazzos approached Jake, invading his personal space and shoving him in the chest. "Measure it and check, then get on with it. We haven't got all day."

Jake, a strong lad with a football background, wasn't going to be intimidated. He stood his ground. "No problem, Tony M. Can do. But I can't sign off on the MOC on Mario's permit. You need to tick that box!"

11

LIAM WAS SOUND ASLEEP in his father's North Adelaide renovator when Zoe was picked up for her ride back to the Adelaide Hills. It had been a mentally draining few days and his body welcomed the chance to tune out and recuperate. He woke mid-morning, showered, and dressed, and then made himself a pot of tea. He pottered around the house looking at his father's handiwork. The result was a mix mash of outcomes. He had obviously used trades where required but the inexperienced handy man had left telltale signs in the paintwork and some of the finishes.

Solar panels had been installed, but there was a selection switch that seemed misplaced, a mystery that might only be solved in his dear dad's mind. The front sitting room with an open fireplace had been converted into a master bedroom, oversized in the context of the house, while the third bedroom was a pokey old storeroom and laundry conversion barely large enough to contain a queen bed. The add-on extension that spoke of Dad's amateur carpentry ventured into the back yard. It contained a bathroom and a relocated laundry, along with a covered veranda, more like a caged sitting room. The yard featured several large lemon trees with fruit in abundance and an old, one-car garage at the rear of the property. The neighbours had built two storey mega mansions that occupied their entire blocks and looked over into the back paved courtyard. There was nothing wrong with the place, but the changes didn't really flow together. The end result was a patched together house and it would be a challenge to market the place.

There was a lane access at the back into the garage, which housed Zoe's car. She was driving Dad's old Mitsubishi, only because it was convenient. Liam's twenty-first birthday present for his sister was to fund an upgrade into something more suitable, using a portion of his part of the inheritance from his parents' shares and cash savings. He opened the side gate and walked down the dog-leg laneway coming out opposite the The Lion; a North Adelaide traditional hotel.

Returning to the kitchen after doing a lap around the block, Liam sat down to make a few calls. The first call to Sarah, caught her on the way to tennis. They updated each other and he wished her well for her game, ending with kisses over the phone. He then called the plant, dialling up the shift supervisor's number. Frank was still on day shift – his last one before switching to a couple of night shifts in their two-day, two-night, four-off shift roster schedule.

"Hello, Liam. Are you checking in or something?" Frank enquired.

"Sort of. Sounded like you had a mess yesterday with the agitator. How did it all end up."

"I left them still talking about MOCs and permits. Jake took over and apparently, he went toe-to-toe with old Bullyboy. Anyway, the job got done and the new agitator was in by midnight. We're up and running again and should finish the second last batch today."

"Did you find a spare agitator?"

"Jake told me they used the universal unit, and they questioned Brazzos and Statler about needing an MOC. But they apparently checked the measurements and Brazzos gave a verbal authorisation."

Liam sighed and shook his head. "I'm not surprised. It would have been just as easy to document a short risk assessment. Did Ernesto get involved?"

"Nah, he stayed well out of the way, too scared to say anything. Jake made Brazzos sign the permit in lieu of an MOC number. You should have seen his face – if he was any madder his head would have blown off."

"Okay, that sounds good. Seems like it all worked out." Liam was about to end the call, then remembered, "You said it was the second last batch. Are you also doing the rework batch? The paperwork should be in the control room."

"Don't sweat the small stuff, Liam. We have this and another batch to finish, then the rework batch will follow. We should have it all done by mid next week."

"Thanks, Jake. I'll leave it with you and see you in a couple of weeks."

—

Liam walked into Adelaide's CBD, a leisurely 3km walk. He did a bit of window shopping and then had a look through the State Library and the South Australian Museum. They had an exhibition featuring the history of the local South Australian Football League, and he enjoyed himself looking over the history of the early state champions: Basheer, Ebert, Robran and many others – even the later state champions that were a part of the expansion of the national game. He had a bite to eat at the cafe in the library before walking home, enjoying the quiet ambience of the inner suburbs.

Zoe drove Liam's car home late in the afternoon and parked out the front, where there was a three-hour parking limit during the day. Visitors often had to juggle their cars, or park down the end at the Kingston Terrace in an open area near the parkland. They sat and made small talk before Zoe took a shower and got changed. She returned in a little black dress that showed her legs and hugged her figure.

"You look great, sis. Happy birthday." Liam got up to embrace her. "I have a gift for you from Cora at the Golden Grain."

"That's random," she chuckled. "They were nice people, I remember how good they were to us when Dad was sick."

She opened the small parcel to find an elegant necklace with a key. A note read: *'All our love, happy birthday dear Zoe. This is the traditional Filipino gift for turning 21. Love from Cora, Ben and Tina.'*

"That's so nice and thoughtful. Make sure you thank them for me." She fumbled with the clasp as she put it on. Liam loved his sister dearly and couldn't help but smile at her as she held back a few tears. She gathered herself. "Shall we go?"

Liam laughed as they walked out the back gate and down the laneway, arriving at The Lion inside a couple minutes. Zoe had already booked a table. She showed Liam through the hotel – an old master in the area. The grand architecture of the building and an elegant formal dining-room were the traditional features of the old Lion. Recently, the management had added casual, less formal spots under umbrellas with festoon lights out the back while retaining the initial cobblestone pavement. They stopped as they passed the famous Lion Wine Room. Zoe was in her element as she explained, "You can find all sorts of wines here, and they hold regular masterclasses and wine tasting events. It's kind of cool."

They found their seats out the back and Zoe ordered the Shaw and Smith sauvignon blanc for both of them. The setting was charming and the weather kind. Once the wine arrived and had been poured, Liam raised his glass in a toast. "Cheers, Zoe. Happy birthday."

After a quick clink of their glasses, Zoe responded, "Thank you. I'm really glad you came over. It's been a hell of a year, but ... '*we won't dwell on it, just another step in life's journey*'." Another clink of glasses.

"Cheers," they said simultaneously, smiling at each other. They enjoyed the meal and chatted the evening away, relaxed as always in each other's company.

—

CJ arrived for a morning cuppa the following morning, parking in what they called the wasteland off Kingston Terrace. While Zoe finished getting ready, Liam showed his friend around the house and got an update on what CJ thought of his parents' bed and breakfast.

Zoe found them chatting away in the back sitting room. "Time to go, boys," she commanded as she walked out the patio door.

The boys duly followed. They headed off for a lunch at The Kentish - another North Adelaide pub a block down from The Lion. As they entered, they saw everyone in the pub was decked out in the teal and black colours of Port Adelaide. The place was a buzz, full of anticipation of the big clash against the Fremantle Dockers. The Port Adelaide fans were always expecting to win, but this season had started badly without a win to date.

After lunch, the patrons filed out and walked together to the game at the Adelaide Oval, an informal battalion of the Port Adelaide army. Zoe had a season ticket and still had access to her father's pass for one more year. They had secured a guest pass for CJ and were on track to be seated well before the start. The best part of the day was the pre-siren communal singing of Port Adelaide's war song, *Never Tear Us Apart*. It was an adaption from the official song for the Liverpool football club *You'll Never Walk Alone*. Everyone stood tall and held their scarves aloft between each hand, swaying from side to side. The trio belted out the song along with 40,000 other rabid Port fans. It always brought goose-bumps to Liam's arms.

The game started badly for the home team as Fremantle were on fire and had several goals on board before Port Adeliade had scored. The Fremantle rucks were dominating, and their small forwards were everywhere.

Liam looked at CJ with a heavy sigh. "Might be a long day, my friend."

The crowd was boisterous and already unhappy by the winless start to the season. The love affair with their long-term coach was rapidly going south. Several fans were calling for his head and even some *boos* rang out as the home side made repeated errors. The crowd was seething, and you could sense a mutiny in the making.

Liam went off to the bathroom and to collect another round of drinks. On return he passed around the drinks and turned to CJ. "I learnt two things back there."

"What would that be?"

"Firstly, the patrons aren't happy. He, the coach, will need a miracle in this second half, or else he won't be able to walk back across the bridge. I reckon a lynching party is being organised in that bar." CJ nodded in agreement and Liam added, "Secondly, I found a cure for the stage frights at the urinal. You know when it's three-deep, and you're all lined up for ages. Then when it's your turn, and you step up and the wee doesn't come."

"Sure, happens to me every time." CJ laughed. "Always with a queue behind you watching and keen for their turn."

"Well, there I was with that stage fright sensation again, and about to backout and try later. For some reason I thought about my work bosses, the new dickheads Bullyboy Brazzos and the Muppet Man Statler. I took a breath and relaxed and peed all over them." Both boys laughed. "Maybe they are good for something after all."

The Port players must have been given a fair old bake at half-time, as they resumed with much more purpose at the start of the second half. The run and dare was like the Port Adelaide of old, and they slowly eroded the deficit.

"We can do this!" shouted CJ as the crowd rose in anticipation late in the match. The Port Power captain was still dominating, willing his team towards victory. In one final courageous act in the face of closing opposition, he bounced out of the tackle, took the ball, and snapped a goal from the 50m arch. The ball sailed through the goal posts as the final siren echoed around the stadium.

The crowd went berserk, as the theme song played around the ground. The coach stormed onto the ground, fists pumping high – a miracle was delivered. The fickle crowd saw him as a saviour and the un-official lynching party was placed on hold, for another week at least. The players flocked to their captain and the crowd embraced each other, hugging and kissing strangers. Liam, Zoe, and CJ were jumping up and down, too excited to speak even though they wouldn't be able to hear over the noise and the ongoing mayhem in the stands.

The walk back to The Kentish was a dream. "Can you believe what just happened?" laughed Zoe, with the crowd still singing and praising everyone, even the coach.

They queued to get into the crowded bar, with wall-to-wall fans in high voice. Smiles all round, pats on the back, three cheers for the Power. It was going to be a long night. Another rendition started: *'We've got the power to win, power to rule, come on, Port Adelaide aggression ...'*

12

THE WORK SAFE VISIT was scheduled for Tuesday and Billings was super attentive when Sandy arrived on Monday morning. "Good morning, Sandy," he chimed with a cheesy grin. Sandy thought Brazzos may have already spoken to him over the weekend, and maybe he was forced to acknowledge her worth. She nodded and moved into her office.

Billings followed her, and once she was settled at her desk, he asked, "Is everything ready for the Work Safe visit tomorrow?"

"Yes and no, it depends on how deep they dig on their focus topics." Sandy waited to see how he would react. She'd tried to give him the focus topics two weeks ago, but he hadn't been interested and waved her away. She'd just left the inspection preparation letter on his desk.

"Mmm," mumbled Billings, "explain the issues again, please, if you would."

Sandy, surprised by Billings's servility, thought it was a rare moment to reinforce her PSM role. She gestured for him to sit at her visitor's chair. "They've indicated they want to review our permit to work system, so they'll be interested in your system upgrade, the SWMS and the retraining activities."

Billings nodded and, feeling a bit more comfortable, enquired, “Do you think that will satisfy them?”

“Probably,” Sandy said. “However, we are well behind with permit audits so that may be an issue, and they may make that a finding. But generally, it should be good. I think you should stay away from your plan of all the operators becoming permit writers. It’s an aspect that can be reviewed later, and if you proceed it will need a lot more training and coordination.”

“Fair enough. What else?”

“There are four things on their inspection list, and they will have four separate auditors reviewing one apiece. The other topics include our Vessel Integrity programme, the Management of Change processes, and Operator Training.”

“When did we get this list and who will be responding on each?”

Sandy smiled at her chance to rub salt into his wounds. “The list arrived three weeks ago, and I raised it with you at one of the weekly catchups. You said you would look at it later, so I left a copy on your desk, if you remember?”

“Oh yes, of course,” Billings replied with a frown as he struggled to recall.

Sandy stayed silent while he went through his own mental gymnastics of how to get out of this. Then she spoke before he could dump it all in her lap. “I’ve spoken to Stuart Jennison, and he’ll look after the Vessel Integrity programme and get his maintenance planner involved. I will try and cover the MOC issues myself, but we have some big holes that could be a problem. Jim Statler will cover the Operator Training, and I have suggested you respond to the Permit system.”

A concerned scowl etched onto Billings’s forehead. He

wasn't ready for a Work Safe audit. He had been spruiking the upgrade to the permit system so he was the best person to talk on the subject. Thinking quickly, he suggested, "I'm not sure I'm the best to deal with these people. You know them better. Maybe you would be better to cover the permits as well."

Sandy knew this was coming and was prepared. "I can't do it, Barry. I'm already slated to cover MOCs, and I think it'll be a full-time effort to avoid getting any improvement notices. Besides, you're the person championing the permit changes. It will be good for you, and they are interested in talking to all the leaders."

Billings didn't respond and Sandy knew from past experience that he was still trying to find a way to get out of it.

He prances around when it's his stage, but a limp dick under scrutiny, she thought to herself. *I bet he finds a way to be absent tomorrow.*

Billings stood and made to leave. "Okay Sandy, we'll see."

Surprised, Sandy smiled and offered her thanks. "Two more issues, Barry, if I can have another five minutes."

He sat back down and gestured his acceptance.

"Firstly, the MOC coordinator role with Ernesto."

Billings shrugged. "Yes, what about it?"

"We didn't make the change from Liam to Ernesto with an official MOC document. That will be a problem. We can fix it now, but it will require you to raise the change request and get Tony Brazzos to approve it."

Billings sighed. "Why the rigmarole? Can't you just check it off?"

Sandy should have expected that response. She mentally counted to ten to diffuse her anger before responding, "MOC is a cornerstone of process safety, and the coordinator role is crucially important. We have it documented in the procedures and you're the element leader in our process management structure." Billings didn't reply, just looked at Sandy blankly, as if she were speaking in a foreign language.

Sandy added, "If we don't get this basic issue sorted, then the audit will crash down all over us. If we can just get it formally approved today, then it might even look good. At least it's a story with which I can work."

Billings nodded slowly in agreement but was troubled to explain. "I don't know how to raise it. Can you help? I'll talk to Tony and get him to get it done. What was the other thing?"

"Work Safe will also want to talk about the next Safety Case, and I had left a request for Tony Brazzos to discuss this matter with them. They will be here on Wednesday morning to review this in detail. Have you had a chance to follow up with him on that?"

"Sorry, no, not yet. Can you do that as well?"

"I can try, but they normally want to liaise with either the CEO or the site manager. I thought Tony would be better than Paul De Zaale." Sandy knew Billings had forgotten the request, so added an extra barb. "Can you ask Tony if he's available? It'll help a lot if he can meet with them."

Billings was now in a bind. He didn't answer Sandy, opting to simply walk away. Sandy felt like a troublemaker, but these people needed to step up.

—

In the plant, the T-campaign had come to a halt with late staff withdrawals over the weekend. Statler was fuming and in the morning meeting with his team, he yelled at them all, sparing no one. He was covering for O'Donoghue and was concerned that these delays were now going to be attributed to himself. It would make him look bad as they still had two batches to finish and then the rework batch. He left the shift team to juggle the operator coverage and to increase the priority for finishing this campaign. His urgency was not reflected by the shift team, who collectively knew it was always futile making product this late in the season. However, the matter became a moot point when the hot baths sprung a leak and needed welding repairs.

13

TUESDAY MORNING CAME AND the Work Safe team were set up in the conference room with a couple of spare offices assigned for break-out interviews. Albert Cohen, Work Safe's lead investigator, introduced his team of four, which included himself. Albert was also the Work Safe contact for Agro Alliance and had worked with Sandy for several years. He was a tall man, affable with years of experience in workplace safety.

The plan was for each inspector to catch up with the subject matter spokesperson from Agro Alliance and then follow through with the specifics in the field. As expected, Billings hadn't fronted, and had arranged for his new deputy, Natalie Marron, to fill in.

Sandy met the MOC inspector, and they set up in one of the breakout rooms. With her experience in process safety, she managed all the questions with ease. She was able to show the inspector the procedure and the electronic database which Liam had meticulously maintained. Somehow Billings had convinced Brazzos to progress the coordinator documentation and Sandy was feeling a bit better, until they wanted to meet Ernesto.

A full day of interviews and investigative reviews were exhausting. The visit was concluded with a close-out meeting where the Work Safe team gave their preliminary feedback. Tony Brazzos had been invited but elected not to attend. Cohen noted with disappointment that both the site manager and the safety manager hadn't taken the time nor the interest to attend, but was allayed when Natalie indicated that she had apologies from both.

"Sorry, Mr Cohen. Mr Brazzos was unfortunately called away for an urgent issue, and Barry Billings was in that as well. He sends apology and they'll catch up with you tomorrow."

Sandy wasn't so sure, sensing a coverup. *However, time will tell.*

Albert summarised the Work Safe teams' findings, commenting that there was evidence of systems in most areas, but the team had found several action items that would require a follow up. He indicated that there would be a summary of the actions in their final report and there was no formal Improvement Notice at this stage.

Stuart Jennison, feeling confident that he had done well in his area, took the lead, acting as the group spokesperson. "Thank you, Albert. Can you explain some of the detail of the main issues you found and what do you mean by 'no notice at this stage'?"

"The issues are of some significance, and we expect that you will address them in a timely manner," Albert replied. "As such, and in the spirit of this inspection, we don't feel that we need to use the legislative process. However, if they remain unaddressed, we have the right to escalate them with formal Improvement Notices."

Albert proceeded to outline the issues, prioritising the main concerns and leaving the smaller administrative matters for their report.

"Firstly, the permit system seems to have undertaken a substantive upgrade, and we are pleased that you're adopting formal risk assessments." Albert gave Natalie Marron an encouraging nod. "However, some of the permit writers seemed confused with the changes. We acknowledge the recent training, and we assume there will be follow-up reinforcement and closure of any gaps. Several of the permits that we checked failed to reference any MOC information, leaving out vital information. In some cases, we couldn't even find the relevant change authorisation. Additionally, your permit self-audit programme seems to have fallen into disarray in the last few months. There was no evidence of any self-audits, nor any feedback. This may have been conducted, but we found no evidence and the people we questioned were vague on details. There was more, smaller attention to detail issues, which we will cover in our report."

Natalie sat quietly, having been thrown under the permit bus by her boss, while Albert switched to the Vessel Integrity programme. Looking across to Stuart Jennison, he added, "The maintenance planning group seem well organised. We note that you have most of the trade persons engaged in planning now, which can be good and bad."

Albert continued, "It's not our place to judge the efficiency, but we acknowledge the increased focus. However, the scheduling of Asset Integrity inspections has slipped behind your own agreed schedule. Most are recent, and therefore they may be within your tolerance of acceptance, but again there was no evidence of this, nor any documentation of the control of change on this aspect. This is quite serious, and if these inspections had been delayed for more than a month, we would have issued a Notice and probably would have enforced a shutdown."

Jennison was stuck for words, so Sandy filled the breach. "Yes, Albert, the T-plant campaign has only recently been extended, and the team is aware that inspections are due. There were discussions about the approval to extend out the inspections and it is disappointing that we haven't followed up with the documentation."

Albert smiled back at Sandy, knowing full well this was an attempt to smooth the situation. "I accept your word on that, Sandy, but from an auditor's perspective if there's no evidence then we can't assume anything. Even an email trail that highlighted the discussion may have assisted, but this is just another example of detail." He looked across at Stuart. "I trust you understand and appreciate this point."

"Yes, we need to be better. Point noted," Stuart responded meekly.

"And while we're talking about Asset Integrity, we couldn't find a register for your slings, ladders, or lifting equipment. If they exist, no one could tell us where it is. It certainly wasn't in your maintenance management system. One of the fitters indicated that it used to be in the storeman's office, but now all that is up with purchasing. That's a problem you need to sort out straight away."

Albert switched tack to discuss the operator training programme with Jim Statler. "Your operators seem eager and they were very responsive. They also seem to be quite new and inexperienced. We couldn't find any documentation on their training or their competence assessments for the task. When we asked them, they indicated the training was under supervision of their shift supervisor. They didn't seem to know all the technical detail of why they took certain actions." Albert continued to stress the importance of solid understanding by all operators of critical safety issues and that the systems that relied purely on supervision were not robust.

Jim Statler frowned as he struggled to fully comprehend the message. "We've had a significant restructure, and we're still working through the training details."

"Maybe so," countered Albert. "That might work for non-hazardous activities, but it's unacceptable for a major hazard facility and for situations with high-risk work. You should have a documented training plan, a skills matrix and action items to ensure all persons are competent for their task." He paused briefly. "The team seemed genuinely capable, but we can't be assured that they're competent. This issue was bordering on being a Notice. I'm sorry to be so blunt, but this is life and death stuff we're talking about."

Sandy was silent, internally pleased that these new managers were getting a PSM lecture. *This is just the message these guys need,* she thought. *I'm so happy, maybe now I might get some cut through and attention.*

Albert then looked her way. "Sandy, your MOC system had good structure. We found ample evidence of self-audits and good change management risk assessments. It seems that your coordinator was on top of it." He looked down at his notes. "That was Liam O'Donoghue, I believe."

"Yes Albert, Liam is a stickler for detail and has been doing a lot of work in this area."

"Maybe, but it seems to us that it has variable coverage.

We found several work permits on things that, to our eyes, looked like changes. Most were small but the detail on change management was absent. Liam may be an agent for the system, but it doesn't seem to work unless it's under his nose."

Sandy knew this was a fair observation and she had been telling the managers this for months.

"Furthermore, Sandy, the recent switch of coordinator to Ernesto Gonzales is a problem. The paperwork seems to be completed, but we wonder whether Ernesto really has the skillset for the role. He seemed totally out of his depth when questioned."

Another pause, with Sandy unable to answer nor disagree. Albert added, "I know it was not your decision, but my question is for Mr Billings and Mr Brazzos. They were the signatures on the MOC, and I would like to ask how this appointment is demonstrating good governance on change management. The MOC coordinator has a responsibility to ensure oversight on changes and particularly where high-risk activities may be involved. From my perspective, despite how well-meaning Ernesto may be, he struggles with the basic change management concepts. It appears he's just a paperwork administrator when we would expect much more."

Albert took a sip of water and looked around the room. "Finally, while we were doing permit checks, we found an example of a permit which had issues across all our focus areas. A high-level switch was apparently faulty, and a work order was raised to remove the switch and insert a blank in its place." Albert frowned as he gained Sandy's attention. "No MOC was raised." Then directing his attention to Natalie. "The permit made no reference of the obvious change, nor any indication of any authorisation." Then switching his attention to Stuart. "The tradesman didn't understand that it was a safety critical item, despite a tag on the device to that effect." And then finally addressing Jim. "And you allowed the plant to operate after removing the safety device."

Jim recoiled in surprise then cautiously said, "We had the level control working and there's still a relief valve."

Sandy dropped her head into her hands as Albert resumed a lecture about layers of protection and reduction of risk to an acceptable level. "Jim, firstly, relief valves and high-level switches are completely different. Secondly, if your safety design stipulates a high-level switch and you claim this as a layer of protection, you cannot, I repeat CANNOT ..." raising his voice, "operate without it. THIS IS FUNDAMENTAL. If your supervisor didn't immediately shutdown when I requested him to do so, then I would have issued a PIN on the spot and shut you down myself."

The Agro Alliance team were subdued. Albert sighed, took a breath then offered, "This is all a lot to take in, but frankly it's quite simple stuff that should be bread and butter for Major Hazard Facilities. We'll let you reflect on our feedback. I look forward to meeting Mr Billings and Mr Brazzos tomorrow."

14

CARSALES.COM HAD A FEW interesting options to consider. Liam had poured over the site for a few days and had Zoe set up for a day of searching. Tuesday morning and she had the rest of the week off to spend with her brother. Breakfast of toast and tea awaited her when she came into the kitchen. Seeing Liam's preparation, she smiled and asked, "Where to first, boss man?"

Liam had his computer open and was making separate notes on his forever handy notepad. "There's a few I've marked out, but they're all over the place. This might take a few days, or longer if we don't find anything."

Zoe smiled. "I'm all yours, but you do know that this idea is totally too much, totally over the top."

"Not really. The sacrifices you made with Mum and Dad were over the top. So please let me show my appreciation. Besides, you can't be part of your Adeliade scene in Dad's old Mitsubishi."

Zoe looked over Liam's shoulder at his notes. "What sort of car are we looking at? I assume I'll get some say in this decision? You have one marked in Morphett Vale."

"Yes, an Audi. It could be your stye and it has low mileage."

Zoe was thinking about her aunt and uncle in Victor Harbour and killing two birds with the one stone. “Why don’t we look at that one first, leave now and then trek on further south and catch up with Aunty Julie? I’ll give her a call now. She should be home and that way we can free us up later in the week.” Zoe loved her aunt and uncle, and had committed for a catch up this week for her birthday anyway.

“Alright,” answered Liam, “do that and I’ll call these people in Morphett Vale, and another small BMW on the market in Glenelg. We can get to both by mid-morning and still have lunch with Julie and Joe.”

Zoe went back to her room to grab her bag and make a call, while Liam went around to the wasteland to retrieve his car. Fifteen minutes later, they were on their way.

Zoe advised Liam that they had a booking at 12:30pm in the bistro at the Crown Hotel in Victor Harbour. “It’s Julie’s favourite place. Apparently they eat there at least once a week. Maybe we can do the walk across to Granite Island or catch a horse drawn ferry. It’s been a while since I’ve done that. Dad used to love it, so that would be kind of fun.”

“Absolutely, Zoe. Let’s book it in.”

The BMW in Glenelg was disappointing. It smelt of stale cigarettes and that was an immediate no for Zoe. “Sorry, that was a bummer, but you never know without looking,” Liam said. “Hopefully, the Audi will be better.”

“You know I don’t need a fancy car. Why don’t I take yours and you get a new one?”

“That’s not in my plan. Don’t worry, we’ll find something, that was just the first.” Changing the subject, he added, “How often do you get down to Victor Harbour?”

“Not as often as I should. Last year I took take Dad down

there every two or three months, but since his funeral I've only seen them once, in January."

Julie was their father's older sister, and they were always close. She'd moved to Victor Harbour after she married Joe as he ran a bakery in the seaside town, while the rest of the family stayed in Adelaide. Zoe and Liam would spend some part of every summer holiday with their aunt – a tradition that was set in stone. Julie and Joe had both retired in the last twelve months and they purchased a caravan and were now regular 'grey nomads'. They went up the middle to Darwin in November last year and only got back in January.

Zoe screwed up her face as she looked at Liam. "Don't get me wrong, it'll be good to see them again, but I'm expecting the twenty questions."

"What do you mean, twenty questions?"

"You know: What are you doing? Any boyfriends? Ae you going back to uni? Etcetera, etcetera."

"Good, it saves me pestering you as well. But can you add another one to the list? What are we going to do with Dad's house?"

"I really don't know, Liam. Is it urgent?"

"No, not urgent, but it isn't a destination place for either of us, and we could cash in and make new plans." Liam wasn't pushing, but it was an issue that needed further consideration.

Zoe agreed but was hesitant about the timing. She had so much on her plate and wasn't ready in her mind. They debated the pros and cons while they looked for the Morphett Vale Audi, which the owner had left at his workplace at the Morphettville racetrack. The inspection was quick and unhelpful. The car was boxy, according to Zoe, and the price was too high for the mileage.

With the searches now abandoned for the day, Liam drove on towards Victor Harbour. The discussions continued about selling the North Adelaide property. They agreed that it could wait, but that they would get a couple of agents around in the next week while Liam was still on vacation. He had his eye on the fuel gauge and signalled into a BP at Mount Compass. They were only twenty minutes from Victor Harbour, but Liam hated running low. He still remembered the near disaster on his way over in Ararat. After filling up and paying, he returned to the car with a couple bottles of water. He passed one to Zoe and asked her to get his travel diary from the glove box.

Zoe laughed. "Don't tell me you're still filling out that travel diary?"

"Too right I am. Important stuff."

"My brother, a class one weirdo. Some things never change. Do you always fill this out?"

"Without fail. I don't get back on the road until it's done, even if I must move away from the bowser to let someone else in."

Zoe just shook her head.

They arrived at the Crown Hotel just after 12:00 noon and parked out the front, opposite the park. The view over Warland Reserve was exactly as Liam recalled, remembering days when there were stalls and attractions in the back corner near the horsedrawn tram station.

Even though they thought they were early, they hadn't beaten their relatives, who were already at the table enjoying their midday refreshments. Hugs and kisses all round as they reunited. "So good to see you both," Julie proffered as she squeezed Liam.

"Sit, you two. Let me get you a drink. What would you like?" asked Joe after shaking Liam's hand and giving Zoe a peck on the cheek.

Liam looked at Zoe and she nodded. "Thanks, Joe, that would be good. Just a pale ale for me and a white wine for Zoe, sauvignon blanc, please."

Over lunch, they caught up on the travel to Darwin and then the twenty questions began. "Zoe, what are you doing now?" Julie started. "Are you back to uni?"

"I'm working up in the Adeliade Hills at a winery, learning marketing and doing work in the tasting shed." Zoe noticed Julie's furrowed brow, so she pre-empted the follow-up question by adding, "It's good for now, but not long term. I just need a short-term option, and it's a load of fun. I think I might go back to uni next year and study science. Since Mum was sick and then Dad, I would like to get into medical research. In Dad's case, there's not a lot known about the causes and the current focus is on treatment, so that seems like a place to start."

Liam suspected this was her plan and just sat back in silence but beamed at his bright and talented sister. His turn was next as Joe asked him about his work. "The work was good, Joe, but recently there's been a big change of leadership and I think the place is falling apart."

"How long have you been there now?" asked Julie.

"Just gone three years in January. I'll stick it out and see how it goes. I might be looking for a change."

Zoe jumped in, saying, "But he may have to get that cleared by Sarah, the new lady in his life."

Julie gave a small cheer and extracted the details, Zoe smiling as Liam took the heat. But her turn was coming, when Julie rounded on her, "And what about you, Zoe? Have you got a young man on the go?"

The smile evaporated and Zoe shook her head. "No, not at the moment. I haven't had time for that with Dad, and now ... I still have things to sort out. Maybe in time – not looking but I'm still open. Maybe the Port Adelaide captain might come available."

They laughed through lunch and dessert. Joe insisted on paying – a gift for Zoe's birthday, with a promise of a shopping day with Julie to follow. Afterwards, they all strolled across the park and over to the causeway. Zoe and Liam said farewell to their uncle and aunt and purchased tickets for the horse drawn tram. A round trip with nothing to do, other than relax and remember their childhood.

It was middle of the afternoon when they got back from their trip across the causeway, time enough to grab a couple ice creams and start the hour-long journey back to Adelaide.

As they came back into the Adelaide CBD, they were driving along West Terrace when Liam spotted the Lexus dealership. He slowed and turned in. "Let's have a look at a Lexus, sis."

"No way! They'll be too expensive."

"Maybe, but let's have a look anyway."

As soon as they parked and within moments of getting out of their car, the Lexus salesman was strolling towards them. "Hey guys, can I help you with anything?"

Liam nodded, noting the Lexus name badge 'Mitch'. "Maybe. We're just looking at options. I'm helping my sister consider trading in and upgrading. What have you got, not too big, reasonable price ...?"

Mitch waved them to follow him. "This is a new car yard but we do have some used cars nearby. But while you're here, let me at least show you some of our Lexus options."

They followed him into the showroom and looked over several cars; most were too big and too expensive. Mitch then took them to the smallest on the range: the IS 250. "This size might be your best option. You can get it in a range of fit outs, sports, luxury, or a combination. We have an ES version if hybrids are your preference. Have a seat and check it out." He opened the driver's door and stepped back to let Zoe take a seat.

Zoe was beside herself with excitement but was playing it cool in an attempt to withhold her eagerness. "Not bad. I'd need to have a drive, but how much does the basic model cost?"

They took the black demo IS250 out for a drive, and Zoe instantly felt the difference in handling compared to her father's Mitsubishi. "It drives well, but look, it has a sunroof and it'll be way out of our league."

"I'm not so sure. Let's see what the final price is and how much they can do for a trade-in," Liam said, thinking this might still work.

Back at the car yard, they did the salesman dance with Mitch on the price and trade-in, not getting to anything definitive. "Take the car overnight, drive up to the hills tomorrow and come back with your Mitsubishi and I'll get the boys to look it over," Mitch suggested.

Zoe's eyes nearly popped out of her head. "What do you mean, just take the car?"

Mitch smiled at her. "To be honest, Zoe, the best sales

representative is the car itself. After 24 hours, you will want it. I can't give you a fixed price yet, let's say $49,900 and then the trade-in to be discussed."

The siblings looked at each other, musing over the offer.

"Take it, leave your car and keys here. I'm relying on the car selling itself. Come back in tomorrow and let's talk. Absolutely no obligation."

15

THE HOT BATHS WERE repaired and the leaks had been re-checked. After extensive work, they were finally returned to service mid-morning on Wednesday. Along with the labour shortages over the weekend, the pre-emergent campaign had fallen behind schedule by four full days. Jim Statler was in a state when he found that there was still a batch to process and then the rework material to consume. How was he going to explain this to his boss? Brazzos had been angry yesterday when the hot baths were out of action.

Jim called his maintenance counterpart. "Stuart, what was the problem with those hot baths? We've only just got them back today."

"They were in a bad state and needed more than just patching and welding. We had to rebuild the complete back of one unit. That all takes time, I'm afraid."

"Shit. It's not good. Tony will blow a gasket." Jim went out to the plant to make sure the operators appreciated the urgency and were starting up again.

When Brazzos arrived at the plant that morning, he decided to drive straight into the plant to talk with Statler, annoyed by the lack of progress with the T-plant campaign. Supposed delays and issues about hot baths had him fuming. *I'll kick some arse,* he thought.

The gate guard stopped him and asked for a pass. Standard protocol for all cars. Brazzos wasn't happy and angrily berated the guard. "Are you joking!? Don't you know who I am?"

"Yes sir, but my orders from security are to have a pass for all vehicles that are not making a delivery."

"That's bullshit. Talk to whoever and get this gate open. I'm not in the mood for this sort of shit. You can tell Statler I have a delivery for him."

The guard retired back into the gatehouse and called Barry Billings. He took a few moments to answer, while Brazzos blasted his horn. "Mr Billings, I have Tony M at the gate, and he wants authorisation to take his car into the plant. Can you arrange a pass?"

"Just let him in, for goodness' sake. I'll get a pass to you this morning." Billings hung up, exasperated and not wanting to debate the issue.

I'm just following protocol, the same protocol that you guys lectured the guards about last week. The guard was still mumbling to himself as he raised the security barrier. *Obviously two sets of rules, one for everyone and one for the toffs!*

Brazzos drove through, only to come to another barrier. Some operation was about to be conducted, and the unloading operator was positioning a barrier to restrict the area, temporarily blocking the roadway. Brazzos blasted his horn again, wound down his window and shouted at the operator.

The gate guard heard the commotion and peered out his doorway, smiling to himself. *What a tosser!*

The unloading operator walked towards Brazzos's car and began to explain he was unloading some flammable material and had to block the roadway. He indicated that it would take around forty minutes and suggested that Brazzos reverse up and park, then walk around through the internal plant if he wanted and if he had his helmet.

"That's not good enough, buddy. Just stop what you're doing and let me through or else I'll have your job."

The operator stood his ground. "Sorry, but I have my orders. You will have to talk to Statler." Then he turned his back and rolled his eyes at another nearby operator, indicating that this bloke was a wanker.

"What's your name, buddy?" Brazzos spat. The operator pretended he didn't hear and walked off.

Brazzos was fuming and called Statler. "Get down here and sort out this prick!"

"What's the problem, Tony?"

"Don't give me *what's the problem*. Some prick acting like the sheriff in a cowboy western has blocked the road and won't let me through."

"If we're unloading then that's the safety requirements, and it's an important—"

"I don't give a shit!" Brazzos cut in. "This turd isn't in charge. I want you to come out and put him in his place. Open the road and let me through. Do you hear me? It will be your job as well as this idiot's if I don't get action." He ended the call and blasted his horn again.

Statler came out of his office, flustered and annoyed. He approached the unloading operator and engaged in a stand-off, arms waving and pointing. A few minutes later, after shutting valves and disconnecting the delivery tanker, he pulled the barrier back to let Brazzos drive his car through. Brazzos glared at him as he drove by, but the new sheriff just glared back.

Statler was carrying a spare helmet and safety vest, knowing Brazzos would be without his company issue, and thus avoiding a potential public conflict if he was wanting to visit the T-plant. Brazzos had stopped his car on the road outside the plant, middle of the road with no consideration of parking on the side, got out and slammed his car door.

"Who the fuck was that prick? I'm not happy." He snatched the helmet and vest from Statler. "Now show me what's going on here."

"Well, we've had some issues with the hot bath repairs. They're back online now, and we are heating up."

"Always problems. When will this campaign be finished?"

"We still have one batch and the rework to go, so maybe tomorrow or Friday."

Brazzos stormed off towards the plant, with Statler trailing behind. He burst into the control room to find the shift supervisor and the T-plant operator sitting at a table having morning tea. "There's no time for coffee breaks. You guys are days behind with this campaign. Get your arses into gear and get it finished. I don't want any more delays." Turning to see Jim Statler standing at the door, he added, "Do I make myself clear? No more delays, this needs to be wrapped up by tomorrow. Got it!?"

The supervisor and the operator shrugged their shoulders behind Brazzos's back, while Statler offered a weak nod. "Yes Tony, no more delays."

"Good." And with that, Brazzos stormed out and drove off, leaving the helmet and the vest on the side of the road.

Clarry, the supervisor, sidled up to Jim. "Wow, what was all that about?"

"Mmm, I think that was what you call 'shit flowing downhill'." Statler sighed and shook his head like a defeated man as he eyed Clarry. "Best we get this campaign finished."

—

While the Brazzos histrionics were playing out, Sandy approached her boss to check on the plans for the Work Safe visit with Brazzos. Billings just got off the phone and saw Sandy standing at the door. "What do you want now?"

Sandy halted with the abruptness of Billings's remark, her face dropped in shock. "Just checking about today's meeting with Work Safe. Are you ready?"

"What the fuck, this is all your fault?" he yelled back.

"I beg your pardon! What are you talking about?"

"This Safety Case crap. They are just making paperwork and getting in the way of progress. And you ..." He pointed aggressively at her. "The likes of you just kowtow down to them. *Yes sir; three bags full, sir.*"

"I don't appreciate your language or your tone. You can't talk to me like that." Sandy was fuming, with tears not far behind.

"I don't care what you think. I'll tell you what to do and you need to shut up and listen."

Sandy's mouth opened and closed, too stunned to speak. *Two days ago, you were buttering me up, then you didn't have the guts to show up yesterday, and now this tirade completely out of the blue. I'm not having it.*

It was classic Billings. His management style was erratic and unpredictable at best. He had no process safety experience and was hardly suited to the detail of a major hazard facility. It had always puzzled Sandy how he was seen as suitable, and it spoke poorly of the governance by De Zaale and Brazzos. They were probably in the same ignorant headspace as Billings. However, this current outburst was bizarre. Sandy had no capacity to feel sorry for the man but now began to think he might actually suffer from some sort of disorder. She wouldn't be surprised if he has a multiple personality disorder.

Sandy glared back at Billings. "You're not well. I'm not taking this. Sort the meeting out yourself. I'm going home."

"Get back here, you bitch. You can't go home unless I say so." Then, as Sandy walked off, he repeated, "GET BACK HERE!" turning several heads in the adjoining offices.

Sandy packed up her belongings, cleaned her desk, and left the Safety Case binder in her top desk drawer. She marched out without talking to anyone, holding herself together until she got to her car. As she drove out, she called the head office in St Kilda Road. When the receptionist answered, Sandy asked to be put through to HR.

She waited a few minutes and was already at her car when a voice came down the line. "Hello, this is HR, Michelle Buchanan speaking."

—

Brazzos was back in his office when Suzi reminded him that he had a meeting with the Work Safe inspector later in the morning.

"Shit, I don't have time for them now. Get Billings on the line and have him sort it out. I'm too busy."

Before Suzi could even pick up her phone, her target appeared at the door. "Mr Billings, good, you're here. I think Mr Brazzos wants to talk to you."

Billings barged past Suzi's desk and entered the inner office, slamming the door behind him. "Tony, this is shit, my team is falling apart. They fluffed around in yesterday's Work Safe inspections, and that Hudson bitch is not helping."

"Settle down, man. What's the problem?" Brazzos watched him closely, thinking he was about to have some kind of panic attack.

"I was talking with the team that met with Work Safe yesterday, and they reckon the feedback was bad. It's not my fault. Hudson has been running with the systems, and I think she's been deliberately undermining them and me." Billings was pacing up and down at this point.

"Are you sure? Seems to me she knew her stuff, and didn't she prepare all the documents last time?"

"That's exactly the problem." Billings sighed as he slumped into the Brazzos visitor's chair. "She should have this fully under control, and now she keeps spruiking about needing more help and doing extra analysis. She won't listen to me and refuses to do the stuff I need."

Brazzos could sense that Billings was floundering. "What do you want me to do about it?"

"Back me up and let's get rid of her. I can't work with her."

"That sounds drastic, Barry," Brazzos said, silently

amused at this meltdown in front of him. “What about the Safety Case? Won’t we be vulnerable without her?”

“Nah, we’re already vulnerable with her attitude and all her fluffing around.”

“I’m listening, but it still sounds a bit drastic. When is this Safety Case due and who will finish the work? Can you?” Brazzos looked at him directly.

“I’ll get Natalie Marron to step up and maybe we can get some consultancy assistance. It’s not due until November, so we still have six months.”

Brazzos raised his eyebrows. “Listen, Barry, settle down. I’ll think about it, talk to HR, and get back to you later.” As Billings got up to leave, Brazzos added, “We have some meeting with that Work Safe inspector today. What’s that all about?”

Billings took another deep breath. “It’s just another Hudson love affair with Work Safe. They want to tell us how we should be preparing the next Safety Case. I think Hudson has set them up to push her own barrow.”

“You’re getting worked up again, Barry. I’ll get Suzi to cancel the meeting. Can you get Suzi the name and contact for this Work Safe joker?”

“Thanks Tony, I’ll get that to her now. Thanks again.”

As Billings walked out the door, Suzi buzzed on the intercom. “Michelle Buchanan on the line, boss.”

16

THE WINE TASTING PARTY was arranged for the Thursday afternoon at Shaw and Smith in the Adelaide Hills. In the end, it was just a party of six. CJ, Liam, Zoe and three of her girlfriends. CJ's parents were apparently too busy at their B&B but probably felt out of place with the youngsters.

On the day before, Liam and Zoe made the deal with Mitch, trading in the Mitsubishi and taking full ownership of her new black Lexus IS250. They spent the day driving around Adelaide enjoying themselves. They could have taken Duchess for a run to Victor Harbour again or up to Hahndorf, but the former had been covered earlier in the week, and the latter would be tomorrow's event. Duchess was Zoe's name for her new car, founded on research on the internet where they learnt Duchess to be the mother of the famous Black Beauty. They elected to visit the old town of Gawler, an hour drive north to let the Duchess stretch her legs.

Zoe was over the moon with the car and Liam was as pleased as punch himself. He had budgeted $30,000 and when they offered $15,000 for the Mitsubishi, the wash-up was just $4,900 over his budget. *What the heck, it's only money, and she deserves it,* he reasoned with himself. *A few extra dollars from the inheritance is well spent, especially remembering the look on Zoe's face when she drove it out of the yard.*

Naturally, they took Duchess on the drive for Thursday's wine tasting and headed early for lunch at Hahndorf. They decided against The German Arms, wanting to try something else, something different, something non-German. They choose an Italian restaurant instead: Geppetto's. It was a balmy day and a table for two on the kerbside fitted the bill. It was a celebration and Liam treated Zoe as the final part of his birthday package. They ordered some Italian wine and toasted each other.

"So, are you happy with the car, Zoe?" he asked her.

"Really happy, thank you so very much."

"Well, you deserve it. Just another step in our journey." Liam raised his glass again. "Here's to a bright year ahead."

As lunch was served, Zoe asked her brother, "Have you missed work, or have you spoken with them this week?"

"Honestly, I haven't missed it at all. I spoke with them once and I probably should check in again. After lunch I'll make a call. I'll check that the T-plant campaign is finished. I'm a bit concerned about the recent maintenance switch of the agitator. I only hope they did a full risk assessment, but something doesn't feel right."

Surely the campaign would be done by now. Mario had the list of the post campaign maintenance requirements that he should be progressing. All the safety critical devices needed to be checked, and the vessels inspected. The operators should be starting a spring clean through the plant and finishing the 5S programme. There was plenty of work and lots to sort. Despite the notes, he feared that nothing – or very little – would get done. The boys gravitated to the minimum effort unless someone was calling the shots and pushing them along. The off-season could last several months, and the crew, operators and maintenance inevitably took it easy. Plenty of time to get it done.

Liam knew this mindset was a trap. It had caught him out in his past two seasons, leaving him panic stricken when the bosses inevitably wanted an early start to the campaign. Not this year; he was organised. Lists and notes were issued and hopefully Mario and the supervisors were on the ball. He started to think he should get back to keep it moving.

Zoe snapped him out of his daydreaming. "When we're finished here, I need to drop into work and arrange a few things. Maybe you could do some shopping or find a spot and make those calls. I'll come back and pick you up at 3:00pm and then we will go to the wine tasting."

"Sounds like a plan," Liam said. "And while we're making plans, I've been thinking about Dad's house. Let's get an agent to value it for now. You stay in it for twelve to eighteen months until after you decide what you're going to do. University or whatever. Let all the dust settle and we can review and look to sell next year."

Zoe smiled. "I'm glad you suggested that. I've been unsettled and don't want to rush anything. At the same time, it's ours to share. Don't you want your half to do something now?"

Liam nodded. "Of course that would be good. However, I'm a bit unsettled myself. The work situation is crazy and I might need to look for other opportunities. So, again, let's pause and regroup. Let's agree to discuss it in a year."

Silence crept over them while they considered their options, until Liam thought aloud, "You pay the rates while you have rent free access, and I'll continue renting in Melbourne for the moment."

"How's the house sharing working out? You've probably told me but who are the flatmates?"

"The house is a big old four-bedroom weatherboard house in Oakleigh, and the flatmates are mates from my uni days or from football. I went to uni with Ross and I played footy with Adrian and Rick."

"Are you playing again this season?"

"Maybe, not straight away. I know that's not the attitude. But work, Dad, and everything, I'm not in the right head-space at the moment."

The lunch wrapped up and Liam took off for a stroll down the main street while Zoe drove over to Shaw and Smith, only a few kilometres away. Liam had been calling Sarah at least twice a day but had completely ignored the plant. Quite normal, he rationalised, and besides, he was on leave. But now work was intruding into his thoughts again. He grabbed a Coke from a nearby shop and found a seat in the community area. *I should check with work, check the status.*

Liam called the shift supervisor's phone and got hold of Jake. "Hello, Jake, are you back already? I'm just checking how everything's going."

"Of course I'm back. You must be on vacation or something. Time doesn't stand still back here in the funny farm."

"Sure, I lost count of the shift roster. Is this your first day back?"

"You got it. You croweaters aren't as silly as you look."

"Ouch, have you finished the campaign yet?"

"Nah, still going. The Bullyboy is hopping mad, chewed

out the Muppet Man a few days back. We had low staff numbers last weekend, lack of interest I guess, and then the hot baths were out of action for a few days."

Liam frowned. "What was the problem with them?"

"Surprise, surprise. They were rusted out in several areas and sprung leaks. If you don't do the maintenance, then you know what happens."

"Sure do. The karma bus runs over you."

"I have the keys as well. Frank and I told that Jennison character last year in no uncertain terms and also the Muppet Man several times that they were on their last legs. But no, they know best. Don't you think I had a lot of fun pointing that out to them."

Liam laughed at the thought of Jake's revenge. He wasn't wrong. With maintenance now subcontracted out to this new group – 'Asesoria' – progress was terrible. They spent more time planning the next week's schedule rather than attending to today's breakdown. The hot baths should not have fallen into the never never land.

"How much more of the campaign to go?" asked Liam, refocusing himself back into the now.

"Not much. We should start the rework batch this afternoon. I have Johnno on overtime today and he has them in the bath now."

"I'll leave you to it then. Make sure Johnno follows the notes. We all love Johnno, life of the party, everybody's best friend, but keep him grounded with the instructions. Once this batch is finished, you can get Mario to start on the maintenance list."

"Yes, yes." Jake was about to hang up but remembered, "Before you go, tell me about the gossip on Sandy. No one's seen her this week, and apparently the staff up the front heard about some big bust-up. You're close to her, so what's up?"

Liam chewed on his lip. "All news to me. She wasn't happy last week, that's for sure. I'll give her a call."

After hanging up, Liam sat and thought about his friend and how unhappy she was last week. *She wouldn't bail without telling me. Something must be up.* He looked at his watch and with only fifteen minutes before Zoe was back, he resumed his window shopping. *I'll ring her after Zoe's wine tasting, so I won't be rushed.*

—

Normally the wine tasting event at Zoe's work required ten patrons, but the bosses had made an exception for one of their favourite employees. Zoe had funded the event and welcomed her guests on arrival. It was a forty-five-minute tutored tasting with the wines paired along with a selection from their seasonal cold larder menu. They were set up in an elaborate room with a full view over the vineyard.

Once everyone had arrived, they gathered around the tasting table. Zoe then welcomed them all. "Thank you all for coming. It's important for me to have you here. I didn't want a big party or any fuss, so this is just a small gathering. It's perfect for me and it puts me in a happy place. I trust that you will enjoy our venture on the Classic Wine Flight."

Liam coughed to interrupt. "Thank you, Zoe. It is a stunning view, and I can see why you love working here. Before we continue, can I ask everyone to raise their glasses in a toast to my sister. Happy birthday, Zoe."

Liam had pre-arranged a starter toast which was a surprise for Zoe. The group raised their voices in unison. "Happy Birthday, Zoe."

Liam and CJ looked at each other and smiled, CJ whispering in his ear, "Pity we're spoken for, mate. Her friends are knock-outs."

Liam clinked his glass again with CJ. "I noticed. I might still get a few names or numbers for my flatmates in Melbourne. If ever the girls are in town."

CJ slapped Liam on the back. "You do that."

The event went well, wines were excellent, and the group was in fine form. The forty-five-minute soiree was over before they knew it. Everyone hung around for another forty minutes, the staff not in a hurry to kick them out. Liam remembered to get some wine for Sarah and the Golden Grain crew and bought a dozen bottles of the sauvignon blanc. Then the group retired back to the German Arms for dinner. They collectively insisted on paying for Zoe.

After the dinner, Liam excused himself to make a call to Sandy. He left CJ in charge, watching him being the charming host with four young beauties and totally in his element. Liam grabbed a pint of HB and found a quiet spot out on the balcony. He thought he should text Sandy first, in case she wasn't taking any calls.

'Sandy, it's Liam here. Just texting to check if you are all right. I got a funny message from the plant. Can I call you?'

There was no immediate answer, so Liam just sat with his beer watching the pedestrians below. Five minutes later, Sandy texted back saying she was happy to talk to him, but that she would call him back in another five minutes.

Finally, ten minutes later, Sandy called, and Liam answered immediately. "Hello Sandy, I'm so glad you let me call. Are you okay? What's happened?"

"Thanks for contacting me, Liam." Sandy sounded flat, none of her usual positivity to be heard. "I don't really want to talk to anyone from the plant, not that anyone has bothered to call."

"I rang almost as soon as I heard something was wrong."

"I know. I'm happy to talk to you. You're the only real friend I have there."

"So, what happened?"

Sandy spent twenty minutes explaining the Work Safe visit and the Billings meltdown. Liam took it all in without interrupting and when she finished talking, he was equally flat. "Totally unbelievable. How stupid is that man?"

"Yes, and I don't think I can work with him anymore. In fact, I won't!" stressed Sandy.

"What're you going to do? Is there anything I can do to help?"

She sighed. "There's nothing you can do, and quite frankly I don't know what I will do. After the Billings tirade, I went home and called HR on the way."

"Good. Very good," Liam said, happy she had taken a stand.

"I spoke with Michelle Buchanan, who said all the right things. I don't know if she believes me. She said she would talk with Brazzos. I'm not sure it'll get anywhere. She didn't sound alarmed at all. Her manner was more about how she could control the situation. She suggested I take a week off, so I'm officially on stress leave. I have a sense that her version of HR is about managing the company issues, protecting their interests first, and little about supporting the 'H' in HR."

"Wow, I'm so sorry. The place is imploding. What next?"

"I've told Michelle that I can't work with a bully like Billings, and I've left it with her to sort something." Her voice faltered slightly when she said, "I remember my old mentor and good friend Alexander Scotland telling me: *'Accept what you can't change, or change what you can't accept.'* ... So I think it's time for a change."

"Strange to say, but well done."

"Thanks, Liam. I'll stay on stress leave indefinitely. I'll lick my wounds and look for something else."

"You are, and you will always be, in so much demand. The Agro jokers don't appreciate your skills and dedication. What's going to happen with the Safety Case?"

"I don't know. That will be Billings's problem and almost certainly the shit will hit the fan if he gets involved."

They spoke on for a few more minutes, covering Zoe's birthday and his vacation. Liam wished her well and closed, "Let's catch up when I get back. You'll be the winner in the long run. You can have the keys to my karma bus."

Sandy laughed, her first for several days. "Thanks. You and your bloody karma bus. Thanks again for the call, I feel a bit better after talking to you. See you soon."

17

THE THURSDAY SITE MEETING was short and sharp. Billings wasn't in attendance and so Brazzos asked the others how the Work Safe inspection went.

"Not as bad as I'd feared," Stuart Jennison answered. "I think they were happy with some of our systems, the ones they looked at. They had some issues and they've identified several items for follow up. They didn't enforce any Notices, so that was pleasing."

Brazzos scowled, clearly in a dirty mood. "Maybe, let's see. Billings has a few issues and apparently his staffer Sandra Hudson is away. We may have to cover for this Safety Case exercise. I expect all of you to fill gaps in the interim."

There was silence around the table, everyone apprehensive about what that might mean. Brazzos added, "De Zaale has contacts with the new maintenance management team, and they might be able to get someone to look after the Safety Case. Anyway, it's just updating the old and ticking some boxes."

The table remained silent, reflecting that it might not be that simple. The close-out meeting sort of indicated a lot more system management would be required. Jennison had his own doubts about this Asesoria group. The inside word was that the relationship with De Zaale was the key driver. It wasn't about the new group's performance history. They apparently sold a concept which captured De Zaale's interest. Rumours were rife that De Zaale was earning some retainer for their appointment. Jennison was making his own quiet enquiries to get some background on Asesoria, already finding a South American connection.

"Enough of that for now," demanded Brazzos, then looking at Statler, "What's the update from production? Surely the pre-emergent campaign is finished by now."

Jim confidently reported, "Almost finished. We still have the rework batch to run, and we should have that started today."

"Jim, 'almost' and 'should' are not good enough." He shook his head furiously. "This has dragged on all week. I'll go down there and give them a piece of my mind. I want this done. Done *now*, not almost."

The last regular batch of the pre-emergent campaign was finished late on the previous night shift. The next and last batch of the rework technical was staged ready for Johnno to charge. The T-plant operator had rung in sick, and Jake had called Johnno in on overtime.

There were only fourteen drums in front of the hot baths. Johnno spent the morning loading them and looking for the other two that he needed to make up for the standard charge of sixteen. Liam had mentioned that sixteen were available, so the night shift may have missed the others, or they were playing funny buggers with Johnno.

The fourteen were heating up when Jim Statler came into the control room, catching Johnno taking his lunch break with his feet up on the desk. "What's happening, Johnno? Is everything charged?"

"Not yet, Jim. They're still in the hot baths. Apparently, the rework stuff takes more time, impurities or whatever." Johnno nodded, impressing himself with his answer. "The only issue is we can't find the last two drums. Nothing seems to be in the rework area or over at the raw material store."

"Check it out and get it moving. You can expect a visit from Brazzos this afternoon and I want it all charged and going – fourteen or sixteen drums, but whatever you have."

"The standard batch is for sixteen and the tolerance is fifteen minimum," Johnno interjected. "What do we do if we can't find the other two drums?"

Statler wasn't happy and called out on his way out the door, "Just do a short charge and adjust the other ingredients. I'll get Jake to get you some help. Find these other drums, otherwise just get started." He slammed the door on his way out.

Johnno made his way to the hot baths and started pumping them into the process. Each drum had to be lifted by an overhead crane that was fitted with drum grabs, then transferred across into a decanting station from which the molten contents were pumped into the first vessel. After decanting the first four drums, Jake came up behind him. "What's all this drama that the Muppet Man's going on about? Fourteen or sixteen drums?"

Johnno explained his dilemma with the fourteen drums and that he had looked everywhere for the other two missing drums. "It's not my fault, boss. I don't know where they are. There was only fourteen here this morning."

"Okay. You keep pumping and I'll get someone over to help. I'll check the stores myself. Apparently this needs to get cracking and Brazzos will be down to give you some of his personal encouragement."

"I can't wait," Johnno sniggered. "While you're at it, can you check the batch sheet? It calls for a minimum of fifteen drums. Statler is pushing me to do a short charge. Will we need an MOC?"

"We will if we don't find the others. That will give Jim and Ernesto a task," Jake said as he left to continue the search for the other drums.

Johnno finished pumping ten of his fourteen drums when Oscar, a new employee, came over under Jake's instructions to help. Johnno had only met him once and shook his hand. "Thanks for coming over, not sure how you can help. You haven't worked this plant and I'm nearly done with this charging. Unless you can find the missing two drums, you can just hang around. Maybe move these empties onto pallets to take away."

Oscar went into the control room to put his bag down and read the instruction sheets. He saw that Liam had left notes stating the fourteen drums of rework were to be taken from the rework pad, and another two drums were marked up at the back of the T-plant. As Oscar walked out to check, he saw Brazzos had turned up and was remonstrating with Johnno at the hot baths.

"How come you are still charging this last fucking batch?" Brazzos shouted.

Johnno braced himself with a deep breath. "Rework sludge takes longer to melt, sir. We're going as fast as it is melting, and we're still looking for two more drums."

"This is a circus!" Brazzos fumed. "Get this batch charged. I want it started. Whatever you've got, just get it started."

Jake had arrived amidst the commotion. "I've double checked everywhere, and there appears to be only fourteen drums."

"All right then, make it fourteen. But let's go!" demanded Brazzos.

Jake nodded. "I'll tell Jim to arrange an MOC and we'll start the batch as soon as that's done."

Once Jake headed towards the production office, Oscar walked over and bravely interrupted. "I might know where the other drums are. They might be at the back of the plant, but the notes say they may need longer to melt."

Brazzos turned around and glared at Oscar. "What? Why are you guys just finding this out now? We don't have time. Just get these into the plant and get started. Forget the other two and forget that MOC baloney. I want this started now, or else I'll have your guts for garters. You understand?"

"Okay," answered Johnno. "Whatever, you're the boss." Oscar just looked at them, bewildered.

Brazzos stormed off as Jake and Jim came out of the production office. Brazzos saw them and yelled, "Get this going!"

Johnno went over to Jake to boast that he may have found the other two drums at the back of the plant. "I'm getting Oscar to get them now."

They agreed to try and get them melted and proceed as quickly as possible, leaving Johnno to get it done. Johnno, pleased he'd scammed the ownership of the find, took over and told Oscar he wasn't needed anymore. He thanked him and said he could go back to the day group. Oscar just shrugged his shoulders and left.

—

Johnno put the last two drums in the bath and continued decanting the others. The eleventh drum ran into difficulties. It looked like there was some solid material that hadn't fully melted, dreaded dregs. He rolled the drum on its edge but couldn't really see anything. It was dark inside the drum but it wasn't that much heavier than an empty drum anyway. He thought it would be okay, so he proceeded with the rest of them. He wasn't surprised to find that each of the remaining drums also had a small heel left unmelted. When he got to the last two recently found drums, they were still quite solid. Johnno had the agitator stirring and the vessel was hot and all ready to go.

He went for a smoke and coffee break while waiting on the last drums to melt. Jake found him in the smoke shelter twenty minutes later and asked how the charge was going.

"All good, boss," replied Johnno. "Just waiting on the last two drums to melt. It seems quite sludgy, maybe mixed with rust, dregs or other solids," he guessed, not really having any idea.

"Keep it in the hot bath until it melts, then charge as much as you can of the drum. We need at least fifteen drums for a charge."

"Yes, sir." Johnno saluted his boss.

Jake was still not happy with Johnno, thinking, *Frank's told me that he can be a lazy bugger. Frank always had to push him. I'm glad he isn't on my shift.*

Jake had had enough of Johnno's cavalier attitude and was losing his patience. "Don't get cocky. We must get this batch finished tonight. It's the end of the campaign and everyone's waiting for it. So, get cracking. Get it charged and started, and then Clarry's boys will finish it off."

Johnno didn't seem too fazed, put out his third smoke and wandered back to the plant. He checked his watch, still a few hours to shift change. He figured that these last two drums weren't going to melt in time. He thought to himself, *This hassle isn't worth it. Brazzos is on our back. I don't want him or Statler back down here spitting chips. I'll call it quits and let's get started. It was their call anyway.*

He took the last two drums out of the bath and decanted what he could – barely 100mm from each – before turning off the baths, leaving the sixteen drums collated on pallets to return to drum washing or the rework pad, and headed into the control room. He started the batch on auto and went back to the smoke shelter. He had an hour before it would be ready to drop and he still had time for a coffee before doing his three o'clock readings. After that he would take a sample and drop the batch. If all went well, he would have it in the second reactor and finished before shift change. *Jake may even be pleased, and he can tell Frank that I was on top of everything,* Johnno thought.

Jake followed up with Mario about some other maintenance work and then finished checking with his other plant operations. He had time for a cuppa with Willo in the gatehouse before shift change. Paul Wilson was on shift again and watching his screens when he heard Frank's knock on the door. "Come in, Frank. I'll put the kettle on. All quiet amidst your troops?"

"Yeah, pretty good. Bloody Johnson is giving me the shits though, lazy bastard." Jake looked at the clock on the wall:

4:15pm. "I've time for a quick one, then I need to ride Johnno on this last batch and get my report done for shift change."

A few minutes later they heard a noise, maybe a steam vent somewhere, and before they could comment, they were shaken by an enormous bang. The shockwave knocked them onto the floor. The security office back window cracked and imploded, while the files and the security radios flew across the room. Stunned, they looked at each other while the screens above them showed a massive orange plume spewing all over the T-plant and part of the production office block. Their first instinct was to remain on the floor and allow the earthquake or shock wave to pass over, but the orange plume was an ominous sign of more pressing problems.

In the front offices, Brazzos was walking past Suzi's desk when the building shook and items fell from her desk. "What the hell ..." Suzi's head whipped around, thinking it was an earthquake, while grabbing at her desk.

Then the site evacuation siren sounded everywhere, and five seconds later his phone rang.

18

LIAM SLEPT IN, RELAXING mind and body. Zoe and he had nothing planned for the day, perhaps a counter lunch then a follow up with real estate agents, or some shopping, or maybe nothing. Zoe had hinted about a trivia quiz at The Kentish in the evening. His phone rang, breaking his slumber. It was Sarah. *That's strange,* he thought. *She's on morning shift this morning. I wonder what's up?*

Sarah hardly waited for Liam to answer when she started, "Liam, have you heard? It's on the news this morning."

"Slow down, love. What are you talking about?"

Sarah struggled for words, her voice faltering as she tried to explain. "I don't know, that's why I'm calling you ... Apparently, there was an explosion at a West Footscray plant, and I think they said Agro Alliance. Liam, they said someone was killed."

"What? When was this?" Liam went to get up but slumped back on the bed. The unease that had been sitting in the pit of his stomach was rising and making him feel sick.

Sarah took a breather. "Thank God you're over in Adelaide. I don't know much else. I saw a report on the television when I was in a patient's room. They said it was yesterday, I think.

I was worried, even though you're safe. Phew, I just wanted to hear your voice. I know it's silly but ..."

"I love you, Sarah. Silly you. Thanks for the call, I'll find out what's happened. Love you."

"Bye, and Liam, stay safe." They signed off.

Liam bounced out of bed, still in shock by Sarah's news. He was smiling and felt the love and energy that Sarah had shown him, despite the shock of the news. Their relationship was tracking well; maybe it was the real deal. He made his way into the kitchen. *Shit, explosion, Agro Alliance, someone dead. Must be the synthesis plant – where else could an explosion occur?*

Zoe was already up and doing her breakfast thing, forever an early bird. "Morning, sleepy head. Do you want a cuppa?"

"Yes, sure, thanks." Liam walked into the kitchen half dazed. "I just got a call from Sarah. She says there's been an accident at my work and that someone was killed. It's on the news apparently – Melbourne news, I suppose."

"What!?" Zoe came over and gave her brother a hug. "Sit down and give someone a call, find out what's happened. I'll get you a bagel and a cuppa."

Liam sat in his chair slowly, eyes stuck on the table in front of him. "I feel sick."

He gathered his thoughts, ate his breakfast, and considered his options of who to call first. He should call Jim – but then again, he would rather talk with the supervisor or one of the operators, or maybe his mates in maintenance. Maybe all of them, but where to start? They would all undoubtedly be busy.

What will I say? Who was killed? What should I do? His thoughts continued to bounce around in his head, adding to his procrastination. *Enough!* He made a call to Jake on the supervisor's phone.

Jake answered immediately. "Hello, Liam. I guess you've heard the news."

"Just got a message now, I don't know much," Liam stuttered. "Some sort of explosion and someone was … killed. Can you … talk. What happened?"

"I haven't got long. It's mayhem here. The short story is that the T-plant formulation vessel ruptured and blew Johnno off the deck and covered him in tech. Shit, Liam. It was shit. The only good thing …" Jake stopped, choking on his words.

"I'm sorry, Jake. You were there. It's okay, tell me later. You do what you need to do."

"Thanks, Liam," Jake sobbed. "I'll need to talk to you later. Listen, the only good thing was … that Johnno was killed instantly. He wouldn't have suffered." Jake hung up.

"Wow, wow, wow," Liam exclaimed. He looked at Zoe as he struggled to say, "It was in my plant and one of our operators, Johnno – he was the one that was killed. I was just talking to him on the day I left to come here." Liam walked to the back door, hiding the tears from his sister. *Johnno, what have you done? Why Johnno? Shit shit shit.*

Zoe was almost in tears herself for her brother, beside herself on how to help. "Liam, I'm so sorry. You might have to go back. How can I help?"

"I don't know, Zoe. I guess so. I can't think straight. I'm going to have to talk with my boss or others before I know what to do." He looked up at his sister. "I might have to …" He left his sentence hanging while he stared blankly at nothing.

Liam made another cuppa and took it outside in the

courtyard, pacing up and down in thought, before he finally sat down and called his boss. Statler answered, “Thanks for calling, Liam. I guess you’ve heard the news.”

“Yes. I can’t believe it. It sounds bizarre. Do you know what happened?”

“An investigation has started. The plant is shut down and the police and Work Safe have set up barriers. I will need you back here. Sorry about your leave, but we’ll need your help.”

“Of course, I’ll head off this afternoon and come in on Sunday.”

“Thanks Liam, that would be good,” Jim replied, surprising Liam with a rare compassionate tone.

Statler spoke with Liam for another half hour, explaining and answering questions as best he could. The initial theory was that the new agitator had broken away from the vessel and it had knocked Johnno, while the contents of the vessel sprayed out and covered all and sundry, Johnno included. The source of the pressure build-up was the main mystery, but the sample pot vent and the scrubber lines appeared to be blocked and there was a pressure spike on the control room recorders. Jim speculated, based on what Mario and the supervisor deciphered, that the blockages led to a pressure build up and coupled with a potentially loose or poor fitting of the agitator, the agitator coupling failed.

Liam had a hundred questions; this all sounded too simplistic. *It’s a non-pressure vessel for one, and I’ve never seen pressure spikes before. Why was the sample pot or scrubber blocked? What force was required to launch an agitator from its coupling. Our fitters have never left loose or poor fittings. There’s something missing. I’ll find it; Work Safe should. I’d better get back.*

He went back into the kitchen, left his cup in the sink, and then went in search of Zoe. She was coming back from her bedroom and saw Liam at his door. "Did you find out anything?"

Liam sighed. "Not much. They confirmed that the operator was Johnno. This is all surreal. I have to go back. I'll pack now and get on the road by lunch time. Sorry to leave in a hurry."

Zoe pulled him into a hug. "Don't be silly. Of course you must go back. Keep me posted. Promise?"

"Thanks, will do. I'm sorry that this puts the real estate agent idea on the back burner. Let's think about it and talk later."

—

On the road, Liam called Ben at the Golden Grain and got his booking changed, explaining that an emergency had arisen and he was heading back to Melbourne early. It wasn't a problem, and Ben was only too happy to accommodate the change. He called CJ to debrief, apologising for leaving early and arranging to meet up soon, possibly in Sydney. He would call Sarah later, after her shift had finished, most likely at his break in Bordertown, if not then when he got to Horsham.

For the next hour, he kept reviewing the facts as he knew them. They made no sense. There was something wrong, something drastically wrong. They had processed hundreds of batches and there were no signs of any pressure, none that he could remember. He vowed to check the recorded history and to look closely at the trends from the pressure transmitter. Maybe it was the rework batch, but that didn't make sense either. There were no problems with any batches in the past couple of seasons when he had overseen the rework process, and none from any records or discussions with the operators. In fact, he recalled, even the rework batch mid-campaign when there was a shortage of tech, and there were no problems then. It made no sense, but it was a mystery that had led to the death of Johnno. He felt for Johnno; a lazy lad and not the best of operators, but still a nice enough person. No one deserved this.

Liam's thoughts turned to the bosses. Brazzos, Billings and Statler. They would be shitting themselves. De Zaale would be angry, and they would all be looking for someone to blame. *Fortunately, I'm not there and they can't make me their scapegoat. I bet they're more worried about a loss of face rather than about poor old Johnno.*

At a loss to rationalise everything, he called Sandy – he just needed to talk. Sandy had heard the news on the radio and was equally shocked. She didn't know any of the details and didn't feel that she could call, having already estranged herself from the place. She welcomed Liam's call as he provided a little detail and background – the little he knew.

Sandy was equally as puzzled as Liam. The T-plant was low on the Safety Case scenario schedule. Reactor 1 was a scenario because of the flammables, but reactor 2 was not. It was a fibreglass vessel with no pressure control. In fact, she reminded Liam, "It's an atmospheric vessel connected to a scrubber."

19

BRAZZOS AND DE ZAALE had been in collaboration since the news reverberated across their mobiles. Brazzos rung De Zaale even before he knew any details, agitated as he escalated his concerns. "Paul, we've got a problem down here. Some sort of explosion and we have sirens everywhere. Now I see police and an ambulance coming up the road. Now two fire trucks."

"Okay, you find out what happened, and I'll make calls at my end." De Zaale left his site manager to do the site manager stuff while he went into emergency mode. Within minutes, he had Buchanan chasing up HR issues, working through her relevant contacts and coordinating any support issues that these Aussies may have needed. He had marketing guys working with their media contacts to get a jump on any news narrative, and then he rang his legal contacts.

De Zaale and Agro Alliance used a high-flying law firm at the top end of town, one of Melbourne's Collins Street practices. They specialised in take-overs, mergers, and business practices, but after taking De Zaale's call, they referred him to another firm they had worked with previously. He made a call to RK Legal, a specialised firm with expertise in defending companies in cases of industrial accidents, workplace manslaughter, safety breaches or Work Safe prosecutions.

RK Legal were also based in the Melbourne CBD and when De Zaale called, he explained his situation and was put through to a partner Angelo Tambakis. De Zaale went straight to the point; "Tambakis, thanks for taking my call. Our legal firm suggested I call you to discuss our situation." He explained that an industrial accident had only just occurred and although he wasn't fully briefed, he feared a nasty outcome. "It appears that there has been an explosion at our plant in Footscray and there may be injuries."

Tambakis replied, "Hopefully it isn't too bad. You were right to call as soon as you could. If there's any serious issues, we can address them immediately. Always easier to set up protocols now rather than try and recover from a worsening position."

They spoke some more about the costs and making contact again as the situation evolved. Tambakis was about to hang up when his assistant interrupted and gave him a message. "Paul, I've just been handed a message. The news stations are reporting an accident at Agro Alliance on the news and saying people may be injured."

"Shit. Hang on a minute, Angelo. Let me check on the other line. Can you hold?" A couple minutes later, De Zaale was back. "Angelo, they tell me there's one person dead and no other casualties. Police, ambulance, fire brigade and Work Safe are all in attendance."

"Okay, okay." There was a pause from Angelo as he gathered himself. "We need to act immediately. I want you to tell your people at the plant not to answer any questions. Tell them, whoever asks, that you're reviewing the details and won't be able to say anything at this time. Tell them you'll be fully cooperating but that you'll get back as soon as possible. Also tell your people no written correspondence to anyone on any subject, even internally, no emails, nothing. We need to get all of this under 'legal privilege'."

"Will do. I'll get that sorted immediately."

"Paul, make sure you reach everyone, managers, guards, staff at all levels. We need to call a meeting tomorrow morning at the plant and make a forward plan."

"What time?"

"Let's make it 10:00am and we should have the relevant managers only. Work Safe, and maybe the police will want to take photos and start an investigation. You can't stop them, but no interviews for now. Work Safe or the police will trick people into saying stuff that isn't relevant. We need to control the narrative. Tell them to give you twenty-four to forty-eight hours to let the staff recover from the shock, and that you will make them available as soon as you can."

"That should suffice for now," Tambakis finished. "I'll see you in the morning and I'll bring one of our engineering consultants. She can conduct our own independent investigation, and she will need access to everything, but it will be under official 'confidential and legal privilege' copy."

De Zaale was relieved these people were taking control and had obviously done this before. "Many thanks, Angelo. See you tomorrow."

—

As soon as Jake picked himself up from the gate house floor, he told Willo to go into emergency mode. Willo knew the drill and immediately hit the evacuation button. Then straight away he called the fire brigade and an ambulance. Jake burst out of the gatehouse and sprinted back toward the plant, looking straight into what looked like an orange nightmare. There was no fire, but he still hit the sprinkler system as a natural reaction. At least it would be a blanket in case a fire or another explosion was in the wings, and it would chill the molten lava that had erupted from the T-plant. Operators and other staff were emerging from their areas, Jake yelling at them to follow the evacuation protocols. His first thought was for Johnno; *Hopefully the lazy bastard would still be in the control room.* He raced to the control room door with his heart pounding madly and his adrenaline rushing. The room was empty. *Fuck, fuck, fuck, where is he? Probably on the plant deck. No, please don't be on that deck, mate.*

Looking towards the plant, nothing but an orange coating everywhere. There was no sign of him at the hot baths and he could see the reactor vessel split in two and the agitator thrown askew across the landing, jammed into the plant support structure. He stood at the face of the mess, feverishly scanning for movement and yelling out for Johnno. Then he saw a body on the bottom floor to the left of the stairway. The agitator was dangling above, like an arrow pointing to the obviously dead Johnno.

Nervously checking the surrounds, Jake entered the cascade of the sprinkler system. He reached Johnno, and his worse fears were realised. He lay there lifeless, covered in molten orange lava with a huge gash on his cheek. *Mate, what's happened here? No, no way. What the fuck!?*

Overcome with grief and being drenched in the sprinkler

deluge, he checked Johnno's shirt, cold to touch from the downpour. He grabbed his collar and dragged him back to the control room entrance, then slumped on the ground next to Johno. Head in his hands, Jake was at a loss, hearing sirens at the gate. He summoned some strength and went out to the roadway waving to the approaching ambulance and fire brigade.

Jake's nightmare continued as the ambos checked over the body before pronouncing him dead. The fire brigade turned off the sprinklers and conducted their checks to ensure the area was safe. Soon after, a police car arrived and one of the officers spoke directly to Jake, who just stared blankly shaking his head. Jim Statler came over to Jake and put his hand on his shoulder. "Come on, Jake. Go with this young fellow," he said, signalling to one of the paramedics to look after him.

Statler then addressed the police officer, reporting that he was the production manager. He told her that he had called the site manager, who was briefing others in the administration block as required. When the officer asked him what had happened, Jim shook his head. "I don't know exactly. Just a loud bang, shook everything in the office. And this mess in front of us, looks like a process vessel has erupted."

The police officer excused herself and retreated to her car to make a call to her despatch. The paramedics were still at Johnno's side, on standby as any medical intervention would be futile at this stage. They left Johnno in position with a sheet covering him and joined Jim at the police car. The police officer advised them that the police chopper was in the air, and they had already enforced a fly restriction zone over the area for the moment. The news choppers would be up almost immediately but would be out of the area for an hour at least.

Jim just nodded, words escaping him. The paramedics advised that there was nothing more they could do and that their despatch had cleared them to leave. Their protocol was to hand over to the police, leaving them to contact the coroner and coordinate transport of the deceased person.

The day shift staff at Agro Alliance were all stunned and filed out of the plant with a collective heavy heart. The incoming afternoon shift was equally dismayed, while everyone stayed in the changeroom or canteen awaiting advice. Jim had contacted Brazzos who reluctantly agreed to close the plant for the day, but Jim needed to arrange skeleton crew to cover overnight. Everyone else was dismissed. Jim had to complete the mandatory incident notification report to Work Safe and he stayed waiting until they arrived for their own initial assessment.

In the interim, the coroner arrived. Two staff: one man and one woman in an unmarked white van. Surprisingly, these coroner assistants were small and light, hardly available to lift a big kid let alone a heavy adult. They struggled with Johnno, who while not large was still quite stocky and heavy. Jake was required to help, his nightmare going from bad to worse. With Jake at one end under Johnno's shoulders and the two coroner lightweights with a leg apiece, they lifted the lifeless Johnno into a body bag. Jake stepped back while the coroners zipped the bag, thinking, *What a nightmare. Are these guys for real?* The lifting party then put poor Johnno into the back of the van. Jake immediately walked away, only to be called back by one of the coroners. She said that the deceased had to be taken back out and turned around.

"You're fucking kidding me!" exclaimed Jake.

"Sorry, mate," the coroner said. "Even though the ambulance officers have pronounced him dead, we officially need to get a doctor to do the legal verification. We'll take him to an emergency ward, and a doctor can come out to make that call. Our protocol is to have the body's head closest to the rear access."

Jake was dumbfounded, blinking rabidly, while Statler just shook his head.

It was dark by the time Albert Cohen arrived, and there wasn't much he could achieve. He was able to connect with the police officers, take some photos and ensure the site was safely secured and isolated. Albert instructed Statler that it was now a protected zone – a crime scene, if you will. Nothing could be touched or moved until after Work Safe had completed a full investigation, planned for the morning.

—

Albert returned early the next morning with another colleague, Vanessa Campbell, and a specialist consultant they used for industrial accidents, Daniel Bourke. They had an arsenal of safety gear, cameras, clipboards, and notepads, and set themselves up in the production block meeting room. Jim gave them access and the basic induction on safety alarms, then left them to do their work, with Mario as their assigned escort, contact and go-between. Initially they were focused on reading the requested production reports and then spent time taking photos at the accident site.

The T-plant resembled an orange paint ball site and was still fully barricaded off, while other sections of the

Agro Alliances business were slowly returning to normal operation. Jim had made his morning rounds and was on his way to an emergency meeting with Brazzos when Liam called. The news had filtered over to South Australia, but this gave Jim the chance to recall his plant supervisor. Liam seemed shocked at the news of the fatality but was more than agreeable to return and assist. Brazzos had arranged a meeting for 10:00am and needed all his management staff in attendance. Jim was talking with Liam while he walked, thinking to himself, *It's good that Liam's coming back – he can take the technical lead. I can't be late for this Brazzos meeting!*

With everyone assembled, Brazzos welcomed Paul De Zaale and introduced the visitors from RK Legal team. De Zaale gave an overview of how sad he was of this very unfortunate accident and that they were all to cooperate as best they could to determine the cause. De Zaale stipulated that despite the loss, they all needed to pull together and that RK Legal was here to help. He invited Angelo to brief the team.

Angelo was a large man with a barrel chest and dressed in what looked to be an expensive suit, a matching expensive shirt, but he had no tie. He looked to be around 190cm, or 6ft 4inches in the old, and commanded attention with an imposing presence and a booming voice.

"Hello everyone, my name is Angelo Tambakis, and I'm a senior partner with RK Legal. RK stands for Rick Kelly, our founder, and we have been practicing in legal defence for industrial accidents for fifteen years."

The room remained quiet, with several just nodding or waiting patiently for the guidance to follow.

Angelo continued, "Let me introduce Consuela Garcia." He pointed to the lady with her hand in the air. "She's our point of contact for everything, and I'll get her to do the personal introductions with each of you after our briefing."

"Also, the same as Work Safe, we have our own specialist in investigating industrial accidents, and I introduce you to Sue Carpenter, who's seated next to Consuela. Sue will require an induction and an escort."

"I'll get Jim to arrange that," Brazzos called out, pointing to Jim Statler.

"Thank you, Tony," said Angelo, resuming control of the briefing. "This is a terrible event, and everyone will be in some state of shock. While that's understandable, it also leaves everyone quite vulnerable."

Angelo paused for a drink of water, then stressed, "What I'm about to say may sound wrong, but we also need to protect the company. Unfortunately, the accident has happened, and we must work out why. BUT," pausing again for impact, "and let me emphasize, BUT, we must be careful to focus on the facts and the facts alone."

Angelo pranced around the room and with a captive audience. "We have a few basic rules. These are golden and I stress that everyone must follow these, from here forth.

"Firstly, all correspondence on any matter, but in particular anything related to the accident, must be written with the following words on top." He strode across to the white board and proceeded to write: 'Confidential and under Legal Privilege.' Scanning the room while he waited for this to fully register, he continued, "I will have Paul or Tony circulate an internal email to this effect, which will also provide some legal standing to protect subsequent documents as well. This allows us some control over what is disclosable to the authorities. Unfortunately, anything already written or in the public domain is disclosable. We are effectively drawing a line in the disclosable sand."

Angelo again scanned the room. "It's important that everyone understands this first and most important point."

Having secured a room of nodding heads, he continued, "Secondly, everyone should cooperate with the authorities. It conveys a sense of remorse and believe me, it helps. Otherwise, they tend to think there's something to hide and that often prompts them to keep digging and dig deeper. It's a fine balance, but don't get too cooperative. Only give them what they request and only answer what they ask. Do not speculate and do not add extra detail. Keep your answers limited strictly to the scope of the question, nothing more."

Angelo paused once again while the information sank in across the room. "This is important. Little comments that might not mean much, may trigger cross-thoughts and lead to tangents and avenues that we can't control. Our control is already weak under this sort of investigation, but we can limit the damage by sticking strictly to the question. Do not stray. Again, is this clear?"

"Very clear," stated De Zaale, adding his authority to the RK Legal position and to reinforce the point for his staff. *I like these guys. Firm, strict, no nonsense.*

"And finally," Angelo resumed, "you have the right to be excused from questioning. I'm not sure this will be needed. It's done for people that may be separately accused or prosecuted. My very brief understanding of this incident is that this is unlikely. If it were required, we would need to set up separate and independent counsel."

The briefing continued for another thirty minutes as a monologue from Angelo. It left the room sombre and fearful to say anything wrong, precisely what RK Legal and Paul De Zaale wanted. Angelo's final requirement was that anything that was handed to the authorities or taken by them for their investigation must be recorded, and a copy sent to Consuela. Anything and everything.

The meeting closed and the Agro Alliance staff filtered back to their workplace. Brazzos and De Zaale retired to the De Zaale office. With a stiff drink in hand, De Zaale began, "What's your take on all this, Antonio?"

"It's a shit fest." He shook his head. "A major fuck-up somewhere, and my guess is poor maintenance."

"How can you be so sure?" asked De Zaale.

"I'm not really sure, but things don't just fall apart if repairs are done correctly."

"What are you inferring? Repairs?"

Brazzos shrugged. "Well, last week we had to replace the agitator on that vessel, and it looks like it's blown its mount in this accident. It might be early days and that might be too simplistic. But that's the first impression."

"Alright, Antonio." De Zaale refilled his glass. "Let's follow the RK Legal guidance to the letter and get through this. Did we lose much production?"

"One batch, maybe 10,000 litres," Brazzos replied. "That's a shame."

20

LIAM ARRIVED AT HORSHAM late in the afternoon, happy to find he was assigned his normal room. He took a quick shower then called back to the office to catch up with Ben and Cora. He wanted to relay Zoe's appreciation for her present and give them a couple of bottles of wine from Shaw and Smith. Declining their offer of a drink, he told them he was planning to have a steak next door and go to bed early. He would be getting up early and he wanted to be back on the road before dawn.

Sitting in a front booth of the Victoria Hotel, nursing a pint of pale ale, he placed a call to Jim Statler while waiting for his steak. He advised Jim that he was well on the way back and would call into the plant tomorrow afternoon to catch up with the supervisor. *Probably Frank would be back on shift,* he thought. Jim updated Liam on the Work Safe visit and said they had taken many photos and several samples and they would be returning on Monday. They had allowed the maintenance team to disconnect some items to further secure the site. The agitator had been taken down and moved into a marshalling area in the back of the maintenance workshop, which was also secured and restricted. Jim sounded pleased to have Liam back in the fold, probably freaking out with the technicalities.

"How are the operators taking it?" Liam asked. "Has there been any follow-up with Johnno's family?"

Statler hesitated. "Yes ... a bit hard to say. HR is dealing with Johnno's family, so I don't know anything else yet."

Liam thought to himself, *Translated, that means I don't know, nor do I care. Brazzos is probably breathing down his neck.*

Liam was unimpressed and slowly shook his head. "What about the shift team?"

"It's knocked them around a bit, but we're all back at work now and that should help them focus on something else."

After dinner, he retired to his room and called Sarah. She was happy he was coming back early but remained concerned for him about the impending stress of his work. They chatted away on other topics and promised to get together on Sunday. He texted Sandy and arranged to talk with her tomorrow afternoon after he visited the plant. He laid on the bed resting, struggling to fall asleep. He had the TV on in the background as white noise. Finally, the sound of shunting trains in the yard behind the Golden Grain induced slumber and he drifted off.

—

After a restless night, Liam was fully awake at 4:30am. He was up, showered, dressed and heading out of Horsham by five. Heading east into Melbourne, he had to fight the rising sun, so he planned a refuel stop and a bite to eat at McDonalds in Ballarat before the sun rose into his eyeline.

Being a weekend, the traffic was light. He made excellent time and parked in the Agro Alliance visitor's park at the front, right up next to the gatehouse.

Liam didn't recognise the guard; a temporary from a security company. He signed the out-of-hours attendance book and showed his employee badge. After he swiped through the turnstile, he headed to the changeroom but couldn't help but notice the orange smear and the twisted roof of the T-plant in the distance.

Frank was the supervisor on duty and he was at his desk when Liam walked into the office block. Frank looked up and stood to offer his hand in welcome – a standard custom Liam and the supervisors performed every day. "Good to see you, my friend. Glad you're here. Hopefully you can make some sense out of all this madness."

"To be honest, Frank, I couldn't rest. I had to get back." They shook hands. "How is everyone? It must have been horrible."

"I was very happy that I wasn't here," Frank said. "Jake took it hard, and everyone is still a bit shell shocked."

"No doubt. Any word from Johnno's family?"

Frank just smiled. "Do you know what? You are the only one in this management team to ask. The boys have got around them. But they're all a bit numb. It'll take some time."

"Has anyone collected his things? And what about his car?"

"All good. His brother came and collected everything. It's good of you to ask," Frank answered.

Liam put his bag at his desk, grabbed his notebook, and returned. "Can I look around?"

"I'm not stopping you, but the official word is that Work

Safe have taped off the area and it's still supposed to be secure." Frank grabbed his helmet and the two walked to the edge of the plant.

Liam gasped when he saw the scene. "What a mess."

"They took the agitator out because it was still hanging on the structure with its cable attached like an umbilical cord. The rest is the same as it was on Thursday afternoon." Frank showed Liam where Johnno was found and walked with him as they sombrely navigated around the site.

Frank pointed out the drums still on pallets and the stray helmet that was once Johnno's, which from a distance looked like it was cracked. As they walked over to the control room, Liam asked, "When are we allowed to clean up and get access?"

"Don't ask me, mate. We're last to be told. It's mushroom management here at the best of times, let alone in times of a crisis. You know that!"

Dean from maintenance and a synthesis operator, Rod Sheldrick, were coming down the road. They approached Liam and Frank, and followed as they all entered the T-plant control room together. While Liam was looking around, Rod broke the silence; "Hey, Liam, what's going to happen?"

"Sorry mate, I don't know. Your guess is as good as mine. Apparently, I have a meeting on Monday with an independent investigator and we'll supposedly be trying to work out what went wrong. I think Work Safe are running their own investigation and Statler told me yesterday that Workcover will be sending another team to take statements." Liam looked to Dean. "Deano, any idea of what the problem was? Statler was saying something about a fault with the agitator repairs."

Dean flared back. "I knew it. Slimy bastards trying to blame the fitters."

"Hey, don't get excited, I don't know anything. I think they're jumping to conclusion that the agitator went sailing. That's all."

"Maybe, but that won't explain why they successfully processed two or three batches between the repair and the accident." Dean fumed, starting to work himself up further.

"You're right, Deano. Let's see what the investigation reveals."

"Bring it on," Dean snapped his reply. "I smell a rat, and I'm looking at your Muppet Man and that Bullyboy from up front."

"Not sure what you mean. Let's just wait and see." Changing subject, Liam looked across at Rod. "Have you spoken with Johnno's family? How are they coping? What about Jake and the boys on his shift?"

Rod shook his head in silence. "They're all in shock. This is not good, Liam. The boys are shitty with management and like Deano said, we don't trust these bosses. I reckon they will be banking on a cover up. Can I have your word you'll get to the bottom of this?"

"One hundred percent, there will be no cover-up on my watch." Liam offered his hand to seal the agreement.

Rod accepted it and slapped him on the back. "Good, glad to hear it. I think we might look at getting union coverage. Since the Bullyboy has arrived, we've had no pay rises, he treats us like dirt, and there's a string of little issues that's irking us. He's taken the TV out of the main control room and expects us to be on patrol 24-7."

Liam nodded, knowing most of this. Rod continued,

"And now if they try to jam this down as an operator error ..." he stopped before adding, "we won't take it."

"The supervisors aren't happy either," Frank added. "We'll watch events closely as well."

"Solidarity, my friend," shouted Rod, slapping his hand down hard on the control room counter. He pointed at the poster on the wall: 'Safety Starts With You'. "These muppet managers wouldn't know the first thing about safety."

Liam thought Rod was becoming a self-proclaimed steward. He walked towards the control panel. "Fair enough, you'll have to do what you must do. It might be a bit premature, but I hear what you're saying. All out of my control or my influence, I'm afraid."

As Rod and Dean walked to the door, Rod turned and looked at Liam. "Maybe. Just get to the bottom of this mess. You promised."

Liam stayed at the control desk, pouring over the displays, pulling up trends and taking notes. He first looked at the pressure trends. There was nothing of note; a small spike hardly of any significance, at the point of the incident, when the alarms triggered at 4:18pm on the eventful Thursday. He expanded the range and scrolled back slowly over the preceding days, looking for trends on previous batches. Nothing, no spikes at all. For the next hour, he pondered over the screens scrolling back and forth. Everything looked normal. *What am I missing? There must be something. Maybe it'll come with fresh eyes again on Monday and a walk inside the plant.*

—

On the way home after a stop in the synthesis plant and the laboratory, Liam called Sandy. She'd been eager to help but her self-imposed exile was a brooding concern. "Hello Liam, thanks for the call. I assume you've been to the plant. What have you learnt?"

"Not much, I'm afraid," Liam answered. "It's still a mystery. I could only look at the screens and trends. There was nothing obvious. The plant is still blocked off and we won't get access until Monday."

"I wish I was there to help but I don't think I'd be welcome."

"Billings has lost the plot. It's madness, Sandy. I know you're better away from here but they don't appreciate the experience you have." Liam was puzzled how Sandy's situation had escalated. "I spent some time talking with the operators, the lab techs, some of the maintenance crew, and Frank the shift supervisor. The feeling is sour. Not just this accident with Johnno, but the boys aren't happy with management."

"Nor am I," Sandy replied.

"Things have certainly changed – there's real feeling now. The place has had a family feel for decades. Now they're talking about joining the union. They also reckon no one has shown enough empathy for Johnno or the shift guys at all."

"Well, I can tell you I don't feel the love either. I spoke with that Buchanan lady in HR again, and she said she's still looking at it. I got the short shift and was told to be patient."

"Maybe it's a work in progress."

"Maybe, but I doubt it. Just something in the tone. She still sounds like she's more focused on management control than on people support."

Liam was speechless, only managing, "Wow."

Sandy offered to help if there was anything to review or to be a sounding board if needed.

"Thanks Sandy, that may well be required. I'm meeting up with an investigator from RK Legal and I'll keep you in the loop."

"RK Legal – who are they?"

"De Zaale has engaged them to assist us in the legal side of things. Good business practice. Apparently, they already have us quarantining our correspondence and they'll be coaching us on interview techniques."

Sandy knew the routine. "All very normal and quite appropriate, I'm sure."

"Absolutely, no doubt. I'll call you again on Monday." As he was about to hang up, he added, "Pity they don't act as intuitively and with the same urgency on the people issues. I bet they were probably more upset about the loss of a batch of the precious pre-emergent sales than they were for Johnno."

—

Liam left the plant and pondered on his three options: head home to an empty house at Palmer Street, see his flatmates at the local football, or drop in to see Sarah at her tennis club. It was a no brainer as he headed to Bentleigh, hoping that her match might still be going.

21

MONDAY MORNING CAME AROUND all too soon. The Work Safe crew were in their makeshift office promptly at 8:00am as Liam arrived at his desk, Statler still not yet to be seen. Liam had met Albert Cohen previously and made his way over to reintroduce himself. Albert then introduced his colleagues, and they shared a morning coffee and some small talk.

Statler walked in shortly after and nodded to the group as he headed into his office, making a motion to Liam to join him. Liam looked at Albert, commenting, "Looks like I'm needed. Have a good day, everyone."

"Shut the door behind you," Statler barked as Liam walked into his office. After ensuring the door was fully closed, Statler approached Liam and told him in no uncertain terms, "I don't want you to fraternise with them. They have a job to do. Just let them get on with it."

"Mate, slow down," Liam retorted. "It was just introductions and coffee."

"It doesn't matter. One thing will lead to another, and they sneak some snippet and run with it." Statler suddenly recalled that Liam was away when they'd had the legal debrief. "Look,

RK Legal are acting for us, and their instructions are clear. Only answer questions directly put. Don't make any speculation, don't offer up anything not requested. The plan is to keep our contact with them to a minimum. Got it?"

"If you say so," Liam replied, shrugging in defeat.

"I do say so. You can act as their intermediate, their official contact, but stay strictly in your lane. No straying."

"Anything else, boss?"

"Yes, all future correspondence must be headed 'confidential and under legal privilege'. I'll forward De Zaale's email which also provides universal coverage so you can't forget. They can have any past documentation but only provide them the stuff that they specifically request. Furthermore, you will need to create a register of everything that is disclosed or given to the authorities, and you will need to make a separate copy of everything and send it to RK Legal – their contact is Consuela or something like that."

"Got it." Liam made to leave but Statler remained blocking his exit.

"Two more things. I've told RK Legal that you are our contact person, and they will have their investigator here this morning. You can be open and honest with her."

"Okay, you told me that on the phone. What's her name again?"

"Sue Carpenter, and she should be here soon. The last thing is that Workcover have a separate interest, in addition to Work Safe. I told you this on the phone as well. They're sending their own investigator this afternoon. I'll find out the name and let you know."

Liam smirked. "Who's Workcover? And I take it I'll be their contact point as well?"

"Workcover is the claims arm of the process and they're apparently the legislative arm that makes any charges, while Work Safe is the authority. It's all a bit confusing but you're the 'go to' man for both."

Liam didn't respond and opened the door. *More like a safety barrier so that the Muppet Man doesn't get involved.*

As Liam returned to his desk, he saw Mario enter the production block escorting a lady. "Here he is," Mario claimed, pointing at Liam. "Liam, this is Sue Carpenter from RK Legal. I've been told to make the introduction and to leave her with you."

"Thanks Mario. Nice to meet you, Sue." Liam extended his hand in welcome just as Statler came out of his office and nodded to Sue.

"Welcome. I'm Jim Statler the production manager. I'll leave you in the capable hands of Liam." Then turning to Liam, said, "I'll be off site for an hour or so, then I have meetings up the front. I'll catch you after lunch."

With that, Statler was gone, leaving Liam and Mario to host all the visitors. Liam looked at Mario and they both shook their heads, then laughed. Both were probably thinking the same thing: *Couldn't get out of here quicker if he tried.*

Mario had previously shown the Work Safe team around last week and was renewing acquaintances ready to continue his escort role. Liam and Sue joined them and made introductions all round. Albert tapped Liam on the shoulder and asked if they could talk somewhere in private.

Retiring to Jim's office, Liam asked, "How can I help you, Albert?"

"Mario gave us the training notes for your pre-emergent process, and I thank him for the prompt follow-up. However,

I wonder if you could give my team a rundown of the key steps in this T-plant process. It may even be of some assistance for your investigator, Sue."

Liam didn't hesitate. "Certainly, give me a couple minutes and let's convene in your meeting room."

"Thanks Liam, I appreciate your support." Albert left, knowing that Liam was genuine, and he felt confident that he was also a person determined to get to the root of this accident.

Both Liam and Sue entered the meeting room, Liam carrying copies of the operating procedure 'Synthesis of pre-emergent herbicide, T-plant'. He handed them around, looking directly at each person. "I know Mario has already given you some training notes, but here's the actual operating procedure as an aide in the overview of the process. I won't dwell on all the technicalities. Albert has asked me to give you a helicopter summary and please, I should advise you that the detail about components and the separate process steps is proprietary. But don't hesitate to ask any questions as we go."

Albert thanked Liam and assured him, "Don't worry, Liam, everything we discover or use is confidential and is retained only for our investigation. The detail is never disclosed to the public unless it's determined to be critical for public safety."

Liam proceeded with his summary. He outlined that the pre-emergent herbicide is generated from a technical base and progressed through a three-step process. They start with a synthesis reaction in a pressure vessel. Liam explained that the technical base was a by-product of research during the second world war and was accidentally found useful as a herbicide. It's solid at temperatures below around 50°C and therefore requires melting in hot baths. The molten tech is decanted into the first reactor where it is then mixed with a solvent. This results in an exothermic reaction, which is managed with temperature controllers using the cooling water system.

"Excuse me, Liam," Vanessa from the Work Safe team interrupted. "Is the solvent flammable and is this process a scenario in your MHF Safety Case?"

Liam acknowledged the question, knowing they probably already knew the answer and thinking it could be a test. "Yes, right on both accounts. I can get the Safety Case if you need, but I suspect you have your own copy. Sandra Hudson has coordinated a HAZOP study on this part of the process and the specific controls are outlined in the back of this procedure." Liam demonstrated by turning his copy to the appendix section. "The process requires extraction fans to be running, to pull off any fumes, and there are controls on the agitation, vessel levels, pressure and temperature."

The group began flicking through their copies while Liam continued. "Importantly, the agitator must be running to ensure good mixing. It's an exothermic reaction and both the reaction efficiency, and the dissipation and removal of the heat require good mixing."

"How do you determine that the agitator is operating?" Vanessa asked.

"There are a few ways. Firstly, the system must have the agitator switched on, a control signal back from the starter must be made, and secondly, we have feedback from the amp draw on the agitator motor that must be above a set level. If the agitator isn't turning or just spinning in an empty vessel, then the power draw is very low. Once the liquid level is above the agitator blades, the power draw increases significantly."

"Thank you," Vanessa replied. "And Liam, it also says here that the agitator can trip on low seal tank level. What does that mean?"

"We have an oil seal on the agitator shaft to keep fumes from escaping from the rotating shaft. The seal is made with a circulating fluid from a seal pot – a small 'tank', if you will. If the level in the seal tank drops low, then the performance might be compromised. So, we shut down."

Liam continued to explain that the reaction phase was monitored and completed with the controlled addition of alkaline material like caustic or soda ash to control the process pH at a level just above neutral, mainly to consume any hydrochloric acid produced as a by-product of the initial reaction.

Liam paused, having finished outlining the first process. "It's a fairly simple process and produces two layers of product. The bottom organic layer is our herbicide product which we call 'T-tech'. It is later used in formulations where we add surfactants and other solvents to make the end-use product more effective for the farmer. The top layer is largely water based and has a mixture of salt, water, and some partial emulsion of the tech."

Liam went on to explain that the next step is where they separate the two layers, directing the organic product into reactor 2. The drop into reactor 2 was stopped when the emulsion layer was detected, and the rest of the aqueous phase was directed into a separate recovery tank. At that point, Liam suggested to pause for a break and grab a coffee.

Albert agreed. "Good idea. Thanks."

While everyone went out to the small production office coffee station, Sue approached Liam. "Thanks for all this. You sure do know your stuff. How long have you been here at Agro Alliance?"

As they followed the Work Safe team, he answered, "I've been at here just over three years now and have been looking over the T-plant for a couple of years. What about yourself? What's your background?" Liam detected a sense of self confidence in her eyes and in her manner. She was short and lean, dressed in jeans and a jacket. Liam assumed she was in her late forties.

Over coffee, Sue gave Liam a potted history. Her experience was in petrochemicals, and she had worked for a few companies across Australia and around the world, with long stints in England and the Middle East. After returning to Australia as a technical lead, she was recruited for project expansions, settling first in Sydney and later Melbourne. She was a chemical engineer the same as Liam, graduating from Melbourne University rather than Monash.

She had a calming manner, yet Liam thought it might just be disguising a sharp and critical inner persona. He was impressed and was looking forward to working with her. *I think I might learn a lot from this lady.*

Albert approached them. "Sorry to interrupt. Liam, you mentioned Sandra Hudson and the Safety Case. Will she be available today?"

"I don't know, Albert. She's on leave at the moment and I'm not sure when she's returning. I've only just got back from leave myself, just this last weekend."

"Mmm ... she's a good engineer. Maybe we can arrange to catch up and we would like to talk with her if that's possible.

I believe you know that Workcover will be here this afternoon and maybe I can sit in with you to discuss the list of interviews."

"I'll check this morning and get back to you this afternoon." Liam finished his coffee and took his and Sue's empty cups to the bin. He asked Albert, "Do you want to put Sandy on the interview list?"

"Possibly, but because she is our MHF contact, we need her, or her manager to attend a close-out meeting today. If she's unavailable, could we get her boss – is that Barry Billings, or the site manager Mr Brazzos to attend?"

"Yes, Barry Billings is the head of the safety team. I'll send them a message and see what I can arrange." Liam was laughing internally. *This is going to be good.*

The group gathered back in the meeting room, Liam resuming, starting back on the synthesis process. "I should have explained that we do a series of analytical tests during the synthesis process in reactor 1, before we call it complete. Overall, it takes around an hour. Unfortunately, there is an unwanted by-product of the process, an impurity. While it's only in trace amounts, it is regulated by the ag chem authorities. Hence, we must remove these impurities below the regulated level before we can sell anything."

Pausing to check everyone had understood, Liam went on with his summary. "The destruction is done in the second reactor, with the addition of hydrochloric acid. This process is not an MHF scenario because it's not highly toxic, nor does it involve any flammable substances. The vessel is made of fibreglass and has a rupture panel designed to relieve at around 25-30 kPA. The vessel itself is nominally sound for up to 200 kPA. We have the same control systems for level, temperature and mixing, similar to reactor 1. The addition of the acid can sometimes result in a slight temperature rise, but it's marginal at best."

Liam paused once more to allow the group to absorb the information, and provided some time for the group to read over their copies of the procedure.

"We mix for around another hour and do some more testing, as it again settles into two phases. A technical phase and an aqueous phase, the latter mainly from the acid. We send the tech layer to a stripping vessel to remove any traces of water, and the aqueous layer is neutralised with soda ash and sent to the effluent plant. That concludes the technical manufacture. We formulate the tech in another vessel once we have accumulated enough material over several batches."

The group remained silent, seeming to understand. "Any other questions?" Liam asked.

"No, not now," Albert again responded as the group lead. "That helps a lot. I'm sure we'll have more questions later. I think we might now do a plant walk through and look at the trends in the control room."

"Okay, then I'll get Mario to escort you and he can assist you for anything you may need. I'll leave you to it. Hope you all have a good day."

"And you," responded a chorus of voices.

Before setting off for the day, Liam managed to get another word with Albert and confirmed that he and Sue could gain access to the restricted area, provided they didn't disturb anything. Albert indicated that they had already taken photos from last Friday and expected to finish taking samples and additional photos today. He would report back at the close-out meeting to update when and if Agro Alliance could have free access to start their clean up.

The Work Safe team filed out, leaving Liam and Sue alone. "Hopefully I didn't overextend your RK Legal protocols there. Didn't say too much, I mean," Liam said.

"It was good, don't worry." Sue managed a smile. "Everything was disclosable with the procedure anyway. I like your style. I believe it's always better to be friendly and cooperative. This reminds me, you should set up a register of things that have been officially disclosed, that procedure and the training notes can be the first items. Keep a copy of everything yourself and email another copy to RK Legal, attention to Consuela Garcia."

"Will do. I've been told already. I'll mark them up today. Could you give me Consuela's email details at some stage?"

Sue nodded. "Certainly. I've been doing this investigative stuff for a while now, and trust me, you're doing fine. Remember, if you are overly defensive, abrupt or in any way un-cooperative, they sense it and dig deeper. They think you have something to hide."

"I agree. Where would you like to start?"

"Let's not just follow Albert's team. Let's talk with some operators or other staff first and then look over the plant after they have finished." She paused and looked at Liam more attentively. "Before we go, what is your gut telling you? What are your initial thoughts?"

It wasn't a difficult question. Liam had been pondering this for a while but he was still uncertain. "It's still a puzzle. I wasn't here last week and can't really assess the situation. I was in on Saturday and checked the screens. There's nothing obvious."

Sue smiled and calmly redirected him. "Okay, nothing obvious. Then what's different? What should we focus on first?"

"Good questions, hard to say. Everything is routine. Normal business, batches, end of season rework, operators, all the same as for any campaign."

Sue acknowledged him with a nod but persisted, "Things don't just explode, erupt, or go awry if everything is routine. Wouldn't you agree?"

"Sure. So, we should look for the anomalies. What is different."

A reassuring smile broke out on Sue's face. "That's as good a place to start as anywhere."

22

BRAZZOS CALLED AN IMPROMPTU manufacturing meeting, needing to have his managers all coordinated in order to maintain control over the T-plant accident investigation. He was nervous that the Work Safe inspectors were trying to find a scapegoat and they would be making life difficult for everyone. It was already embarrassing enough that this death on his site had ruined his safety record. He knew De Zaale would be mad. There were rumours that Agro Alliance might be extending its reach internationally, and he wanted to be a key figure in any expansion. As the managers filed into the conference room, his predominant thought was to get this wrapped up quickly, limit the damages.

Brazzos waited until they were all seated. "Obviously this accident is a terrible event. We all need to pull together and we need to be on the same page. I want to reiterate the messages from RK Legal: cooperate, but only to the extent of what they require. Don't offer or speculate on anything else. Are we all clear?"

The attendees sat silently, some nodding in agreement. Brazzos revisited it again. "I will take the nods as confirmation, but I can't hear nods. I want you to verbally agree as well. Are we all clear?" He glared at each manager in succession and didn't move onto the next until he had a verbal confirmation.

"Let's go around the room and get an update from each of you. Let's start with HR. Do you have anything, Michelle?"

Michelle Buchanan had been a bit subdued over these past few days. Brazzos had become a bit standoffish lately, and with the accident she had to cancel their next superannuation lunch. The accident itself was giving her extra work. There were complaints coming in from the shop floor and then last week the bust-up between Billings and Hudson was a problem she could do without.

She looked around the room before answering, "We have the EAP on site today and anyone that requires counselling or support are free to access their service. Otherwise, the family have been in and collected the poor bloke's things. There's not much more we can do at this stage. I've heard that several staff want leave to go to the funeral, although we don't have a date yet." Michelle took a breath and was happy to be finished. She thought the touch of 'the poor bloke' had actually covered up the fact that she had forgotten 'the poor bloke's' name.

Brazzos was pensive; all this investigation was giving him an uneasy feeling. Surely he had nothing to worry about. "What is EAP, and how long will that continue? The staff can take annual leave for the funeral."

Michelle could sense Brazzos's edginess, but after all, it was still a death on his watch, and a bit of empathy wouldn't go astray. "EAP is the Employee Assistance Programme we have, and we engage with a specialist company that provides assistance in instances like this one. I recommend we keep them here this week. At least while the investigation is in progress and the plant is in a mess."

With a pause and nothing more from the HR lady, Brazzos was bouncing on his feet. "What about the funeral then?"

Michelle felt the heat of the Brazzos glare. "The staff will be expecting a personal leave day, and in most situations, it is warranted. It would be a bad look to insist on annual leave. It's your call, but I would not recommend you go that way. The shop floor is already grumbling and that would only add to their grievances."

"What grievances? They're pandered enough." Brazzos shook his head, thinking to himself how unappreciative these Aussies were. "Go with the personal leave for his direct workmates and annual leave for anyone else."

Michelle was joined by the rest of the managers in thinking it was the wrong hill to die on. He was being pig headed, and undoubtedly it would all blow up in his face one day. Who were his direct workmates? His shift, or the shift that he was working with on overtime on the day of the accident, or the whole shift team, or his cousins in the day group, or his close friends in maintenance? It was a fine line to draw, but Brazzos wasn't thinking of the people or the politics.

Brazzos had moved on around the room. Keith Dwyer from the laboratory had nothing of significance. The test results from the batch in progress at the time of the accident were available. They were non-remarkable and would undoubtedly be shared with Work Safe in time. Barry Billings from the safety group also had little to say. He was awaiting the feedback from the investigations and in the interim his team was concentrating on the permit upgrade and the 5S implementation. He omitted any discussion on the Safety Case, not relevant at this time, he thought.

Brazzos turned to his maintenance manager. "Stuart, what have you got? Do you have any thoughts about the accident?"

Stuart shook his head. "Sorry, Tony, I have nothing new. I've asked all my boys, and they're stumped. They can't believe it was a maintenance issue. Dean is adamant they had tightened the agitator when they set it up last week. Besides, it doesn't really explain why they made two complete batches in the interim."

"Maybe, could it have worked loose or was the vessel an issue?" countered Brazzos, annoyed that the team was providing more questions than answers.

"I doubt it. There was nothing unusual. We don't inspect the non-pressure vessels, so we have no detail on file."

Leaving that to linger, Brazzos reflected to himself, *Still might be the cause.* "So then, Jim, what have you got?"

"Work Safe are on site and I have arranged O'Donoghue to coordinate everything. He has the RK Legal instructions and has that Sue lady with him today. They are all going over the plant as we speak."

Brazzos was still pensive and started to pace around the room. "So, it's a waiting game."

More silence, no one bold enough to offer any comment. "One other thing, Tony," Jim interrupted the reflections. "O'Donoghue rang me just prior to this meeting and said a Workcover investigator would also be coming this afternoon, and they'll want to discuss a list of interviews. He also said that the main Work Safe bloke, Albert Cohen, wants a close-out meeting this afternoon and has requested for Sandra Hudson to be present. O'Donoughue told him she was away, to which they apparently then requested yourself and Barry."

Billings arked up. "No way. Hudson is not going to be involved. She can't—"

"Don't get worked up, Barry," Brazzos cut him off, and looking over to Michelle Buchanan, asked, "What's the status with our Miss Hudson?"

Knowing she had left this matter in her 'too hard basket', Michelle made up the ruse. "She's claiming stress leave, indefinite stress leave, and she's claiming irreconcilable differences at work."

"The bitch," Billings spat as he was about to explode.

"We can't tolerate that, Michelle," Brazos said, while glaring at Billings to shut up. "You need to sort that mess out. She doesn't dictate to us, and she can't be allowed to contact Work Safe. When all this is finally over, then we can part ways."

Brazzos returned his attention back to his production manager. "Okay, find out the time for this close-out meeting and I'll see this Mr Albert. Find out what this 'another Workcover investigator' means and get back to me. Anything else?"

"Well, O'Donoughue also said they'll be discussing our access to the site at this close-out meeting."

"That's nice of them. They'll let us know when we can go into our own plant ... I don't think so."

—

While the Work Safe team resumed their inspection of the damaged plant, Liam and Sue headed to other parts to talk with staff that were around last Thursday. Unfortunately, the shift team was a new group, none of whom were on site at the time of the accident. They'd only heard second-hand rumours or scuttlebutt, none of which were useful. Sue said to take everything in, let it settle, and the facts would sift themselves out eventually.

They visited the maintenance shop and spoke with Dean, several fitters and a couple of the electricians. Nothing significant was forthcoming. Dean was defensive and reassured Liam that the maintenance on the agitator was solid. Those nuts were tighter than a fish's arse. He blushed and apologised to Sue, who smiled and assured him she had heard much worse.

The laboratory technicians that were on deck on the Thursday had tested Johnno's samples. Sue and Liam met with a young technician, Xia Nguyen – a Vietnamese lad who'd immigrated to Australia several years ago. He had joined Agro Alliance as his first job in his new country, well before Liam had started. Everyone referred to him as Aussie Joe. Liam introduced him to Sue, and Aussie Joe beamed and said he was pleased to meet her. "Just call me Joe."

"Joe, tell us about the day of the accident. What do you remember?"

"I remember Johnno bring sample into lab, same as normal. I test. All good, normal. I tell Johnno that it okay. He leave to drop the batch. All normal. Then a few minutes later, *bang*. Everything shake, glass fall everywhere, windows shake. I fall to ground, right here where we are now."

Liam asked, "The sample Johnno had, nothing unusual. You tested it and was it normal?"

"Yes, all normal. I give Johnno the all-clear to go to the next step. I wouldn't say all clear if it wasn't normal. Test results are here. I can get them if you like."

"Thanks Joe, that would be helpful," Sue responded. "Tell me though, you said the 'bang' was a few minutes later. How much later or what time was it? Your best estimate."

"Mmm. Let me think." Joe walked over to the other end of the lab to get the test results and returned. "Maybe twenty-five to thirty minutes. Could be forty minutes, but definitely not more. I get ready to hand over to afternoon shift when bang come."

"Okay, that's very helpful," Sue said with her calming tone. "We might need to talk to you again. It was nice to meet you." They shook hands and left Aussie Joe smiling as they walked out.

Exiting the lab and while they still waited for the Work Safe team to vacate the T-plant, Liam took Sue to the gatehouse. "If we're lucky, the guard might be Willo. He works most weekdays and was here last Thursday."

"Good, let's see if Willo's here," Sue said, still maintaining her calm and easy-going attitude. "That timeline that Joe mentioned – thirty to forty minutes, after testing complete – does that make sense to you?"

"I was thinking about that myself. Probably. We know that the acid charge was already started on reactor 2, and an efficient operator pushing the batch along would have got to that point in around twenty minutes. Johnno was never in a hurry, so thirty minutes would fit the bill, even forty."

Liam explained it was only a couple of minutes to walk

back across the road from the lab to the plant and write up the batch sheet, then another five minutes to set up and a further maximum ten minutes for the drop to reactor 2, that also included splitting the rest into the recovery tank. The acid charge would be initiated almost straight away after that.

Sue was contemplative and stopped outside the gatehouse to write some details in her notebook. She looked across at Liam. "Let's get the exact time of Joe's testing and confirm the time of the accident, which we have as 4:18pm. Is that right?"

"That's right. 4:18pm." Liam opened the door and stepped back to let Sue pass into the gatehouse.

"Thanks Liam," she said as she stepped past. "And for my benefit, from where would Johnno have activated the acid charge and why was he on the plant deck at the time of the accident?"

Liam gave a knowing nod to himself, acknowledged the questions, and made a mental note to follow it up. *This Sue lady is sharp.*

"Willo, I'm glad you're here. Let me introduce you to Sue Carpenter. She's working with us to investigate Johnno's accident. Have you a minute for us, to answer a few questions?"

Willo stood and shook hands with Sue. "Of course, any time. How can I help?"

Sue asked him to go over his recollection of the timeline and events of last Thursday while she took some notes. Willo recounted that he was at the security screens when Jake had come into the office, a standard practice. He and Jake were old mates from their past football days. They often shared a pot of tea just before shift change. He remembered some sort of noise in the plant and then there was the explosion.

Other than that, he couldn't help. Willo told them that Jake immediately ran out into the plant while he called emergency services and secured the front gates to stop any traffic. He remained out the front with a radio waiting for the ambulance to arrive.

"Thanks Paul, very helpful," Sue said, again in her usual charming manner. "Just one other thing. What was the noise you heard in the plant, the one you said you heard before the bang?"

"Call me Willo, everyone does. I don't recall the noise exactly. You might ask Jake. He seemed a bit perturbed by it. To me, it was just loud plant noises. You know, this place creaks and groans all night at times."

After saying their goodbyes to Willo, Liam suggested a bite to eat. "We can go across the road to the Sons of the West cafe. They do a good sandwich or have the standard fried food if you prefer. Then after lunch we can walk through the plant."

"Sandwich sounds good to me," said Sue. "Let's also make a note to investigate what that 'noise' was."

—

The close-out meeting was held in the front training room. Mario diligently escorted the Work Safe team there after they wrapped up everything in the plant. Work Safe had taken hundreds of extra photos and collected an abundance of more samples, mainly from the ruptured vessel and surrounds. In the afternoon, they had focused on the computer trends and were given copies of screen data for almost every transmitter in the T-plant. They had visited Xia

Nguyen in the laboratory and been given a copy of the batch test results. Mario, under Liam's instructions, had made a note of everything that was provided and had a duplicate made in each case, leaving the list and a wad of papers on Liam's desk.

Albert and his team were all set in the training room, each nursing a soft drink sourced by Mario from the canteen. Tony Brazzos entered along with Jim Statler and Barry Billings, all of whom looked like they would prefer to be elsewhere. Liam thought that he should have been invited, but when he asked Jim, he was told that they were strategically keeping him at arm's length.

Albert stood up to greet the Agro Alliance managers. While he had met or dealt with Jim and Barry on previous occasions, he had not previously met Tony Brazzos. He extended his hand in welcome. "Mr Brazzos, I assume. My name is Albert Cohen. Thank you for coming to the close-out meeting. I'm sorry about this unfortunate accident."

Brazzos accepted the handshake, not willingly, but rather to avoid aggravation. He bluntly went straight to the point. "So, what's your verdict?"

Albert had a wry smile when he answered, "Way too early to have any conclusion yet. We always have a close-out meeting with the company each time we are on site. I have prepared a summary. It gives a list of the things that we requested and received, and an outline of the areas that we have investigated today." Albert had copies, which he provided to Tony, Jim, and Barry.

"Hmmph," grumbled Brazzos. "What's next? When can we get into the plant? Jim tells me there's some delay. What's that about?"

Albert ignored his gruffness and calmly responded, "In serious accidents, we have the right to quarantine and preserve the accident site in order to conduct a thorough investigation."

"Yes, I understand that," Brazzos interjected with a scoff, "but you had this blocked off Friday and all weekend as well. We need to get on with our priorities, clean up, repairs, rebuild, etc. We have plenty of work to do."

"I understand, I do. I have a manufacturing background myself. But we must do our due diligence."

"Yeah, yeah, yeah. When can we get the plant back? That's all I'm asking."

Albert remained very patient, knowing he was initially going to release the plant at this close-out meeting. However, he decided a change of track was warranted in light of the uncooperative tone. "Very soon, Mr Brazzos. I would like to consult with my colleagues and the seniors back at my office. If all is good, I can call you or Sandra Hudson tomorrow and arrange the detail."

"Don't bother calling me," Brazzos snapped. "You can tell Jim here and you can forget about Ms Hudson. I will be expecting that we can get in and start the cleanup tomorrow."

Sensing an escalation, Albert remained calm and stood his ground. "We'll see." Then holding Brazzos's stare, added, "One other thing. I am serving you a formal Notice." Brazzos frowned but maintained his glare as Albert continued. "This is a formal restriction. You will not be allowed to rebuild the T-plant, nor operate it, until you have completed a detailed assessment of the cause of this accident. You will be required to submit this assessment to Work Safe."

Brazzos was so infuriated, he was about to blow a gasket. Jim and Barry were watching from the sideline expecting the Brazzos volcano to erupt at any minute. "What a load of crap!" shouted Brazzos. "What sort of nerve do you pen pushers have!?"

Albert knew Brazzos was volatile; tales from previous encounters relayed by operators and Sandy. "It is standard process, Mr Brazzos. You don't need to get all worked up. We serve such notices on all places that have a serious accident, and let me remind you," he raised his own voice for emphasis, "your plant has contributed to a fatality."

"Whatever!" shouted Brazzos. "But it is our plant, and we will make the call on how to re-build it, not you." The Brazzos lava was now rising. "And I fucking well know what I'm doing here. I will decide, not you. Am I making myself clear?"

Albert, enjoying this mini title fight, was trying hard not to smile when he ducked the Brazzos verbal swing and countered with his own jab. "You can think what you want. This Notice is legally binding and it is duly served. We are not telling you how to rebuild your plant. We are telling you that we will not let you operate your plant until you demonstrate to us that there are sufficient controls in place. Controls that are both implemented and functional to prevent a repeat of this fatal accident. And ... I will tell you! We will decide when and if we are satisfied."

"I'll see about this," Brazzos grunted, insisting on having the last word. He stormed out of the room, leaving the Notice on the table. Billings followed his boss without looking back, leaving Jim with the cleanup.

23

MONDAY NIGHT AT PALMER Street was a pizza and beer night for the flatmates. Their diverse schedules had them rarely at home at the same time. They had come to call the Monday pizzas their committee meeting: a semi-formal chance for them to discuss matters of the house, but inevitably it turned into an opportunity for Ross to air his grievances or to espouse some plan or idea he'd been developing. Monday was the easiest night to get together and the other three looked forward to a beer and a catch up, generally ignoring Ross.

Liam picked up Sarah on his way home and swung by the pizza shop – his turn to buy this week. The pizza roster was well established, and Ross had it recorded on his phone. Ross was the de facto accountant of the group, a self-imposed role that satisfied his peculiar obsession with splitting costs. Liam first met Ross at the orientation week at Monash University. They were alone in the chemical engineering department, while everyone else was over at the union building chasing free food and drink. They struck up a friendship that lasted well through the course and beyond.

During the first day of lectures, Liam had suggested

they grab a coffee or a bite to eat at the engineering cafe, under the library. Liam shouted Ross a coffee and a muffin as a welcoming gesture and Ross offered to return the shout next time. A few days later, they were again seated in the cafe and Ross had offered to get the drinks. As he stood to go to the counter, Liam had requested a milkshake instead. Liam always recalled the confused look on Ross's face as he processed the request, and he would never forget the simple response: 'Sorry mate, that's an extra dollar. I'll get you a coffee.' Thereafter, Ross was very particular in splitting bills and always reconciled what each person had rather than to share the cost evenly. It was a quirk that bothered most people, and certainly irked Liam's football flatmates, Adrian and Rick, who both taunted Ross whenever the subject arose.

Ross was a recent addition to the house, filling a gap the footballing mates had when Rick's brother moved out. Liam had taken the previous vacancy five years earlier, extracting himself from the Monash halls of residence at his first opportunity.

Palmer Street in Oakleigh was a quiet residential street with a series of 1960s houses, some weatherboard, and some brick veneer. Large gum trees stood in most front yards and fibrocement garages were tucked at the side towards the back of each home. Twin concrete strips served as the driveway in every home. The front fences varied from cracked brickwork to rose bush borders. Retirees and rentals made up most of the occupants and car spaces in the street always seemed to be at a premium. Often the flatmates would be forced to park a few houses away if they missed one of the few available spots in their driveway.

Liam was usually late and left to battle his chances of

a parking spot on the street. The norm prevailed on this pizza night, but he lucked out with a spot opposite, outside Eddie's place. Sarah grabbed the pizzas as Liam locked the car. Eddie was sitting in his regular spot, a rocker at the back of the front balcony. Liam waved to Eddie, who raised his stubby in response in a toast to Liam, smiling with his semi-toothless grin.

Liam followed Sarah into the house. "Old Eddie hardly changes. I wouldn't be surprised if he were stuck to that chair."

"Pizza delivery," Liam announced as they walked through the lounge room towards the little kitchen. Adrian and Rick were lazing on the couch watching the start of *Australian Survivor* on the television and hardly acknowledged the pizza arrival. Ross appeared from his room as Liam left Sarah to spread out the pizza boxes while he dropped his bag into his room.

Ross, unable to resist commenting, questioned, "Another mouth to feed?"

"I heard that," yelled Liam from the passageway. "Don't stress, Ross, we bought an extra pizza, just to stop your worrying."

Adrian threw a cushion at Ross. "Settle down, penny pincher." As he rose to serve himself, he yelled to Liam, "Liam, mate. We need you to settle the latest bird brain idea from Roscoe. Maybe Sarah can be the arbitrator."

Rick, still on the couch, interjected, "We don't need no arbitrator. His idea doesn't stack up. It's not in our house agreement. Roscoe can whistle dixie for all I care."

Liam returned to the kitchen laughing at the banter, knowing that Ross was never going to win the discussion.

Rick was about to graduate in Law and would wrap it up with some of his legal logic if necessary. Adrian and Liam generally didn't care about Ross's financial control strategies, but they often supported Rick in any vote. "Okay, shoot, what's this idea? By the way, I see 'old Eddie' is still in his office."

"The old bugger never moves," Rick said. "It's like he's a sentry guard. The only thing that puzzles me is how he gets his beer out of the fridge. I never see him move, just drinking his VB stubbies all day."

"He moves alright," Adrian laughed as he explained that he saw Eddie mowing the lawn last week. "Strangest thing I ever saw. He had a beer stationed on the front veranda and another at the letter box. He mowed up and down, taking a swig after every lap. I almost had to take a video."

They all laughed and started to move back into the lounge room with a pizza on a napkin and a beer from the fridge. Sarah sat on Liam's couch, a spot vacated by Adrian who waved her to sit. Ross started, "Since we're all here, I want to put a variation to our Foxtel agreement."

"What agreement is that, Roscoe?" Rick asked, taking a bite of his pizza. "We three share the Foxtel cost as you piked at sharing the cost when we had it connected. So, we decide what to watch."

Ross's expression remained flat. "I know, Rick, don't get ahead of me. I was just saying you make me pay five dollars a week if I want to watch anything, even if I'm watching it with you guys."

"And what's the problem with that?" Rick countered, with both Adrian and Liam in silent agreement.

"Well, I was thinking that I might not need to pay for a full week if I only want to watch one show, say the football.

Could we work out a pay per show rate, say one or two dollars at a time. What do you think?"

They collectively laughed and even Sarah had to stop herself. Rick settled it. "Look, Roscoe, we all – us three – pay the bill and it comes to about five dollars a week each. That's the going rate, you can take it or leave it."

"But that's your choice. I was just—"

"Choice or not, we pay for the connection," Adrian interrupted. "The deal is the deal. Your choice is to take it or not. Do you want us to take a vote?"

"No, no, not necessary. I was just thinking."

"Meeting over," announced Rick.

They continued the dinner of beer and pizza, chatting away about the day's events, the latest news and watching the rest of *Survivor*. Ross retired back to his room to catch up on some work, supposedly. At the end of the show, Rick and Adrian left to catch up with some of the boys who were playing pennant squash, leaving Sarah and Liam alone.

—

Liam sorted the empty pizza boxes and collected the stubbies into a plastic bag. He would walk them out to the bins when he took Sarah back home. Returning to sit on the couch, he asked Sarah if there was anything she wanted to watch. Nothing sprung to mind so they elected to put on some music and chat. Liam was loading a folk music CD he'd recently purchased as Sarah started, "Tell me about your day. How's the investigation going?"

Liam didn't normally like to discuss his work but felt it useful to revisit his day. Sarah seemed genuinely interested and Liam thought that talking it through might clarify the issues that were muddled in his mind. “You’d like the contactor investigator we have working on the case. Sue Carpenter. She’s super smart, very perceptive and has a manner that cuts through any crap.”

“Sounds like a superwoman,” Sarah said with a nod. “What’s this CD you put on? Very folksy! Not your normal Pink Floyd or Dire Straits.”

“Yes, just found this guy recently. Good calm music, great background. I like it, and I thought you would like it as well.”

Liam wasn’t sure whether Sarah was of the same opinion and relayed the story of how he came across the Irish folk singer Enda Kenny. The boys at the footy club were having a golf day during pre-season down the peninsula, back in January, while Sarah was away in Bali. “I went down for the afternoon, just a catch-up after golf, along with Adrian. We ended up having dinner up in the hills, at a place called the Pig N Whistle. Great pub, an English style with a cosy inside area and an outside area sprawled across the lawns and pavers. The food was great, best wiener schnitzel I’ve ever had, big platters and good English ales. The guy behind the jump was a character with a pommy beret, perfect for the place. This night after the dinner, around 7:30pm the joint had a function going in a small shed out the back, open to anyone. They call it MOTH, which stands for ‘Music on the Hill’. Apparently once a month the organisers bring in different local artists and other guest musicians.

“Anyway, Adrian and I stayed back while the others all bailed. It was folk music, and this dude Enda Kenny was the main act. He’s an Irish folk musician who’s lived in Melbourne or parts of Victoria for half of his life. He writes all his own stuff and is a phenomenal storyteller. He just has this gift, probably ingrain being Irish, music sweats out of his pores. He also has the patter that goes with it, good stories, a few jokes. It was a rollicking good night. By the end of the night, he had the whole shed singing along, and even Adrian was singing."

Liam laughed as he recalled the night. "Anyway, at the end of the night I spoke with the bloke, really nice guy and I bought this CD. Like I said, it makes me feel good."

"Okay, leave it on and I'll see. Look at you, Mr President of the Enda Kenny bandwagon. Now get back to your superwoman story."

"Yeah, I was thinking today that I'm governed by superwomen. The main people in my life seem to be superwomen, they all start with the letter 'S'. There's you of course, this new lady Sue, there's Sandy who's fantastic, and my sister."

"Your sister is Zoe. She starts with a 'Z'."

"I know, but that's just minor detail. I count it as a sort of an 'S'. Hence, I am surrounded by these Superwomen."

Sarah laughed and told him to calm down. Liam grabbed another two beers and nestled next to her while he recounted his afternoon.

After Sue and Liam finished their lunch, they took the opportunity to look through the plant. Mario and the Work Safe team had relocated themselves into the T-plant control room. They had to put on gloves, disposable overhauls, and gumboots before slowly progressing around the bottom floor, stopping for Sue to take photos at every stage. There was not a lot to see other than a blanket cover of orange sludge. The pumps, pipelines and instruments seemed to be intact. The sample pot, which also acted as a low relief pot, was blocked with solidified tech, but it was impossible to say whether it was blocked before or after the incident. Liam presumed afterwards.

Liam saw that sixteen drums were positioned on pallets at the decanting station and mentally reconciled that against Johnno's paperwork. He was explaining the melting and decanting steps and absent mindedly rocked the empty drums. He found one that was still nearly full, then another and several others with an unmelted heel in the base. This was wrong. The paperwork signed off sixteen drums decanted, yet in his estimation more than two were left out. Sue took more notes, and they discussed the consequences.

Sarah was very attentive and asked, "So, was that a problem? What did you conclude?"

"It may not be an issue," Liam said, "but it is just a big difference and it doesn't feel right. It didn't fit with Johnno's paperwork. Why would he take a short cut? Why wouldn't he just say fourteen drums?"

Liam explained that the operating procedure required a minimum of fifteen drums but that was an efficiency issue to align with the automated charge of caustic and other ingredients. A short batch could be managed provided there was sufficient material to cover the low-level switch and to cover the agitator for good mixing. Otherwise, interlocks would prevent the batch continuing.

Proper process required an MOC to formally check the interlocks and adjust other additions, but apparently there wasn't any MOC raised, and Johnno's paperwork recorded sixteen drums. Sue made more notes and suggested there must be a reason. They agreed to keep the detail to themselves for the moment and check it further. Sue suggested the drums be moved as soon as the area was released for cleaning, get them weighed and sampled.

Sarah pursed her lips. "If the batch progressed okay, doesn't that mean it was all okay?"

"Probably. Sue just thinks that differences and changes are important. They might lead to answers or at least build towards answers. Ultimately because the batch progressed without the interlocks shutting it down, it should have been okay."

Sue and Liam progressed to the first level and observed the reactor 2 vessel. There was a lateral tear on one side of the agitator mount that had ripped the top of the vessel apart. They measured the rip at 80cm and took several photos. The failure was on the same side as the stairway, which allowed the agitator to be propelled out onto the landing. Was it just bad luck that it failed and split in that orientation, or was the vessel or mount joint faulty? It certainly was bad luck for Johnno who was on that side of the vessel at the time. Had he been on the other side he may still have been injured, but possibly not killed.

They continued through the plant, Sue constantly filling pages of notes. They finished by looking at the agitator in the restricted storage area. It had somehow survived and was virtually undamaged. There were a few scratches from its struggle out of the vessel, but it had remained tethered from fully escaping by the power lead.

Liam checked Sarah's drink and offered to get her another. As he went to the kitchen, he continued his story from outside the room. "While we were in the maintenance area, we called in to chat to Stuart Jennison, the maintenance manager. Sue was particularly interested in the fact that the agitator had been changed recently."

Returning with fresh drinks, Liam explained that Jennison told them it was all good. They had a universal spare which had the mixing blades at the same position on the shaft and the changeout went well. A couple of batches were made without issue, and it seemed to be working fine at the time of the incident. The maintenance crew were still adamant that the agitator was fully secure.

Eventually, Liam interrupted his own story and went quiet for a few minutes.

"What's up, Liam?" Sarah asked. "What're you thinking about?"

"Nothing really, love," Liam replied. "Sue said the strangest thing today when we were talking with Stuart the maintenance manager. He'd told us that the universal spare was the same as in several other vessels and was kept as a critical spare to cover them all. Then she said, 'That's good because not all mixers are the same'."

Liam finished his recap of the day while he drove Sarah home.

Sue had agreed to forward a list of questions, while Liam would provide copies of all the computer printouts, duplicating the material Mario had downloaded for the Work Safe. Nothing was obvious and the failure of the vessel or the agitator mount was too simplistic. It remained a mystery, and what the hell was Johnno doing on the plant at that time?

24

LIAM WAS IN HIS office early on Tuesday, collating Mario's documents from the previous day. They were catalogued into his RK Legal register then individually scanned and sent to Consuela. He was about to send duplicate copies to Sue Carpenter when Jim Statler approached his desk.

Statler stood there, looking as if he carried the weight of the world on his shoulders. "Liam," he started, "I take it you heard that the Workcover fellow cancelled yesterday and he has rescheduled to this afternoon." Liam nodded. "You're the designated contact person, and we need you to talk with him and with your Work Safe guy and convince them to release our plant. We need it back straight away so we can get on with everything."

"Will do, boss. How did the close-out meeting go last night?" Liam was still a bit miffed that despite being the contact person he was being strategically kept at arm's length. *In what world does that make sense!?*

"Hard to say," replied Statler. "They've served us a formal Notice, restricting us from operating the plant again until the redesign is checked and approved. They haven't released the site yet and they were very cagey about their findings.

Brazzos is not happy, and we're knocking heads. You need to get the plant released."

Liam could easily imagine Brazzos trying to brow beat Work Safe.

This is not South America. He would have probably expected to pay the authorities and move on. Knocking heads is probably an apt description.

Statler added, "I've told that Albert from Work Safe to contact you today. If you haven't heard from him this morning, you need to follow up. Push him to release the plant so that we can start the cleanup."

"Okay, sure. I'll do what I can, but it would be better from Sandra Hudson or Barry Billings, surely?" Liam said, quietly testing the boundaries.

"No, definitely not. I don't expect we will see Hudson again." Statler was adamant. "You're now the contact person, so it's you."

"Let me understand this better, Jim. I'm the contact person for the follow-up on the T-plant accident with both Work Safe and Workcover. I'm also the administrator and go-between for RK Legal, and you want me to arrange the cleanup of the plant. I assume Billings and his team will look after the MOC coordinator role, all other Work Safe contacts and the Safety Case. Who will be doing the redesign of the plant and arranging HAZOP and LOPA assessments if Sandy isn't available?"

"I don't know, mate. It may be you as well. You'll be busy."

Liam glared at his boss. "Shit, mate! Frankly, I don't know if I can do all that. I think we will need a lot of help. Seriously, Jim, we will need technical support, expertise in LOPA and a lot of time. You need a superwoman like Sandy, and you're letting her go. It's madness." He felt his anger rising, so he clammed up and made out that he was going into the plant.

Instead, he headed up the front, out of the plant and across to the Sons of the West cafe. He ordered an egg sandwich and a milkshake and slouched into a corner booth. He rang Sandy and vented his spleen for the next thirty minutes. The place was in serious trouble, the managers were ducking and weaving, there was no support, and their answer was to have a pile-on on Liam. He gave Sandy the intel that they were talking about her not coming back nor being allowed to contact Work Safe. Sandy had tried to contact HR again this week, but all her calls and messages remained unanswered. She was already feeling the cold of her isolation. The O'Donoughue-Hudson debrief was interrupted when Albert Cohen came up on Liam's phone.

"Sorry, Sandy. Looks like Albert from Work Safe is trying to call. I better take it. I'll call you later."

Liam hung up and answered the Work Safe call. "Hello, Albert. How can I help you?"

"Liam, I've been told that you're my contact person. I trust that you're aware of that? Mr Brazzos initially told me to call Jim Statler, but he has referred me to you. I thought it would've been Sandy or her boss, but that's your call. Yours as in Agro Alliance, I mean."

"It's a bit of a mess at the moment, Albert. The accident and all, it has us a bit shaken. Sandy is on extended leave and T-plant is my concern, so I'm holding the baby, or the fort."

"Good luck with that," Albert muttered. "Can we meet to go over a few things?"

"Yes, of course. Whenever you'd like. I do have an

investigator from Workcover coming out this afternoon around 2:00pm and I don't know how long he'll take."

"Who is the Workcover assigned investigator, do you know?"

"An inspector called Cameron Oxley, I believe. Why do you ask?"

"I was just thinking. Can I suggest I meet with you at 1:00pm? Then can I also request I sit in with Cameron at the start of your 2:00pm meeting? I want to coordinate with him the interview schedule and avoid doubling up and imposing on your people where possible."

Liam agreed to Albert's plan but remained in the cafe to ponder. The plant was still a restricted zone, pending Work Safe clearance. Not much to achieve there until they could start moving stuff. First priority would be to weigh those drums and get some fitters to disconnect the scrubbing system. Sue Carpenter had her initial review, and he was waiting on her list of questions. Redesign and HAZOP would have to wait until the causes were determined. He felt like he was stuck waiting ... waiting for what? He pulled out his notebook, his constant companion and started listing his own questions:

- *What was Johnno doing on the platform at that time? Normally lazy and mainly found in a direct line somewhere between the control room and the smoke shelter. So why there and why then?*
- *Double check the weights in the tech drums. How low was the batch?*
- *Why did Johnno record a full 16 drums?*
- *How much pressure was there?*

- *Check the power draw on the agitator. * Still a puzzle – batch wasn't interlocked out.*
- *Why did the agitator tear in the one specific direction? Look up details or talk to experts about fibreglass vessel failures.*
- *'Not all mixers are the same.'*
- *Measure the old agitator and the universal agitator to check blade settings.*
- *What was the noise at the time of the accident? Check CCTV at gatehouse.*
- *Check times of lab sample testing against the steps in the process.*
- *Follow up with Work Safe on release of site.*
- *Set up interview list and confer with persons to setup a schedule.*
- ~~*MOC coordinator role – check status.*~~
- *Meet with Sandy to review lists and consider options.*
- *Get Sandy's advice on redesign, HAZOPs, and LOPA.*

—

Liam stayed at the cafe for the morning, trying to prioritise the list and thinking through the details. He took an early lunch: a coke and a meat pie. Facts and observations were spinning around in his head, bouncing hard up against his forehead, forcing a self-imposed headache and some doubt was emerging whether he could sort it out. Additionally, the workload was mounting and bringing its own pressure

He was exhausted by the time he'd made his way back to the office. He dropped past the reception area to let the ladies on the desk know that he was expecting visitors: Albert Cohen and Cameron Oxley.

Lauren and Elise were Agro Alliance's regular receptionists. They smiled at Liam, which was a common occurrence when they saw one of their favourites come through the front door. Elise was the younger and chirpier of the reception duo and warmly acknowledged Liam. "Good morning, good looking. You're not looking your usual sparky self." Realising the plant connection to Johnno's accident, she instantly regretted her words and winced. "Sorry sport, that was dumb, I wasn't thinking. How are you holding up? What about the boys out the back?"

"No problems, El. It's all a shock, most people are still numb. A bit of the lively El is what we all need. A bit of humour to make the world go round." Liam spun a twirl in front of the ladies and gave them a royal bow. "Excuse me, your majesties, I'm just popping in to let you know I have visitors this afternoon."

Lauren was stoked that someone had the thought to let the front desk know. "We're stuck out front, the public face, and often have no clue. It must look bad for the guests and visitors sometimes. A bit of thought, a bit of courtesy goes a long way. We get all our intel second-hand from the boys out the back or the canteen girls. Nothing from upstairs."

Liam got the hot gossip as Lauren made up the visitor passes. He left them with a wave and a significant lift in his spirits.

On his way back to his office, Liam diverted to stop at the gatehouse. Willo wasn't in today, so he presented himself to another new temporary guard, another he hadn't met previously. When asked, Sonjay said that the only thing he knew about the CCTV system was how to switch from one view to another. In total, the site had a dozen surveillance cameras across the site, any three of which could be displayed on three of the four large screens. The remaining screen was set on a loop circulating through all the other views. There were four views around the front administration block from each corner and a fifth in the reception area. Four of the seven other views were at strategic points at the external boundaries of the plant. Another two views were of the car parks and the last was a view down the plant along the main road.

Sonjay demonstrated to Liam how it was possible to flick from one view to another. They locked onto the 'down the plant' view which displayed the main driveway. The T-plant and production offices were in the middle distance. The standard view only showed the edge of the now orange plant. Sonjay thought all views were recorded and retained in history but apologised for his lack of knowledge of how to extract the past recorded history.

Liam left after underlying a note on his list: check the history on the CCTV security footage.

—

Paul De Zaale and Antonio Brazzos were in earnest conversation in the St Kilda Road offices, awaiting their guest from Asesoria. De Zaale had invited his contact at Asesoria, Pedro Cabrera, to meet and discuss expanding their business relationship. Pedro, who was the consummate salesman, headed up the Asesoria marketing team and acted as a principal contact for clients of note. Pedro's South American background and extensive work throughout the southern American continent made him the perfect Asesoria client manager for Agro Alliance.

Pedro was ushered into De Zaale's top floor office by his personal assistant Cynthia, who had collected the guest from the reception on the ground floor. They exchanged pleasantries as the guest looked over the view of Melbourne's Albert Park Lake. It was a prime spot on race day when the F-1 carnival came into town, the street track being used regularly for the season opener. Cynthia offered refreshments and left the men to continue their meeting, which she noted was being conducted in rapid Spanish.

Paul and Pedro had previously cemented a contract for Asesoria to run contract maintenance at the West Footscray plant, a deal that was a good earner for the contractor and had a handy commission for Paul. Brazzos poured everyone a shot of the Buchanan whiskey as they retired to the couches. The afternoon continued on as if they were three best friends; amigos. Pedro was as sharp as his dress sense and ready for upselling Asesoria's capabilities.

The plant incident had circulated throughout the industrial grapevine and was under intense scrutiny by the engineering contracting community. Asesoria was ready and most capable to work on a rebuild project. Pedro allayed all the questions from the Agro Alliance bosses, noting that his firm had construction experience for new builds and rebuilds all around the world. They could readily step up to look at the redesign concepts and would pull in some of the best engineering minds to improve safety, conduct HAZOPs and integrate solutions. He was a master salesman who was confident that being a fellow Columbian was a key asset in this case.

Money was not discussed – that would be established after a few sessions of cultural connection. However, Pedro knew he was sitting on a goldmine. They might have been nice guys – buenas compatriotas – but they were desperate. They needed a quick fix and with a lot of technical input and redesign. Speed and detail were issues which would command a premium. Even if Pedro couldn't do the technical stuff himself, and frankly had no idea of the detail, he knew he would get a crew of highly priced specialists to pad the project. His main focus was to balance the objectives. *Don't kill the golden goose, just milk it for what it can deliver.*

Pedro couldn't contain his excitement when Paul asked if Asesoria could also assist or lead their Safety Case application. All he could think about was dollars. More experts and more premiums. This was going to boost his profile and if it all came together, he may be looking at a promotion.

Pedro explained to his new best friends that this work was highly technical and specialised. They could get it done, of course, but it would require a team. Paul and Antonio were listening and began to feel that they might be snookered by the escalating costs. They were oblivious to their own internal failings and to the disaster that was afoot in the exiting of Sandra Hudson. Oblivious to the irony that they were previously haggling at mounting the work on one person alone, and now they were considering a team of specialists.

"This all sounds good, Pedro," Paul said, shutting down the pitch. "I'll need an outline of deliverables and your proposed cost summary. Our time frame is tight, we need the

Safety Case closed by November and the rebuild completed as soon after as possible."

Pedro, trying to contain his eagerness, blurted, "Certainly. It will be my highest priority, and I will have it to you this week." The time frame was his biggest asset, they would be forced to pay and pay big.

The meeting ended and they agreed to reconvene on Friday over lunch. Paul would arrange something and let him know. As they walked to the door, Paul asked Pedro to hang back for a moment while Brazzos left with instructions to have Cynthia return in five minutes to escort their guest back downstairs. When they were on their own, Paul offered Pedro another shot of whiskey, and they focused on Paul's other serious business.

25

LIAM RAN THE BOUNDARY on the outer wing at Zerbes Reserve, home of his East Doncaster Lions. Just running alone, doing laps. The boys had warmly welcomed him back, a stranger through the pre-season and despite the fact he was a doubtful player this season. He was simply happy to reunite with his mates and build up his fitness. Match fitness was a long way off and his pre-season absence would count against any chances of a game on match day. Not that he was looking to resume playing; that would come in time. He was simply happy to be exercising.

He welcomed the small opportunity to tune out and just run endlessly without any worry, pressure or thought. This was a perfect escape from the mounting stresses at Agro Alliance. His coaches and the club weren't pressurising him for a return, but they kept the door open. Rick and Adrian had been in serious training for months and had figured prominently in last week's opening round of the season. Tonight, the boys were in routine training drills around the centre wicket, stopping occasionally to yell out to Liam goading him as he ran. Lap after lap, Liam ran through the late afternoon fading sun, the outline of Melbourne's CBD in the distance.

The issues from work soon crept back into his thoughts. He had left early as soon as the visitors left and after sending summary notes to Frank on night shift and to Statler. He had enough for one day, and he felt the load of all the drama at work. The Muppet Man had been unsighted all day and there was no sign of any interest or support from Billings or his depleted safety team. Surely this was a joke. How could these clowns expect him to be a one-man show, lead the investigation, be the contact person to all the authorities, but not too friendly – stay in their lane, redesign a plant, and oversee the cleanup. Too much work, not enough hands, no technical support, and no leadership; a recipe made for a disaster.

All afternoon, Statler's words were replaying in his head: *It may be you as well. You'll be busy.* He needed this exercise to vent his frustration. He would run or jog laps until training was finished – that was his target. Then once adequately vented, he would shower, grab a few beers with the boys, and go back over to Sarah's place, catch her before she went into a stint of morning shifts.

—

The afternoon with Albert and Cameron went well. As well as he could have expected.

Albert was no fool. He knew the lay of the land and understood that the Agro Alliance senior managers were floundering with little process safety acumen. That wasn't his concern; it was inevitable that the place would lose its licence to operate as an MHF. Inevitable and almost certain if Brazzos continued his bluster and if they continued to strip experience and talent from the ranks. Albert had interacted with Sandra Hudson on many occasions and rated her as the best process safety specialist in Victorian industry. She was the best bar none and had been sought by Work Safe to aide in industry workshops. They had used her as an exemplar to guide other MHFs.

Albert met up with Liam in the production office conference room his team had been using in recent days. Liam was another emerging talent, rising quickly under Sandra's mentorship. The pair had the basis of a great team, but Albert sensed that the lack of site leadership was undermining the best of their talent.

Albert initiated the conversation. "Liam, firstly, thank you for being available to meet with me, ahead of Cameron. Your attitude and flexibility is both welcomed and refreshing. I am formally releasing the plant for your access. You can start the cleanup immediately. A word of advice from me, though: take it slow and be meticulous when the planning the rebuild."

Liam nodded to himself, relieved that he would be able to give his bosses some good news. "That's good. Thank you, we have a lot of work to do."

"No doubt. I assume you have been informed about the Notice restricting the operation until the re-design is completed and approved. Don't take it personally, it's very standard business," Albert said, and Liam nodded. "I hope you can get Sandra back on this project and please ensure your managers appreciate the necessity of this re-design. Sandra would be the perfect person to lead such a project."

Liam could only agree, and they reflected on her expertise across numerous areas. Albert took the opportunity to test out whether Sandra was still available, and they unofficially shared their confusion over Sandra's absence. Albert asked Liam if he could get a word to Sandra on his behalf. If she were thinking about a career change, they would love to talk with her. She would be an excellent supervisor in their ranks, a perfect mentor for some of the young graduates starting at Work Safe. Of course, she would be excluded from any matters relating to Agro Alliance, but Albert was almost visibly excited at the prospect of snaring a resource like Sandra Hudson. Liam was internally beaming with pride and couldn't wait to relay the interest.

Liam was enjoying the private yet frank discussion and sensed Albert was himself a good mentor. Albert couldn't discuss the deliberations of the investigation, as they still had interviews and technical follow-ups. Liam was trying to read between the lines and he surmised that the investigation was steering towards poor systems, inadequate design, and lack of process awareness. This may have ended with a large fine. It didn't sound like there was any focus on deliberate operator error nor any individual culpability, but Liam was only guessing.

A coffee break and small talk filled the rest of the time. They still had a few minutes before Cameron Oxley was due to arrive. Cameron was a tall striking man, dressed casually in jeans and a business shirt, with a healthy mop of black hair. He introduced himself and they learnt that he had been with Workcover for two years, transitioning after ten years as a police officer. Liam let Cameron and Albert do most of the talking. The plan was established and they listed seventeen names for interviews. The supervisors, plant operators, Mario, maintenance fitters, the maintenance planner and engineers were all expected. The addition of Billings, Statler, Jennison and Brazzos was surely intended to test the management leadership. The surprises were that they were adamant to add Sandra Hudson and Ernesto.

Liam walked his visitors out and returned to write up his notes and send a couple of emails.

He emailed Frank, the oncoming night shift supervisor, with instructions to move the empty tech drums, get them weighed, sampled, and sent to drum wash for processing. He also added a copy of his list of questions and circulated it to the four shift supervisors asking for their review, consideration, and response in the next few days. He printed a copy of the email and discussed it with today's supervisor Dennis, asking him to relay it to Frank on shift change and make sure he got a start on it tonight.

Then he wrote to Jim Statler and copied those that were requested for interview, as well as Consuela Garcia from RK Legal. He outlined that Cameron Oxley was planning to interview on the upcoming Friday and then three or four days the following week, scheduling the people on the list at four or five per day, each for around an hour, maybe more. He drafted a proposed schedule and asked for responses as soon as possible. Liam also advised that they had requested copies of information about the initial design of the T-plant, all equipment inspection records for the plant, specifically the fibreglass vessel, the training records and competency tests for Johnno and all the T-plant operators, copies of the MOC procedure, Johnno's personnel file, and any vision of the plant from the security CCTV system.

—

After football training, Liam drove the thirty minutes back to Bentleigh to catch up with Sarah. The original plan for a Tuesday night at the small cinema in nearby Pinewood was shelved. He was too late and Sarah needed to be up bright and early for her morning shift. Plan B was to watch some television or just hang out at the Hatfield's.

Sarah's parents loved Liam; besotted was how Sarah had described it. *Liam this and Liam that*, a bit over the top. Sarah wasn't complaining, certainly better than the opposite when her previous choices were not of her parents' liking. When Liam arrived, Sarah's mum Daphne greeted him at the door with a hug. Sarah's dad Gerry had put a beer in Liam's hand before the hellos had even finished.

Sarah's mum was making a cake and had been doing other baking, in her preparation for the Easter break. Everyone gathered around the kitchen bench watching Daphne cooking her heart out. Samples were on the offer; Liam first, of course, and much to the annoyance of Sarah and her brother. Gerry had brought out some playing cards and was enticing the youngsters into a game of 500 or maybe 'head and foot'.

As Gerry was setting up on the dining table, Liam helped Sarah's mother with the cleanup. Daphne was singing his praises. "Such a good boy. He's a keeper, Sarah. Don't let him get away."

Sarah was pretending to gag while Liam's cheeks turned red. "Don't give him a big head, Mum."

Liam redirected the attention away from himself by looking at all the items in the sink. "So many attachments, Mrs Hatfield. What are all these for?"

"Cooking requires lots of different things. Mixing, blending, folding, chopping, beating, stirring, whipping, kneading and on and on."

Liam nodded, thinking to himself, *Mmm ... so it seems that not all mixers are the same!*

26

FRANK HAD RECEIVED THE email from Liam and the relayed instructions from Dennis at the shift handover. Jim Statler had authorised some of the day group to work back on overtime under Frank's direction. He had a crew starting the cleanup with shovels and brooms on the ground floor and others collecting debris and sundry items, relocating them to an area assigned at the drum wash station. The afternoon shift maintenance team had reactor 2 secured and suspended on slings while they started the disassembling process. Oscar from drum washing was assigned to collect the tech drums and get them all weighed and sampled.

It was just the start of what was going to be a long job, many weeks in the making just to get it all cleaned and orderly. Each piece of equipment, from pumps to instruments, would have to be disconnected, individually cleaned, and inspected.

Frank felt invigorated in his role as the overseer of this weird recovery project, even if it was just for his shift. He loved the fact that he was calling the shots, with the freedom to assess the order of work and the priorities. Safety was the key concern; it was paramount to get things secured first and then to methodically pull it apart once it was checked. He didn't want the fitters going at it like a bull at a gate. Each part would need to be checked and photographed before moving to the maintenance workshop assembly area.

This was a huge variation to his boring shift routine and made him further yearn for a day role. He had his eye on Mario's senior permit writer role and he was almost assured to replace Mario in time, assured by the prior production manager Eddie Gundy. Frank, like his fellow shift supervisors had been appointed to the shift lead after many years as a senior plant operator. He had worked every plant. He was also a first class permit writer and one of a few that had trained to write confined space entry permits.

Twenty-five years on shift had taken a heavy toll on his body, his health, and his marriage. Frank was tired of the rotating shift lifestyle. It was a young person's game, even then it had its problems. Despite the good money, shift loading and penalties, he regretted his career path. As a young married man on shift with children, it was a constant juggle. He was crabby after nights and yelled at his kids. His wife had to virtually look after the family as a single mum, tip toeing around his moods.

Frank was worn down and needed a change; he needed some normality. He wanted to make up for the lost time he had missed as a father and wanted to be there when it was going to be his time as a grandfather. Eddie Gundy valued him and had worked on this succession plan to replace Mario when he retired. Mario's retirement seemed to be a long-term plan that was talked about constantly, but through his procrastinations it never eventuated. When the new Agro Alliance bosses arrived, they initiated a wave of redundancies across the plant. They took to the place with a new broom, stating that they intended to cull the old inefficient practices and start over with people prepared to toe the line, no more problems with people referring back to the old ways. Mario was given a package and Frank thought that his opportunity had arrived.

But alas, Frank's hopes were dashed and he didn't get the Mario position. Eddie Gundy had been shown the door and the new manager, Jim Statler, wasn't interested in Eddie's plan nor Frank's career change. He didn't even get a redundancy, supposedly retained for his skills with confined space permit writing, while two of his colleagues took the money. To rub salt into his wounds, Mario was hired back by Asesoria and recontracted to Agro Alliance as a contract permit writer. Supposedly all above board, but to Frank it was fully dodgy, dodgy grade number one.

The overtime boys finished for the night and Oscar gave Frank a list of the drum weights. Frank inspected the numbers and determined that the charge that Johnno had performed was equivalent to thirteen and a half drums of tech.

Oscar stood at Frank's desk and apologised. "Sorry sir, I couldn't get any samples. The drums that still had stuff in them ... well, they were way too solid."

Frank looked up, seeing Oscar with an orange board in his hand. "Of course. I might need to get them back to melt again. I'll make a note for Liam. Thanks for your help." Then looking at the object in Oscar's hand, asked, "What have you got there?"

"I'm not really sure. I found it jammed in between the empty drums. It looks like some sort of clipboard, but whatever was on it is well gone. I didn't know what to do with it. What do you think?"

Frank recognised it as the log sheet for the plant and asked Oscar to leave it with him. He gathered some copy paper to make a place to put it on his desk. He thanked Oscar again and watched him walk away, his night over. Examining the mess that was surely the log sheet clipboard, his mind turned back to Johnno. *Johnno must have been holding this same log sheet when the accident happened ... how eerie. This might also be answer to Liam's first question.*

The rest of the night was relatively quiet. Maintenance had only disconnected half of the reactor connections and left after stringing a tarpaulin over the vessel as Frank had requested. Frank rearranged some duties and grabbed a spare operator to run some hot water hoses on the top of the T-plant. They coordinated a connection to a steam-water mixer and washed down the top two levels for the rest of the shift. After a few hours, the orange rain started to turn clear. In the coming nights, they would be ready to tackle the bottom two floors.

Frank retired to his supervisor's desk and sent an email summary of his findings for Liam.

Liam

Summary of work - night shift

1. *Maintenance have removed discharge pump from reactor 2, cleaned and placed in maintenance workshop. The reactor 2 vessel has been secured in place with restraints and work is 50% complete at disconnecting pipelines. The bursting disc has been disconnected and discharge to relief drum was full of tech. Scrubber is still intact.*

2. *Day team have cleared debris and most of the sludge from the ground floor. Will need to repeat after each washdown.*
3. *Tarp set up over reactor 2 and level two work area. Top two floors cleaned down with hot water.*
4. *The tech drums have been weighed, with still two and a half drums equivalent remaining in them. They are positioned in drum wash area. No samples taken. We will need to melt them again for samples.*
5. *Oscar in drum wash found log sheet clipboard wedged in between the tech drums. I have checked control room and original is not in the pigeonhole. I think Johnno may have had it with him doing his readings. Almost sure to be the answer to your question #1.*
6. *I also chatted to our night shift instro/electrician about the pressure spike. Shows at about 30kPa on trend which would correlate with the bursting disc rupture. He said that these transmitters are quite slow, and that the spike could be higher but not recorded. No way of knowing how high.*

I hope all this helps.

PS: I'm not sure why I am on the interview list, and actually I am a bit uncomfortable about that. Is it really necessary?

Frank

27

OVER THE NEXT FEW days, almost everyone on the interview list made representation to Liam to be excused. Brazzos and Billings didn't make any request, rather just returned blunt notes claiming they were unavailable. Early on Thursday, Liam took his scheduling problem to Statler to seek his assistance. He needed to reset the schedule for Workcover, who were expecting their first interview early the next day.

"Jim, I'm just the coordinator, the go-between, in all of this. It's not up to me to say who will or will not attend the interviews. I need management help here. Can you get some legal input and advise me what to do?"

Statler was caught in the middle. He had handballed everything to Liam and wasn't keen to be involved, but couldn't ignore the request. Feeling a sense of obligation, he responded cautiously, "Let me see what I can do. I'll raise it at the production meeting today and try to get you some answers this afternoon. My initial suggestion is to schedule the few that haven't an issue for tomorrow, and that gives us time before next week."

Leaving Statler with the issue, Liam went over to the

drum wash area looking for Oscar, who hadn't been on site in the last few days. He wanted to discuss the clipboard and arrange the remaining tech to be returned and melted. Oscar was a new casual employee doing the dirty work in the drum washing area. He was at the bottom of the pecking order and hence relegated to the tasks that the permanent staff happily left for the casuals. He was stacking a series of washed drums onto pallets when Liam approached. "Excuse me, mate. You're Oscar, aren't you?"

"Ah, yes sir, can I help you?"

Liam introduced himself and explained that he was trying to get the tech drums returned to the hot baths for melting and he wanted to get Oscar to help. He also quizzed him on where the stray clipboard had been found. Oscar directed him to the assembly of tech drums, pointing to a spot in between drums on a pallet.

"That was a good pick-up, and I appreciate your smart thinking to report it to the supervisor. We need more industrious and lateral thinking workers. Thanks a lot, and very nice to meet you, Oscar."

"Do you want all the drums back or just ones with the tech?" asked Oscar, keen to help.

"Just two with the most tech, if you can. Do you know where to take them?"

"Yes, the T-plant hot baths. I know where it is, I was helping Johnno to find the two missing drums on that day ... you know when ..."

Liam's eyes widened. "What do you mean the missing drums? I left notes for the operators. It should have been clear."

Oscar smiled and understood Liam's message. "The plant

was falling behind apparently and Jake asked me to go and help. I don't think that Johnno fellow had read the notes. When I went into the control room, I saw the notes and it was pretty straight forward. I found them and brought them over when that manager from up the front was yelling at everyone."

"Tell me more."

Oscar explained that the manager was really mad, spitting chips at everyone. "He even yelled at me when I reported that I found the missing drums. He nearly blew a gasket yelling at Johnno, Jake, and Mr Statler. He told them to get this damn thing moving. He was sick of the delays. He even told them to forget about the missing drums: 'Too late now, just run with fourteen drums'."

Liam quizzed him some more and asked what else he could recall.

"I'm not sure." Oscar shrugged. "He was just yelling. Said something about forgetting that MOC baloney. I didn't understand and then Johnno sent me back to the drum wash station."

"He said to forget the MOC. Is that right?"

"One hundred percent," replied Oscar. "But like I told you, I didn't know what he was talking about. Ask Jake, he was there and copped a mouthful."

"I will. Thank you, Oscar." Liam left him to arrange the tech drums and made a mental note to talk with Jake tomorrow.

—

Barry Billings found his way to the weekly production meeting twenty minutes ahead of time and cornered Brazzos in his office. He was in a bad mood and remonstrated with Brazzos about the interview schedule. He was adamant that he wasn't going to be a patsy for this Workcover witch-hunt. The accident had nothing to do with him, so he didn't understand why he was on their list. "I'm not going to be interviewed!" Billings demanded.

Brazzos was losing his patience and started to see the fickle side of his safety manager. "Calm down. This isn't all about you, you fool. They are wanting to test the management team. We need to stand united and present as a strong cohesive team. I don't need you getting all flaky when we need strength."

"I don't care. I'm not doing it. You can't make me," Billings stammered, getting worked up and red in the face.

"I certainly can, and if you don't like it, you can pack your bags."

"You can't sack me. I quit." Billings stormed out of Brazzos's office and threw his notepad at Suzi on the way out, passing the other managers who were arriving for the meeting. Statler tried to stop the rampaging, but was shoved fairly in the chest which caused Statler to stumble backwards onto the ground. Brazzos came out of his office and announced the meeting was cancelled. He barked at Suzi to get Michelle Buchanan on the phone and told the others to go back to work.

28

LIAM MET WITH CAMERON Oxley on the Friday morning ahead of the reshuffled interview schedule. He was first cab of the rank for the interviews and had Jake following him in the morning, with Mario and Aussie Joe in the afternoon. Statler had been around to each of the interviewees to remind them to stick to simple answers and not to expand or stray to other non-specific issues. The interviewees were all collectively nervous and each seemed worried about what would happen if they stuffed up. Several pleaded to be excused and most were very subdued.

Oxley was friendly and patient as Liam explained that several on the list were worried and might potentially withdraw. He understood and expected some would take that stance. However, he tried to explain to Liam that they had nothing to fear if there was nothing to hide. The interviews were intended to be simple fact-finding exercises. Workcover had requested the supervisors to get a collective idea of how the shift team operated, the fitters and others to explore the issues around the accident, and the managers to understand the leadership philosophy and structures. Absences would only leave gaps and open up potential speculation.

Liam's interview was unremarkable, with simple detail about the process and explanation of some of the Work Safe observations. Oxley took notes, seemingly happy to fill his brief and move on to the next issue. Liam was again left with a feeling that Oxley was narrowing towards a finding of system failure, an easy wrap up which would result in a big fine. There was no grilling of individual roles, nor was there any sense of operator error. He couldn't be sure, but he suspected the deferred start to the interviews was to allow the Workcover inspector time to consult with the Work Safe investigators. The questioning may be to reinforce their lines of inquiry.

Jake had a similar feeling after his interview, as he and Liam conferred over a bite to eat in the canteen. In time, Liam would report back to Statler after the afternoon interviews were complete. While they were having their lunch, Liam took the opportunity to quiz Jake on the message he'd had from Oscar the day before, paraphrasing Brazzos yelling and demanding to just make the charge and not worry about the missing drums.

Jake smiled at the question. "He really lost it. Ranted to everyone. Stormed off saying we don't need an MOC, just get it started."

"Who was there?"

"Johnno was at the hot baths and copped the initial spray, then that Oscar fellow came over and got a mouthful. Statler and I were off to the side out of the initial confrontation but copped a spray as well when Brazzos walked past on his way back to his office."

"Then what happened?"

"I told Johnno to charge the extra two drums and see

what melted while he continued decanting the other drums. I asked Statler to raise an MOC, but he shook his head and also said to just do a short charge and get cracking, or words to that effect." Jake paused to have a bite of his salad roll. "In the end, it wasn't a big deal. We had enough to fill up past the agitator interlock and get started, maybe a waste in some ways, with an excessive use of the other ingredients was all."

"Maybe," agreed Liam. "But why did Johnno write down sixteen drums? He wouldn't have cared; he could have easily recorded fourteen and noted that was under Brazzos's direction."

"That's right. I don't know the answer to that. I've thought about it. Maybe Johnno was under the pump. I won't lie to you, I was certainly riding him. I had to get the lazy bastard out of the smoke shelter several times, not that he deserved what happened. I think he just cut corners and didn't think otherwise. I was riding him, Brazzos was yelling at him and Statler was pushing him hard. I think he snubbed his nose at us, as if he were saying 'stuff you guys'."

Liam shrugged. "Probably, but he cared enough to do his readings, even if he was late."

"Only to save his own hide, if you ask me," Jake offered. "I was going to write him up if he missed them again, and Frank was always hot on him. He was close to getting a disciplinary note."

—

Statler invited Liam to meet with him and Brazzos late in the afternoon, after the final interviews were completed. Brazzos wanted a recap and an insight into where it was all heading. Liam couldn't be specific but gave his overall opinion of the 'lack of system strategy'. Brazzos asked for examples and seemed happy with the initial feedback. He had been reviewing the interview list with Angelo Tambakis and he confirmed that was RK Legal's impressions as well.

Liam then discovered Barry Billings had quit and that Brazzos wasn't available for an interview. He was insisting that Statler and Jennison attend to provide the company perspective. They collectively agreed that Ernesto should be excused, and Satler was charged with keeping the others on track. Liam expressed his concern that the absence of Billings and Sandra Hudson straight after the accident could be an issue.

Brazzos was adamant. "Don't you worry about that, Liam. I'll get Jim to respond for them. Was there any discussion today about operator error, maintenance mistakes or individual faults?"

Liam was quick to say, "No not in my interview, nor from my understanding with the others." He couldn't resist throwing an extra barb to see where it fell. "I think they were interested in the big rush by Johnno and the lack of an MOC?"

He saw something flicker in Brazzos as he screwed up his face. The moment passed as Brazzos looked directly at Liam, restating his position. "Again, don't worry about that. Let it drop. Let's just let them finish the interviews and move on. Oh, and make sure Ernesto is excused."

"Okay. Can I ask about the rebuild, redesign and Safety Case?"

"Not now. We're still working on that. We'll probably get some technical help from Asesoria. I'll let everyone know once that's sorted. I've got to make a call. Thanks for the feedback. Let's talk again next week." Brazzos was keen to wrap up. He needed to update De Zaale on the Billings exit, which would inevitably lead to another Garcia and Asesoria payday.

29

OVER THE NEXT FEW weeks, Liam meticulously reviewed all the instrument trends. The CCTV vision from the gatehouse was recovered and it hadn't disclosed anything significant other than a small white fuzz in the bottom left corner at the same time as the orange eruption. The interviews were all finished, and all the requested documents were provided and copies were sent to RK Legal.

Sue Carpenter's report concluded that some kind of pressure event had indeed caused the accident, although the source of the pressure could not be fully identified. She suspected that the mixing in reactor 2 was inadequate and that a volatile pocket of unreacted substances suddenly released. The reaction caused a short sharp pressure wave, breaking the rupture disc and stressing the vessel. It was possible that the vessel was weak as it had never been inspected. The rupture possibly occurred on a line of weakness. Sue had specialists review the pressure required to rupture a fibreglass vessel and propel the agitator out several meters. The conclusion was it would have been at least 100kPa and possibly 200kPa if the vessel were solid. In the absence of any new information, it was an open finding and an unfortunate accident.

RK Legal expected that the Work Safe review would result in a similar open finding, and that the Agro Alliance would be found guilty of poor systems and poor supervision These were both standard charges used by Work Safe which had resulted in successful convictions in many other cases. De Zaale and Brazzos weren't happy hearing this summary and were further displeased to learn that each count could attract a fine of up to $500,000. RK Legal suggested that they would engage counsel to try and mitigate the charges, to use the efforts of Liam and others to demonstrate contrition and remorse.

Tambakis had told De Zaale that they would try their best, but the tensions between Brazzos and Work Safe would be an issue, as would the poor feedback on their Safety Case efforts. Work Safe would be keen to take a scalp in the public's eyes and felt no empathy for Agro Alliance's leadership. With all the Asesoria costs and now the potential million dollar finding, this was a grossly expensive fuck up.

The whole situation sat poorly with Liam. The managers appeared to be wrapping it up, paying the money, and forgetting about Johnno. Sue had left issues unanswered and he thought that her 'mixing' comments needed more consideration. The technical experience at the plant was grossly inadequate so Liam sought the opinion of Sandy. It had been weeks and he wasn't satisfied.

"Hello Sandy, how have you been?" Liam asked when he called her to explore his concerns.

"Very good, Liam, very good indeed. You wouldn't believe my luck." Sandy beamed on the other end of the phone.

"Tell me, what luck are you talking about?"

"This week that Buchanan lady called me and offered a six month payout to settle my dispute with Agro – my extended stress leave. I thought they were going to cut me dry, but I guess with the Billings breakdown, they thought I would have a solid case for unfair dismissal. So, six months' pay is in line with a successful claim for unfair dismissal. It's a cheap solution for them and I couldn't be bothered contesting it. I was happy to agree to the payout and the finality of it all has brightened me up significantly."

"That's really fantastic. They seem keen to just throw money at fixing their people problems. Have you heard that they're now engaging a crew of four or five consultants to cover your work on the Safety Case, and they're also using the same firm to help redesign the plant and to provide a temporary replacement for Billings."

"No, I hadn't heard. That's unreal. It makes me laugh. I have to fight my guts out just to get some PSM attention and now when the heat rises, and I've left, they capitulate." Sandy added a bit of anger to her reply.

"Maybe it's what we're learning to be the Columbian way," Liam laughed in reply.

"But Liam, that's not the only news I have," Sandy's voice lifted. "Albert Cohen contacted me and is offering me a senior posting at Work Safe. I didn't hesitate – it's what I like doing and he seems to value my work, unlike Billings or Brazzos. I start in a couple of weeks." She sounded exhilarated, her tone a lot more upbeat now. "I won't be able to deal with anything related to Argo Alliance, of course. I'd love to be a fly on the wall when Brazzos finds out."

"Me too. You'll love that job. I formally acknowledge you as a star."

They chatted for a further thirty minutes, reflecting on how every cloud has a silver lining. Liam finally remembered the reason for his call. "If you have a few more minutes, I want to pick your brain about our T-plant accident."

Sandy was most receptive as the accident was still a puzzle on her mind. She considered it to be business that was left unfinished, albeit not her problem any longer. Liam explained the current expectation of an open finding and the intent to serve charges on system and supervision. However, it was Sue Carpenter's observation of inadequate mixing that intrigued him, and he was wondering where and how to take this thinking forward.

Sandy had no immediate idea, but offered a suggestion. "I'm meeting up with the old guard for lunch on Friday. You remember Alexander Scotland my first boss and Eddie Gundy the production manager? They have a regular lunch date every two months and I join them when I can. Why don't you join us this Friday and we can workshop it a bit?"

"Great idea, thanks Sandy. Where and when?"

"Normally around 1:00pm at the Hobson Bay Hotel in Williamstown, on the rooftop dining area."

Liam took Friday afternoon off as a half day of annual leave. He wasn't going to be hijacked for some obscure training session and was eager to see Sandy and especially his old boss. He worked for Eddie when he first started at Agro Alliance, but a year later Eddie was made redundant and replaced by Statler. It was a strange transition, because as far as Liam could ascertain, the roles were identical. The common belief was that Brazzos had wanted to exit the 'old guard' and replace it with people they moulded in their thinking. Money fixed all his needs. How did the redundancy package operate? A puzzle that HR must have resolved with their wording magic. Liam had never met Scotland but knew he was highly regarded by everyone in maintenance and outside of work. Scotland was on long service leave before the round of redundancies and he seemed to have transition seamlessly into retirement.

Liam arrived at the Hobson Bay Hotel early and located the reserved table on the balcony rooftop. He strolled around while waiting for Sandy to arrive. A dozen tables slowly filled up, as did the series of seats on the long bar that ran along the outside of this open-air alfresco space. It was a wonderful place, serviced with a full bar and extra stools on the western side shaded from the afternoon sun. Liam was mesmerised with the easterly view over Port Phillip Bay. The West Gate Bridge was on the left and framed the impressive view of the skyscrapers of Melbourne's CBD.

Sandy came up behind Liam as he was daydreaming and broke his solitude. "Pretty nice view, don't you think?"

Liam turned and beamed at his friend. "Stunning. Thanks for inviting me." He lent forward to give her a light kiss on her cheek. "I was thinking I must bring Sarah here. I never knew it existed."

"The pub has been here for ages, one of the oldest ones in the area. Apparently it's changed hands several times and was even a fancy restaurant at one stage. I think this rooftop dining is fairly recent, but I'm not sure. It's now famous as the venue for the 'old guard' luncheons."

Sandy ushered Liam to sit while she grabbed some drinks:

a pint for Liam and a white wine for herself. They spent the next few minutes talking about Sandy's new career path while they waited for the others, both of whom walked in together promptly at 1:00pm. Liam rose and greeted Eddie as if he were a long-lost uncle, and then Liam was introduced to the tall Alexander. Sandy shouted a round of drinks and they all settled chatting aimlessly while they studied the lunch menu.

Liam asked Alexander and Eddie how they felt about the redundancy and if they were settled into retirement. "Mine didn't start out as a redundancy," Alexander corrected him. "I was actually on long service leave when Brazzos started at Agro, and I think he just assumed I would retire, or heard whispers that I was thinking about retiring. Anyway, when I came back they had already hired someone else, and he was in my office."

"That would be Stuart Jennison," Liam said.

"Yes, that's right. I met him just the once in my office on that first day back. So, I went up and introduced myself to Mr Brazzos and challenged him as to why there was a new fellow sitting in my chair. He was bewildered then rang his contact in HR in St Kilda Road and they collectively worked out and agreed that I was back from long service leave. Then he tried to tell me that I was retired, to which I told him bluntly that I was not. 'Show me the signed papers and the final pay letters,' I said."

Sandy pricked up her ears, as she hadn't known this detail. "What happened next?"

"Well, they were stumped, completely blindsided. I had never indicated retirement and was back ready to work. They told me to take a couple extra days off while they sorted it out. I told them that I'd had enough time off already, so they agreed to days off fully paid and no deduction on my leave balance. Later that week, I got an offer to consider an alternate role, some fabricated position of 'Corporate Strategy and Engineering Excellence'. When I baulked at that, they finally said they would pay me for nine months and then give me a redundancy settlement. With that in writing, I accepted and never stepped back into the place."

The other three listened intently, shaking their head at the brazen cheek of it all. Alexander added, "The best part was that I was actually intending to retire shortly after I came back from my leave, but I dug my heels in, mainly because I felt insulted and unappreciated."

Sandy clapped her hands. "Well played, boss."

Eddie confirmed he was enjoying his retirement. Life was almost perfect. He was playing more golf, and his handicap had dropped below eighteen for the first time in his life and he was busy gardening or being posted on various grandchildren duty. His life was now focused on the three Gs: golf, gardening, and grandchildren. He hadn't missed the old place one bit, other than the few people who he saw periodically.

Eddie told the group he spent a couple of afternoons catching up with Johnno's parents in the last few weeks, since the funeral. "They are super nice people, devasted of course. I know Johnno was fairly inexperienced as an operator and I've heard he was a bit lazy, but I found him always polite and helpful. He was the sort of bloke that energised his mates. His mates have been great, by the way, and were really pleased that I've visited the family. They reckon the Agro Alliance management team haven't contacted them since they collected Johnno's stuff a couple of days after the accident. Even his last pay and leave entitlements were delivered by mail to his parents, addressed to David Johnson c/o Mr Johnson."

"That doesn't surprise me," Sandy mocked. "The people focus at that place went out the door when they got rid of the 'old guard'."

"Such a pity," Eddie said. "It's extremely hard to build a people culture, but all too easy to lose it. I remember when we used to show farmers through the place. They were all blown away by the attitudes and helpfulness of everyone." Turning to his mate Alexander, he added, "Do you remember when the unions tried to get in the door?"

Alexander smiled. "Yeah, they tried many times and in different ways. Each time they were sent packing. Even the organisers grew to know that we had something special, a nut that they could never crack."

"Well, those days are over now," said Liam. "Union talk is rife, and the nutcracker is being deployed as we speak. The boys don't go that extra mile anymore. Heads down and stick to the basics."

"We used to give the sons and daughters of workers some casual employment when we could," Eddie reflected. "Everyone appreciated it. Not every kid worked out, but the parent generally held them to account and told us to bounce them if there were any issues. It was like a family." Then he changed direction. "I caught up with Phil Buckley's mum a few weeks back. I was helping her take Phil to Centrelink to apply for his disability allowance. Phil was let go, maybe paid out, I think. I don't think current management would have the patience to deal with his brain injury."

Liam shook his head. "No, they didn't. Same as the

operator in the run-off area who broke his arm last year and a few others. You don't want to be injured at Agro anymore. The new mantra is that there are no injuries reported on their watch, hence they can boast about their improved safety record."

"Except for Johnno," said both Alexander and Sandy at the same time.

Sandy redirected the group to the business at hand. "Gents, I invited Liam today, as I indicated in the text that I sent you yesterday, to let him give an update on Johnno's accident and he wants to pick our brains about something related to the accident." The retirees waited with anticipation as she continued. "So, over to you, Liam. You have the floor, or rather the rooftop."

Liam laughed at her quip. "Thank you, Sandy. Firstly, I love this place." Then directing his attention to Alexander and Eddie who sat opposite. "I appreciate the chance to get your input."

Liam gave the overview of the accident and the investigation findings to date, the pressure spike, the torn vessel, the agitator, and the short charge. He took questions and they were collectively brought up to speed with the current status. In recent days, Liam had confirmed that the molten sample of the leftover tech was mainly tech, although very dark in colour. He also explained about the push, the big hurry, during the rework batch and Johnno's shortcuts. The absence of management of control systems to which Sandy added her insight on the recent decline in process safety systems. She explained that even if Agro Alliance had outsourced the preparation of the next Safety Case, they would still have a lot of problems. No good just having a good story; it had to reflect how the place operated and how the people intuitively live the story.

Their lunch arrived and they fell into a conversational lull while they ate. Eddie was first to break the silence. "Liam, you mentioned a noise before the accident or said that Jake had heard a noise. I think that that would have been the sample pot blowing out."

"Yes, that's what a few have said, but no one saw anything, of course. I looked at the gatehouse CCTV view of the main road and couldn't see anything, maybe a small white fuzziness on the bottom corner as the contents blew. That was probably around the rough location of the seal pot."

Eddie agreed and added, "Have you checked the vision from the synthesis tower? It used to point out over the top of the top floor of the synthesis plant for the control room operator to coordinate valving activities with the outside operator. In the background we had a grand view of most of the T-plant, and I remember it because I used it in the infamous 'Lemon Tree' investigation."

Alexander laughed. "I remember that story. It was a ripper."

For the benefit of Sandy and Liam, Eddie explained that the operators had been complaining of urine odour in the T-plant and suspected some people were too lazy to go down to the nearby toilet, opting to relieve themselves in the corner of the structure. "I scanned back through the tapes and found the culprit – an apprentice that worked for Alexander. He was caught red handed, so to speak. Alexander gave him a final warning and I sent an email telling everyone our plant was not a 'lemon tree'."

"That's right," Alexander added, still laughing. "He was

a dickhead anyway and not particularly good at his job. He finished up a few weeks later. Not his calling, he said, but I suspect he was heavy chided by all the operators and maintenance guys."

Liam was writing in his notebook and responded, "Thanks, Eddie. I'll certainly check that out."

"Do it pretty soon, Liam. I don't think there was much memory on that CCTV set-up, and it just over-wrote itself on a continuous loop. Maybe a month at best, from my memory of the lemon tree saga."

Sandy went off to get another round of drinks, leaving Liam to broach the subject of the mixing conundrum. He recounted the words from Sue Carpenter, talking about a pocket of unreacted material, and he explained that he had been thinking about mixers and how they were different. His dilemma was that the agitator on the fateful vessel was functioning and was mixing, so it couldn't be the problem.

"Probably not," Eddie said. "It wouldn't be a problem unless you changed the mixer."

"What do you mean, changed the mixer? We did change the mixer, but it still worked." Liam was stunned that Eddie was so clear. "We apparently broke the agitator on reactor 2 and swapped it out for the universal spare."

Alexander looked at Eddie, half nodded and clapped his hands together. "My boy, not all mixers are the same. Sounds to me that this is potentially the heart of your problem."

"That universal spare agitator is for the formulation vessels," Eddie said. "They are purpose built for the formulation process – they aren't used in vessels where we have reactions. They are designed to simply blend the product to produce a homogeneous mixture."

Alexander picked up the narrative in this two-pronged lecture. "The reaction vessels often need pumping and blending. A more vigorous and turbulent mix. Not all mixers are the same."

Liam appreciated the insight. "So, this difference might be significant. How can I find out more detail? Apparently our records on the plant are sparse."

Sandy interjected as she put down her tray of drinks. "When Brazzos came along, he had Jennison restructure the maintenance records. They brought in a consultant and switched the whole place onto a new electronic database. In their haste to be new and bold, they threw out a lot of old records."

"That is madness, Sandy." Alexander ran a hand through his hair. "Why didn't they just translate them onto the new database, especially the design stuff? What happened to Bussy's files and records?"

Sandy didn't know the answer to the question but surmised they were also boxed up when he was made redundant and his function transferred to the purchasing department. They wouldn't know what to do with them. She suggested they may be archived somewhere.

Liam scribbled more notes – *Check the archive store.*

Alexander started thinking, pondering aloud and mumbling. He looked at Eddie. "What about that bloke we used on the redesign of the synthesis reactor? You remember, he was a mixing expert. From South Australia. He came over and spent time taking measurements and asking heaps of questions. I think he had the history of the T-plant as well. What was his name? Something like a flower. Ohhh ... what was his name?"

"You're thinking of Michael Rosenbloom," Eddie said. "His father started an engineering consultancy, and we used them several times over the years. Michael took over the business when his dad retired. He was a whiz kid, super smart. A bit of a toff, private school boy from a wealthy family, but he knew his stuff."

"That's right, good one." Alexander clicked his fingers, remembering both the name and the man. "That's right. Give him a call, Liam. He'll probably remember the agitator itself and if not, he'll be your best bet at getting to the bottom of any mixing riddle."

Liam was straight back to his notebook. "Why isn't this known in the plant today? Seems like we're working in the dark. Do you have a contact for this bloke?"

"Sorry mate," Alexander said, shaking his head.

Eddie, also shaking his head, offered, "I think it was a family business. Try Rosenbloom, or else google agitation experts."

Sandy smiled. The boys were pulling it all together. *Leadership and experience. It's important to value both.*

30

LIAM LEFT THE HOTEL and headed straight to the plant, an easy twenty-minute drive. He wanted to get there and pick up on the leads that the old guard had provided. Importantly, he wanted to try and get the synthesis plant CCTV vision before it was lost, if indeed it was still available. He was worried that it had now been four weeks since the accident and on the cusp of the memory capability, according to Eddie's recollection. On the way, he phoned ahead to talk with the IT guru at the plant.

Jeff Ogden had been at Agro Alliance for eight years. He had seen lots of change and was the mastermind of the company's IT infrastructure. Jeff was in his late twenties and a geek with computers who stayed sharp and across the ever-changing world of information technology. Jeff had helped Liam on a few occasions with his own computing needs and was a self-recognised dual linguist. Jeff spoke both plain English for technical illiterates and gobbledygook tech language as his preferred tongue.

Jeff answered the call. "Liam, what's up? I assume you know it is Friday afternoon."

"Only too well, my friend." Liam was calling from his car,

still a few minutes from arriving. "I have an urgent request. Sorry for the late call, but I've only found out about this issue, this possibility."

He explained the situation and his concern that the clock was ticking. "I'll be there in five minutes. Anything you can do would be great. It couldn't wait until Monday. I don't want to take the chance that it would be overwritten over the weekend."

"That is, if it hasn't already," Jeff informed.

Liam parked in the front visitor's car park area and raced into the administration building, waving to Lauren and Elise as he went through the reception glass doors. He found Jeff in his office in front of his supersized screen, as if he was a modern gamer. Jeff looked up and beamed. "You're in luck, mate. One day left."

Liam went around the desk as Jeff tracked the timing of the incident. The vision was clear as day and more importantly, it was time stamped. They watched the replay as it panned along towards 4:14pm and saw Johnno walk up the stairs to the first floor with a clipboard in his hand. He walked around and appeared to be taking recordings on the clipboard before heading back to the stairwell as the time stamp reached 4:17pm.

Both Jeff and Liam gasped as they witnessed a large whitish jet of fluid, water maybe, spraying out of the sample pot on the ground floor spraying to Johnno's right, before hitting the second floor above. A few seconds later, the footage revealed the full force of the orange eruption. They could make out the pressure pushing the agitator up from its mounting and then by virtue of the electrical cable attachment, it was pulled towards Johnno. It tore itself out of the vessel, leaving the long scar that Liam and Sue Carpenter had measured, then cartwheeled, blades and all, across the landing.

It catapulted into Johnno with a sickening thud, casting Johnno's helmet into the air as he was toppled over the first-floor handrail, landing with a thump on the ground, dead on impact.

Both Jeff's and Liam's faces lost all colour. "What the fuck …" Jeff exhaled. They sat in silence for a few minutes before he looked at Liam. "Do you want to see it again?"

"No way. That was horrible. Once is enough." Liam sighed, sat down opposite Jeff's desk, and gripped the chair, steading himself to stop the onset of shakes. After what seemed an eternity, he just said, "No, no way. I don't think I wanted to see it in the first place, not that. Can you grab that ten minutes from just before Johnno comes up the stairs until after … Can we grab that and put it on some disc or a USB stick?"

Jeff just nodded as Liam got up to leave. He stopped at the door and turned back to Jeff. "Can you send it to me by email?"

Liam went down from Jeff's office and headed to the canteen where he grabbed a coke from the vending machine and sat in silence. Moments later, he was interrupted by Willo doing his rounds. Willo stopped and took a chair next to his friend, realising something was wrong. Liam looked across at Willo and stumbled through what he had just seen.

"What now?" quizzed Willo.

"I don't know, Paul. I suppose I'll have to share this with the bosses and Work Safe. Not that it changes anything, probably doesn't add much to what they have already. I'll need to check the agitator, that's next."

Liam changed into his hi-vis work shirt from his locker and headed down to his office. He knew that it did mean something. *The footage confirms that the maintenance boys had secured the agitator like they claimed. It also means the pressure event was big, and it was quick. It was big enough to breach the containment of the fibreglass vessel. Most probably north of 200 kPa as Sue had inferred. At least Johnno had no idea, and it was quick, instantaneous.*

—

Liam went to the workshop, passing the maintenance crew as they were heading out. Deano waved to him, and they exchanged some pleasantries about the weekend, none of which Liam recalled five minutes later. The fatal agitator remained in the post-accident collection area, a quiet assassin sitting among an assortment of orange parts and discards. He had seen it before, photographed it and taken the vital measurements. He looked at it with the memory of the CCTV vision that he had just watched and stood with accusatory judgement. *What are you hiding, you piece of shit?*

Spurred on by the need to seek justice, he remeasured and rephotographed the mixing blades. He needed to understand these closely and make a comparison against the old agitator before he could call the agitator expert Rosenbloom. The search for the old agitator was problematic. He hadn't sighted it since returning from Adelaide and it hadn't come up in the investigation, interviews, or any of the conversations since. It wasn't on any workbench, it wasn't in the spare parts store and it wasn't in the assembled works on the side of the workshop.

He called Stuart Jennison, seeking an answer. “Sorry to call on a Friday afternoon, Stuart. I’m trying to find the old agitator that was removed from the T-plant reactor. Do you know what happened to it?”

“No problem, Liam. I’ve left but I can get the fitters to look for it on Monday, if you’d like?”

“I’m in the workshop at the moment, so I was just looking for it myself. But it’s not obvious to me. I just wanted to check something again.”

Stuart was hesitant, a bit puzzled but offered, “The boys told me it had completely failed on the weld of the coupling to the shaft. They thought it was irreparable, we would have discarded it is my guess. They would have thrown it into the scrap metal bin. Other than that, I can’t help you. It might even be a moot point if that bin has already been sent out to the scrapyard. It was getting quite full, I recall.”

Liam felt himself slump – these shafts were expensive. He thanked Stuart and ended their call, making another mental note for his records: *Check with Dean about the nature of the agitator failure.*

He found the metal scrap bin, actually a large skip, overflowing with metal parts and additional items stacked up beside, awaiting disposal. It was like a metal spaghetti with a complex tangle of parts, some heavy, some awkward and some with sharp edges. He thought he saw the tell-tale agitator buried quarter way down the bucket and felt a surge of energy believing that he was on the verge of an important discovery.

Liam tracked down the shift supervisor, Dennis – or ‘Stumpy’ to everyone. Stumpy had earnt his nickname because of his stature of being ungainly, solid, and very muscular. Most people didn't even know his name was Dennis. He dragged Stumpy over to the scrap metal bin and requested he arrange for the afternoon fitters to extract the agitator and have it set aside the orange unit in the recovery section. He implored Stumpy to make it a top priority as he needed to take measurements and make comparisons.

Stumpy, sensing the excitement in Liam's voice and demeanour, promised he would get it done.

Liam smiled and wanted to give him a hug. "Thanks, Stumpy. That's great. Make sure you get the total assembly, shaft, blades, coupling, etcetera, and lay it out alongside the other one. I'll be back first thing in the morning."

"All good, leave it with me. I'm on tomorrow as well and we can check it out together."

Liam left the plant with a spring in his step, one he hadn't felt since the accident. It was after 7:00pm and he had completely forgotten tonight's Friday Night Football. His Port Adelaide was playing Sarah's Hawthorn, and the Hawks were looking good. They were the powerhouse since 2000 but had been in a slump in recent years, before their new coach had reignited them and reestablished them as the new premiership favourites. The match was in Adelaide as part of the AFL's Gather Round where all teams were scheduled for games on the same weekend in the South Australian capital. He had planned to watch the match at Sarah's place, a visiting enemy into their Hawk stronghold, but now he would be late.

He rang Sarah to make his excuses and to share his day. He was excited to tell her about the CCTV footage and his discovery about the agitators.

Sarah chided him for making excuses and trying to

avoid the smashing that the struggling Power were about to receive, even on their home deck. Despite their blossoming love affair, when it came to football, the lines were drawn.

Zoe answered his call and was equally anxious about Port Adelaide's chances. She was at the game waiting for the start in fifteen minutes and the crowd was ridiculously loud. They wished each other well and Liam promised to talk to her the next day. "Hope your team wins, Zoe."

Sue Carpenter and Sandy could wait until Monday, after finishing his inspection of the agitators.

31

PAUL DE ZAALE SUMMONED Brazzos to a meeting at St Kilda Road on the following Tuesday morning, to meet with Angelo Tambakis and discuss matters raised by RK Legal. After everyone was seated in his office, supplied with coffee and pastries, De Zaale opened the briefing.

"Antonio, I've called you here to review the latest information raised by Sue Carpenter and for us to think through our strategy moving forward. RK Legal have received Ms Carpenter's latest report and Angelo felt compelled to call me last night." Then turning to Angelo, he gestured with an open, upturned hand. "Over to you, Angelo."

"Thank you, Paul ... As you are aware at our last review, we believed the investigation was wrapping up, and we think we're most likely heading towards an open finding. There was no clear evidence of cause, and the findings are pointing towards a vessel fault, poor maintenance, and unfortunate circumstances. Not a good outcome because it would still be a failing of supervision and systems."

"I've heard all that," Brazzos interjected, "but how could it be deemed poor supervision? That's a stretch."

"Maybe, Tony, but they will argue you should have had

better vessel inspection regimes, improved integrity inspections, better maintenance procedures, or better something. It doesn't really matter. They will hang it on something."

"That doesn't seem right," Brazzos complained. He thought the issue was straight forward and now all this talk about management responsibilities was clouding his thoughts. Could he actually get criticised in some way? Certainly not if this was back in Colombia.

"Right or wrong is not relevant, Tony." Angelo stood and paced in front of his hosts for effect. "Don't forget that there was a death at the facility and Work Safe will be working hard to make an example out of Agro Alliance. They want maximum publicity and maximum fines to prove they're doing their job. Doing their job at least in the eyes of the public, to impress the hierarchy and the politicians, and to place pressure on all other companies to improve safety practices."

De Zaale brought the discussion back to focus on the next steps. "Okay, it is what it is. Let's get this closed and minimise the impact."

"Yes, exactly," stated Angelo as he resumed his seat. "Our emerging problem is that Sue Carpenter has received information from your man, Liam O'Donoughue, that may reopen the investigation."

De Zaale knew the background and let Brazzos do the reacting. "What!?"

"Yes. Apparently Mr O'Donoghue has found CCTV vision of the accident, taken from another part of the plant. We have a copy here to show you and Sue's conclusion is that it definitively rules out a vessel fault and/or a maintenance error. Let's watch it together and then we can discuss some more."

Angelo opened his laptop, which was preloaded with the footage ready to play. He turned it around on the coffee table towards the Agro Alliance bosses and hit play. Both De Zaale and Brazzos viewed it without discernible reactions and watched it closely a second time before sitting back in stunned silence.

Angelo closed the laptop. "This footage is under privilege and is not available for Work Safe. They asked for CCTV coverage from the gatehouse, but this is from an internal viewpoint. It is a technicality, but my advice is not to disclose this new information."

"I need to check that O'Donoghue hasn't sent it to Work Safe already," Brazzos said.

"Don't worry about that for the moment," Angelo said. "His email to Sue with this footage was requesting her advice as to whether it was disclosable. Sue has instructed him to hold off at the moment, until we review it further. We had a meeting at RK Legal last night and as I said earlier, we recommend that you do not disclose it. Actually, we recommend that you get all copies and destroy them."

De Zaale raised his eyebrows. "Is that legal? Aren't we also expected to provide information that assists in determining the cause?"

Angelo clasped his hands together. "That's why I say it's a 'technicality'. We would argue that the vessel failing is a significant issue, one that we will be addressing in the redesign. Knowing precisely the cause is immaterial. This video shows conclusively that the process got away from you."

"I'm not so sure, Angelo," De Zaale countered. "Why don't we just retain it under privilege and progress the redesign?"

"A good point," replied the lawyer, "but the issue grows

deeper. Sue advised that Mr O'Donoghue is now looking into the cause of the pressure excursion and that he has a theory that it's related to a change in the agitator on that vessel a week prior to the accident."

Brazzos stopped and glared at Tambakis, thinking how this was even relevant. He knew they'd made several batches after that change, and the system operated perfectly. He made these points and got demonstrative in claiming the irrelevance. "Total bullshit!" he exclaimed with an indignant tone.

Angelo held his hands up in surrender. "Slow down, Tony, nothing is disclosable at this point. However, Sue thinks there's a lot of merit in the O'Donoghue theory. The point being that the agitators are significantly different and, maybe, the change may have been part of the problem."

De Zaale entered the discussion. "Even if that is the case, nothing really changes. Doesn't it? The vessel is compromised, and we work a solution in the redesign."

"Let me be frank, gentlemen." Angelo pointed to get their attention. "Without this evidence, the investigation is heading to an open finding. They'll suggest a massive fine on two counts, each of around $500,000. We will plead good reputation, remorse, and whatever else and may have a shot at reducing it, maybe even cutting it in half." De Zaale and Brazzos nodded, and then Angelo continued, "But with this evidence, Work Safe will intensify their guilty charges. There will be no scope for introducing doubt on the vessel integrity or maintenance. Their case will be strengthened on both accounts, and they may even push for higher fines. We will have an extremely hard time arguing any reduction. Our RK Legal judgement is that this evidence may be expensive."

De Zaale looked at Brazzos, pensively but in full agreement with the lawyer. De Zaale gave a curt nod. "We will shut it down, makes sense."

But Angelo had more bad news to bare. "That's just the start. Paul, you should also shut down the O'Donoghue theory. We need to leave the finding hanging around as an open finding. Leave it for a couple of months, or at least until formal charges are laid. Any sniff of any other potential cause could lead Work Safe to re-open the case and then it would all go to hell in a handbasket."

De Zaale frowned. "What do you mean, hell in a handbasket?"

"Sorry, Paul. It's just a saying. It means it could go from bad to worse," Angelo said. "Depending on the cause, it may open up the case for wider charges."

This time, Brazzos was confused, although he was starting to get a bit nervous, anxiety rising in his stomach. "Explain that, please."

"I have no facts, let me make that clear. What I say now may be pure speculation. Let's focus on the agitator change. If it was an error, an oversight, or a careless mistake, then it'll look sloppy and reinforce the current expected charges. But, if it was a change made despite informed judgement or by coercion, then it could lead to individual charges. We could be talking about industrial manslaughter and that would bring larger fines and potential jail sentences."

Brazzos was now sweating, feeling irate. "There's no chance of that. It was obviously an error. Maintenance checked the agitator and measured it all up. They said it was the same. So ..."

Angelo was bemused by the comments; they were overly

defensive. He couldn't help but think he might have missed something. He smiled and said, "That'll be okay then. Our advice is not to go anywhere near this issue. Let the current finding run its course and let's focus on mitigation. Our position is already weak, let's not make it weaker."

De Zaale stood and patted Brazzos on the back as he headed towards his drink cupboard. "We understand and thanks for being so frank. We'll shut it down." Looking at Brazzos with his whiskey bottle in hand, De Zaale reasserted control. "Right, Antonio? Even if we have to let O'Donoghue go."

32

LIAM ARRIVED AT SARAH'S place at half time in the football match – after his Friday with the old guard and the recovery of the CCTV footage. To the footballing world's surprise, Port Adelaide were seventy points in front. Port looked to be the premiership front runners, not Hawthorn. Liam donned his teal and black scarf and knocked on the door, only to receive cat calls and boos from the entire Hatfield family as he made way into the living room. As expected, his good fortune was about to change. Hawthorn scored several goals to scare the Power. Liam was dreading the embarrassment of a record comeback, a Power choking of massive proportion. But alas, for the Hatfield Hawks the comeback was averted, and Liam was ushered to the kitchen while they turned off the post-match celebrations.

The happy banter continued while Mr Hatfield brought out a pack of cards for a couple of hands. Liam excused himself though, as he needed an early night. He needed to get up bright and early back to be at the plant for the agitator inspection in the morning.

Stumpy was ready for him when he arrived at work. "I have it all set out for you. Let's go."

The old agitator was laid out adjacent to the universal spare, sitting as the master alongside a newcomer. Liam took a series of photographs, concentrating on the length dimension and the mixing blades. They measured each and recorded the detail in Liam's notebook. Liam observed that the length of the shaft from tip to agitator blade was nearly identical, but the old unit had a second set of blades at a lot lower, smaller in diameter like junior assistants in the mixing process. *Differences*, Sue Carpenter's words rang in his ears. *Differences and changes are important.* Another difference was the seal configuration on the top of the shaft; the old having a simple oil seal, while the replacement had been fitted with a mechanical seal. He examined them closely and noticed that the new unit also had a spacing bush to align with the nozzle of the reactor vessel. The combination of the mechanical seal and the bush added 150mm to the replacement unit, hence the mixing blades sat 150mm higher in the vessel.

Stumpy waited while Liam made his notes, keen to hear if what Liam had discovered was relevant. "You're doing a lot of writing. What are you thinking? Is this bush thing important?"

Liam thought it over. "I'm not sure, Stumpy, but it is different. Even though it raises the shaft that little bit, the process still had adequate liquid levels and cleared the interlocks. It still mixed."

"What next?" asked the supervisor.

"I'm going to talk with an agitator expert on Monday. I'll mention the different height, the extra small set of blades and the different shape of the mixing blades. See here ..." Liam pointed at the old agitator blades which had more of a pronounced scoop like a rower's oar, rather than a flatter paddle type of the replacement unit. "I'll look in the archives and see if I can find the initial design information."

"Right," said Stumpy. "Call me if you need anything."

The archive store was in the rear of the packaging warehouse, split into two sections. A secure wire-caged enclosure with rows of shelving housed the financial records, all held under lock and key. Behind that in the old warehouse offices were the production and engineering archives. Unlike the precision of their financial cousins, the engineering archives were randomly sorted with varying degrees of information on the box – most were unlabelled. They were all just stacked on benches, under benches or in corners. There was no rhyme or reason for the stacking and the boxes appeared to have been dumped and abandoned.

Liam checked each of the three rooms but was unable to locate a register nor any obvious system to the stacks. He started at the left-hand corner of the first of the three rooms and after several hours had left that room without any significant finding. Half of the records he had searched were ancient and should have been destroyed years ago. The other half were random transportation notes, stock take records, shift reports, production logs or past permit papers.

That was enough for one day. Liam decided it was time to get home and take Sarah out. *The other rooms aren't going anywhere; they'll be a job for next week.*

Sunday was a lazy day. The party at the football club the previous night went into the wee hours of the morning and it was close to 4:00am before Liam got to bed. He slept through well into the afternoon then pottered around the house until the Sunday football game commenced. He had his laptop open while the game played in the background. He checked out the agitator specialists on a Google search. After reading the Mixing Masters website, he prepared an email to Michael Rosenbloom.

He outlined the issue of reactor two in the T-plant at Agro Alliance, referencing Mixing Masters as designers of the original installation. He requested technical advice on the design detail and listed his questions around mixing anomalies that he thought may have been involved in the pressure excursion. Liam signed off with his email seeking a consultation on Monday as soon as possible.

Liam was at his desk on the Monday morning, summarising his findings for Sue Carpenter. He intended to attach the CCTV footage and seek Sue's advice whether it would be disclosable to Work Safe. The dilemma was that Work Safe had only asked for CCTV footage from the gatehouse of any relevant information of the vessel failure. The view from the synthesis plant was certainly relevant and it answered several questions. But technically, the request was not for any footage, specifically the request was for footage from the gatehouse. In Liam's mind, he knew the new vision was relevant, and it should be disclosed, but with the RK Legal overlay he wasn't going to make that call. *I'll cover my position by recommending it be disclosed and request their advice. They said only provide what was specifically requested, nothing more.*

The report was now ready to finalise with a theory that the

excess pressure was a result of a surge of reactive materials after inadequate mixing. The theory needed fine-tuning, and Liam was waiting to get input from Mixing Masters. Shortly before lunch, Liam took the call he'd been waiting for. After Michael introduced himself, Liam felt a tinge of excitement run through his veins.

"Thank you very much for calling me, Michael. I really appreciate it."

"You are most welcome. How can I help? I do remember working on that project with my father, but it was many years ago."

Liam explained the accident and the subsequent findings before focusing on the change in the agitator. Michael took notes from his end in Adelaide and said he had already looked up the project details on his system and had the specifications in front of him. Liam asked if it was possible to get a copy emailed to him, as their records were in a bit of disarray.

"Sending it through as we speak." Then reading from his records, Michael relayed, "That agitator was designed specifically for the reaction process. We recommended a small set of blades to be fitted at the bottom of the agitator shaft. We call them ticklers and then we designed a second set of mixing impellers a meter higher. The tickers don't do any of the heavy lifting in the mixing process, but they do provide some radial movement as the vessel is filling. The serious mixing happens once the level exceeds the mixing impellers; the design number of the impellers is in the detail I've sent you."

"That's interesting. So in your opinion, what would happen if we didn't have the set of tickler blades?" asked Liam.

"Not a lot. They add a bit of initial radial dispersion as the vessel fills, which aids the mixing. Our records note that you guys add the tech material to the vessel and then later introduce hydrochloric acid to react with impurities. Without the ticklers, the mixing and reaction effect is still achieved with the main impellers ..." Michael stopped. "Hang on a second, I've just pulled up some supplementary notes and the ticklers were intended to disperse any carried over bicarbonate or emulsion from the previous process step, ensuring it was dispersed adequately. Hydrochloric acid would react with the bicarbonate and generate carbon dioxides gas, so having it fully dispersed would improve the efficiency of that reaction."

"Uh huh. And if it we didn't have the ticklers?" asked Liam again.

"As long as the tech was mixed by the impeller blades before the acid was added, then nothing. If the acid was added early without good mixing, then once the impellers got the batch stirred up, the acid and bicarbonate reaction might be sudden and excessive."

Liam felt that this was important information, but he was still puzzled. *The process wouldn't allow the acid charge if the agitator wasn't running in the tech liquid.* He verbalised his thinking on the issue to Michael, pondering that if the excessive reaction was potentially evident, it didn't seem to fit the detail that they had discussed.

Michael was quick to set him straight. "But Liam, you said you changed out the agitator. If the new agitator had similar mixing impellers then I would've thought the dispersion would have been adequate. What were the blades on the replacement agitator?"

Liam's face lit up with an idea. "Holy shit. They were the paddle type blades we use in the formulation vessel. Will that be an issue?"

"Bingo!" Michael virtually yelled down the line. "I know those units, we were involved in installing them as well. If my memory is correct, they are hydrofoil design and they have a pronounced vertical blade profile."

"Sorry Michael, can you translate that into English?"

"Put simply, those blades produce a dominate radial flow and have poor vortexing or pulsing circulation. The design of that process requires a liquid coverage of more than 400mm to get any effective mixing."

Liam thought over what he was being told. "So, if we had a short charge or a low level, enough to cover the hydrofoil blades the acid level would need to rise and over these blades by about 400mm before decent mixing was achieved. This would defeat the design intent, which was to ensure that the acid reacts with impurities and any bicarbonate steadily and continuously."

"Exactly, my friend, and if there was a significant amount of bicarbonate then the delayed mixing would initiate the combination in a big rush. A damn big rush, a bit like what you described in your accident." Michael allowed time for Liam to absorb this, then added, "Could you send me photos of the new agitator? You might even consider setting up a lab experiment to confirm the theory."

"I will as soon as we get off this call. Can we also commission you to put a review in writing?"

33

BRAZZOS LEFT THE RK Legal meeting hell bent on squashing this O'Donoghue theory. The email that O'Donoghue had sent to Sue Carpenter had been the subject of the meeting. Tambakis had provided copies to De Zaale and himself, and encouraged Agro Alliance to stop the investigation, put this theory on ice.

When Angelo Tambakis had left the meeting, Brazzos conferred with Paul over the problem. The main problem was that the Work Safe investigation was still pending and that they had O'Donoughue nominated as their point of contact. Tambakis thought it would raise suspicion if they sacked him. The last thing they wanted was for the case to be reopened, have them stick noses into areas not needed. It could escalate the fines. The talk of industrial manslaughter was stupid; how was it even connected? Mixing blades, hydrofoils, surge reactions, just a lot of technical crap. He remained ignorant of the impact that his forced change of the agitator had made, especially without a proper risk assessment; nor how it would be linked back to him.

Brazzos reminded Paul that everything was easier back home. Columbians had their own way of dealing with problems. O'Donoghue would already be gone, and if he continued to talk or complain then he would be dealt with good and proper. Too much dancing around here in Australia. Too many 'what if' scenarios, too much procrastination: *be careful, don't upset Work Safe.*

De Zaale agreed in principle but was keen to distance himself from any backlash. "Antonio, this is your problem. I suggest you deal with it pronto."

Brazzos headed straight to the IT department looking for Jeff Ogden. *First thing, pull a plug on this CCTV footage and squash this O'Donoghue theory.*

He barged into Ogden's office without knocking, surprising Jeff who was on the telephone talking to a supplier. Brazzos pointed at the phone. "Call them back, we have a problem."

Jeff told his caller he would get back to them in a few minutes, hung up and looked at the pacing site manager. "What's up?"

"I'll give you what's up. I hear we have some new footage of the T-plant accident. Is that right?"

"Yes, Liam O'Donoghue asked me to check it out last Friday and said it might be relevant to the investigation or something."

"Maybe, but it doesn't add or change anything in regard to the investigation." Brazzos glared at Ogden across his desk. "I need it pulled. Our legal advice is to kill it. It will only confuse the investigation, and it may muddy the waters and increase our fines. I need this done immediately."

Jeff nodded but smiled. "It doesn't matter – the record has been overwritten already. The system only keeps it for a few weeks, and then it's overwritten. We checked on Friday afternoon. It's gone, apart from a copy that I emailed Liam."

"Good. That's my next stop then." Brazzos left with no further discussion – no thanks, nothing.

Jeff shrugged. *Something's fishy there, Bullyboy. And whoops, there's also the copy Liam took on the USB stick.*

Brazzos headed in search of Ernesto while he called Suzi and demanded that she find the whereabouts of Statler. "I need him in my office in ten minutes," he demanded.

Ernesto was at his desk in the safety department when his uncle handed him a new assignment. He was initially hesitant, but knowing his uncle's temper, he had no choice. His mother had convinced her brother that Ernesto was super smart with computers and needed a job. *Look after him, mi hermano*, she had said. *Blood is thicker than water.* Ernesto knew Uncle Tony was the boss. He left for the plant while Uncle Tony went back to his office.

Ernesto headed down to the production office where he pretended to be looking through the shift logs. He waited for Liam to come back to his desk and made small talk while he laid out his exercise book on the spare desk adjacent to Liam, and he started making notes. Following his instructions, he texted his uncle that he was ready, then waited for the call. Ernesto stood and stepped across to Liam's desk. He waited for Liam to look up and then asked if he could help him with some part of the synthesis process and started a line of questions about an MOC that he was checking.

Liam offered some limited insight. "I only know the basics, but you should ask the supervisor those questions. He would be better."

Ernesto was fidgeting nervously as he waited for his signal. "I will. That's a good idea. But while I—" His phone rang. "Excuse me, Liam, I should get this." He walked away some distance and nodded into the phone. "Si, si, por supeusto, estoy listo." *Yes, yes, of course I'm ready.*

Returning to Liam's desk, he told Liam, "That was Natalie again. I need to action that MOC. Could I log on here, on your PC?"

Liam happily agreed and stood up to let Ernesto take his seat when Statler called. As Ernesto was pulling up the MOC database, Liam tapped him on the shoulder. "I'll leave it with you. The boss wants me up the front. Good luck. Don't forget to ask Jake."

Ernesto was sweating and trying hard to cover his nervousness, head down and unable to make eye contact as Liam walked out.

—

Liam arrived at the site manager's office and smiled at Suzi as he told her that he apparently had a meeting with Statler and Brazzos. Suzi told him that they were expecting him, but to wait a few minutes while they finished something else. Liam sat in the visitor's chair. "No worries, Suzi. How have you been?"

Fifteen minutes soon grew into twenty and Liam started to wonder what the meeting was even about and what was so urgent. Suzi was now outlining her upcoming holiday plans. "We've always wanted to go to Hawaii. It's been a dream for ages, sort of on my bucket list. But Liam, I tell you, it is hellishly expensive and with our dollar dropping."

"I know. Why didn't you just go to the Gold Coast or to Bali? That would be heaps cheaper."

"Sure, but I've been to Bali and it's not my cup of tea. Hawaii is just on the list. You only live once."

"I suppose so. Do you think I should come back later? Seems like they're pretty busy."

"Hang fire, I'll check." She dialled on the interoffice phone and spoke with Brazzos and finished the conversation. "Okay, will do." Looking at Liam, she indicated to the door and advised that they were ready. "You can go in."

"Thanks, Suzi. Enjoy the trip." Liam stretched, knocked at the door, and entered the Brazzos inner sanctum.

Statler was sitting in the visitor's chair when Liam entered. Brazzos got up from behind his desk and ushered Liam to the leather sofa while Jim turned his chair around. Brazzos smiled as he saw the incoming text message from Ernesto: 'Terminado, todo hecho.' *Finished, all done*. "Thanks for coming up, Liam. Do you want a coffee or a tea?"

Liam hesitated, wary of the pleasantries. "No, I'm good. Thank you anyway."

Brazzos sat next to him on the sofa. "Look, I won't beat around the bush. We've had RK Legal review your CCTV footage of the accident. They don't think we need to disclose it."

"Okay, that's your call. It seemed relevant but—"

"Maybe, but not really," Brazzos cut him off. "Listen, it doesn't add anything to the investigation. Not really. Besides, we think it's a bit insensitive to Johnno, so we have elected not to disclose it."

"Fair enough. Your call, as I said," replied Liam.

"Good, that's settled then. Just to let you know I have also instructed IT to remove or destroy any copies, yours included."

Liam paused, thinking that it was all a bit extreme. "It's under privilege, isn't it?"

"Yes, still the RK Legal advice is to erase it, just easier, no mess. So that's what will happen."

Liam shrugged and started to rise.

"Just a few more things, Liam. If you don't mind?"

He sat down again and looked over at Statler who was sitting silent and glum faced, like he wanted to be elsewhere.

"Okay." *This is not good ... something is up!*

34

BACK AT HIS DESK, Liam sat nonplussed. His world had been turned upside down and for what? It made no sense. Initially, Brazzos was ranting over a drama about the CCTV footage, then it was his issue with what he called the O'Donoghue theory and now being relocated. He could rationalise the sensitivity for Johnno's family, but even that was overkill in his opinion. The footage was protected and hardly going to be shared with anyone. It was gruesome enough.

That reminded him that he was supposed to delete his copy. He opened his laptop and started searching as Jake came into the production office. "You still here, Liam? On overtime, I guess."

Liam just laughed. "Not likely." Searching his files, he mumbled, "Where is it?" then sat back puzzled and frowning. *I'm sure I had it saved in the T-pant accident folder. Maybe I put it somewhere else ...*

He searched for the file name and came up short. He looked for the email from Jeff Ogden which had the footage in an attachment. That was gone, nothing in the email file for the T-plant accident, nor in the trash bin, nor anywhere.

Then he searched for the email he had sent to Sue Carpenter. Nothing. Everything relating to the CCTV footage was missing. That was what Brazzos said he was going to do. Maybe he had IT remove the files, but they really couldn't or shouldn't have done that without Liam's password. Surely.

"Something's not right," he said aloud.

Jake was at his desk making his handover report and looked up. "What's that?"

"I was looking for something about the T-plant accident. I had several files saved, but they seem to be missing. Strange thing is I was just talking about them with the Muppet Man and the Bullyboy and now they're gone. I'll check with IT." He picked up his phone to call Jeff, but the call wasn't answered.

Jake walked over to his desk. "Ernesto was here earlier. Maybe you can check with him."

"Ernesto. Surely not."

Jake sneered. "I've never trusted him. He only got the job because of the Bullyboy. Smart with computers but doesn't know jack shit about anything else."

Liam asked Jake to take a seat, and he proceeded to relate his finding of the new CCTV footage, choosing to omit the graphic detail. He told Jake, "I'll double check with Jeff tomorrow, but I suspect Ernesto has already done the dirty work." Jake smirked, amused by all the cloak and dagger antics.

Liam went on to explain that he had a theory about the cause of the accident. The short batch and the poor agitation was validated with his call to Mixing Masters and that he had Aussie Joe in the lab set up to do a test to recreate the accident. He had written all this in a report to the RK Legal investigator, Sue Carpenter, and it seemed conclusive to him that the change in agitator was a key factor. A poor decision without thinking, a collective mistake that resulted in poor Johnno's demise. Liam explained that he thought Johnno probably made the standard drop from reactor 1 and most likely had an excessive of unreacted bicarbonate in the charge into reactor 2.

Jake's eyes widened, astounded by what he was hearing and thought back over his recollections. "Liam, where is that report of the O'Donoghue theory now?"

"Also gone. Brazzos told me bluntly that it was pure speculation, and that he didn't want it progressed any further. He had already called Dwyer in the lab, and they cancelled Aussie Joe's test and told me to erase the 'theory'."

"Shit, and you think that's overkill?"

They sat in silence for some time before Liam answered, "I do. I think it stinks, something's not quite right. Brazzos reckons the investigation is nearly finished and it will end with an open finding, big fines probably. He doesn't want us reopening the investigation because it might leak to Work Safe and blow up the issue, get it revisited and maybe make the fines bigger."

"Fines are fines." Jake stirred in his chair. "Big fat shit. Doesn't bring Johnno back."

"No, it doesn't," Liam agreed. "I tried to argue that the work was all protected by legal privilege and that we needed to know the exact cause to ensure we factor in the appropriate controls into the plant redesign."

"And don't tell me ... He wasn't buying that."

Liam shutdown his laptop and started packing up. "No, he didn't buy any of that. Then the biggest insult is that they're relocating me to work in the synthesis plant, refocus. It would be a good career move."

"Are you going to work for Andrew in synthesis now?" asked Jake.

"No, not for Andrew. Apparently he's being relocated to Queensland. But that's strictly between us for the moment. He may not even know yet."

Jake laughed. "More cloak and daggers. Have they pulled you from the T-plant case as well? Sounds like they're burying something. You're lucky you aren't in South America."

Liam nodded. "Yeah, something is dodgy. Apparently, I remain as the accident contact for Work Safe. Call it continuity, but I am to stop the O'Donoghue theory and with the case coming to a close, I'll be off it completely in the next couple of weeks."

Liam was all packed up and heading to the door as Jake returned to the supervisor station. "Goodnight, Liam. You'll be better off without all this stress."

Liam turned around and shook Jake's hand. "I don't know about that. I thought I was on to something. They, whoever Brazzos appoints – some new bloke from Asesoria – will need help to sort out the design, and where will they get that help?"

"That's above my pay grade," Jake joked. "So what is it you think was the problem with the change of the agitator?"

Liam placed his bag on Jake's desk and gave him the quick version about the wrong blades and the impact on the mixing. They talked it through some more and Liam sat down. Jake recalled the dark nature of the rework batch and that even if Johnno was slack, he may have missed the cut-off anyway.

Liam explained, "Either way, the amount of bicarbonate was a ticking timebomb. The short charge was enough to cover the agitator blades but not enough to mix properly. Only when the acid charge was completed was there enough volume for the mixing to be effective. Then it was all too much, too late."

"What I hear you telling me is ... if the old agitator was in place, it might not have happened."

"Almost certainly not," Liam answered confidently. "The tickler blades would have started a homogeneous mix and the impeller blades would have functioned as designed."

"No way! Did the shortening of the agitator with the mechanical seal and the bush connection play any part?"

The answer was evident on Liam's face. "That only made it worse."

Jake's mouth opened and closed, clearly stunned. "On the night we changed the agitator ..." Then he stopped.

35

THE NEXT MORNING, LIAM made a beeline to Jeff Ogden's office in IT. He waited there while Jeff was completing the morning checks. Liam had been trying to figure everything out. Why was he being sidelined? It was all too confusing, that was until Jake let him know about the Bullyboy and the agitator change. That changed everything. He now knew he was not an innocent bystander trying to resolve a mystery. He held the key to unravelling the lot. Mr Bullyboy was not trying to reduce the fines; he was trying to stay under the radar and avoid an upgrade to industrial manslaughter. Liam knew all his investigations and suspicions were inadmissible, but he was angry and wasn't going to let the South American mafia push their weight around. His plan was to put his case together, slap it on Brazzos's desk and have it circulated internally. Then he would resign and walk out. *If nothing else, it will be my sort of karma.*

Liam was daydreaming a forward plan when Jeff returned to his office. "Hello stranger, lost your way?"

Liam stood and shook Jeff's hand. "A truer word has never been spoken. I believe you had instructions to delete the CCTV footage and wipe my emails."

"Whoa there me matey, back up. Who have you been talking with?"

"Bullyboy made the inference and then when I got to my laptop yesterday, everything was gone. Everything: the CCTV footage, my emails and my summary work on the T-plant accident, everything." Liam sighed. "I was pissed off, really mad. I didn't think you guys could do that without my knowledge or my password."

Jeff stared in disbelief at his visitor who was getting all worked up. "We can't, and we didn't. The only thing I know about this subject is that your Bullyboy asked me to wipe the CCTV footage from the record. I told the fucker it didn't matter because it was already overwritten." It was then Jeff's turn to sigh. "And that, my friend, is the sum total of our involvement. If your stuff has been wiped, it was either you did it yourself by accident or someone with access to your PC or to your password."

"Shit, that means Ernesto," Liam suggested aloud. *The rat sneaking in for his bully uncle.*

"When did all this wiping action happen? Can you recall when the data was last on your laptop?"

"I was working on it yesterday after lunch, then I had to go to a meeting with Statler in Brazzos's office. Ernesto asked me to log onto my PC for him to get access to the MOC database." Liam then put two and two together realising that the delay in the Brazzos office for twenty minutes, leaving him talking with Suzi was extra padding time for the rat to get to work.

Jeff grinned and stood. "Follow me. It's your lucky day."

—

Liam bounced out of IT with a spring in his step. Next stop, Frank, who was the day shift supervisor starting his first shift for the week. Next on his dance card was Mario the permit writer, Dean the fitter and finally Oscar the drum washing casual. They all confirmed Jake's story and even added extra detail. Liam's summary was that the agitator change was pushed through without any risk assessment, that the team conceded to the Bullyboy and the apparent urgency won the day. Even the Muppet Man had pushed them along. These antics were applied to the broken agitator, the shorter shaft, *'it's just a mixer so get on with it'*, and then again with the short charge, *'forget the other two drums and forget that MOC baloney. I want this started now, or else I'll have your guts for garters'.* The boys confirmed that Statler was pushing hard and Brazzos had even made an appearance in the plant a few times ranting and raving, calling people clowns and idiots. He didn't care about MOCs and insisted on getting it started.

Liam took an early lunch break at the Sons of the West cafe, sitting in the corner internally fuming about Brazzos. *I only wish this report could meet the light of day,* Liam pondered. *He needs his comeuppance and needs it good and proper.*

Liam now had Brazzos in his sights and he wanted to share the plan with Sandy. He sat in the cafe for an hour updating Sandy on 'the O'Donoghue theory', and his plan to arrange a laboratory test. "I have my emails and files recovered from IT on a separate USB stick and I'm expecting an email from Mixing Masters," Liam told Sandy. "I have testimony from plant staff about his belligerence. I now know he had my files wiped and we all know that he only thinks about himself. Not about Johnno, not even about De Zaale or anyone, just himself. He deserves the full weight of the karma bus, and I want to be driving it when it arrives."

"Take it easy, Liam. None of this is disclosable to Work Safe, you know that," Sandy reminded him.

"Yes, I know that. I'm leaving this joint and leaving soon. I just want some justice to be served. At least I want Brazzos and the Muppet Man to know they have Johnno's blood on their hands. Even if all I get out of it is for everyone here to recognise them for the scumbags they are."

"It's a grand plan but be careful. People like Brazzos don't play fair."

Liam was almost bouncing out of his seat. "I know. I feel a sense of destiny. I have to try." As he walked out of the cafe still talking to Sandy, he added, "I'm buzzing a bit internally and I just wanted to talk it through with someone I can trust. I should talk to Sue Carpenter, but she's obliged to keep RK Legal in the loop, and that Tambakis bloke is too close to De Zaale and Brazzos." He hung up and walked across the road back towards the plant. *Maybe I'll give Sue a copy of the finalised full version of the O'Donoghue theory after I resign.*

Aussie Joe was at his bench when Liam entered the laboratory. "Hey Aussie, are you busy?"

The always smiling lab technician didn't answer, just laughed. He rarely strung too many words together and did most of his talking with expressions – smiling being the most prevalent. Liam looked at the job sheet on his bench. "Always busy. Testing."

Aussie only answered with a nervous laugh. They stood looking at each other and finally Aussie offered, "Sorry Liam, I couldn't do your test. Mr Keith tell me it cancelled."

"I know, I know. Don't worry. We're good." Liam

reassured him that he wasn't in trouble. "I was interested in what you would have done if it were approved. How were you planning the test? Maybe if you could show me, I could test it myself."

"I can show." Aussie beamed again. "I can't do now, but come back at knock off and I show. I still have everything ready before Mr Keith tell me stop."

"Thanks Aussie. I appreciate it and I'll see you at, say 5:00pm."

Aussie had already packed up and was sitting at his bench waiting when Liam returned precisely at 5:00pm. The spare laboratory fume hood was the fourth in a bank of fume hoods and was rarely used. Aussie had a large glass round bottom flask already set up in a silicon oil bath over a hot plate magnetic stirrer, with a rubber stopper lightly placed in the top opening. Previously, he had collected a range of the needed ingredients, some of the remaining tech which he had reacted to simulate the first step. That was before his test was cancelled. He also had soda ash, bicarbonate soda and hydrochloric acid on the bench. The tech product was sitting on a warming plate, slowly melting in preparation for use.

"What was your plan?" Liam asked Aussie as he studied the assortment of materials.

"I had plan on paper." Aussie handed him his handwritten running sheet.

"This is a rather long list of different ratios and different trials." Liam wasn't sure they had the time to be this extensive, especially as it was now on the prohibited trial list. "We might need to just cut to the most obvious."

While they reviewed the list and discussed the best

option for a one-off trial, the lab manager Keith Dwyer was walking through on his last rounds for the day. He saw the pair standing at the back fume hood and approached them. "What are you guys up to back here?"

Liam turned to face Keith and to protect his lab mate from any criticism. "Aussie was just showing me the trial plan we were thinking of on Monday, the one we were going to use to test causes for the T-plant accident." And then to make it seem just a casual interest, he noted, "It's all interesting. A good set-up. Pity it was cancelled, it might have helped."

Dwyer was sympathetic to Liam's cause and liked how he was always cooperative. Dwyer wasn't a soldier of the Brazzos army, but he wasn't going to be a martyr either. He generally tried to remain on neutral ground. "I'm sorry, Liam, our hands are tied. Brazzos made it perfectly clear he didn't want those tests. The investigation is closed per his instructions. I'd like to help, but it has to be shelved." Dwyer turned his attention to Aussie Joe. "Tomorrow, I want you to pack all this up. Okay?"

Aussie nodded and Liam headed for the door with the handwritten plan inside his notebook, looking back. "Goodnight, see you tomorrow."

36

THE BRAZZOS THURSDAY MEETING was routine until Stuart Jennison brought up that he had received an email this morning on a report that was apparently commissioned by Liam O'Donoghue. He advised that a company, by the name of Mixing Masters, was asked to provide their opinion on the mixing efficiency of the initially designed agitator in the T-plant reactor, compared to that of the replaced spare unit. Stuart summarised the findings which categorically concluded that the poor vertical mixing efficiency of the spare was a high probability to be a major factor in the accident.

"Where did this come from!?" Brazzos exploded.

Jennison was not deterred; he was only the messenger. "It was commissioned by O'Donoghue and the detail seems to refer to O'Donoghue's theory about short batches and poor mixing. I only got an email copy by accident. It was addressed to Liam with copy to Alexander Scotland. Since Scotland has departed, I have been getting his work emails, a diversion that was established when I started."

The team looked to Brazzos to see what was next.

They knew it wouldn't be good and they collectively knew O'Donoghue was bucking the system. It wasn't going to be good and they may all suffer as a result.

Jennison cautiously asked, "What is this O'Donoghue theory?"

Brazzos was not happy. "Don't worry about that now, just speculation. Can you get me a copy of this new mixing report? I need to have a chat with our Mr O'Donoghue." Then looking around the room, said, "This speculation on theories is crap. It's dangerous and it may refuel Work Safe's investigation. It has to stop."

Keith Dwyer commented, "On this topic, I had Liam in our lab yesterday afternoon talking with the techos about some testing."

"I told you on Tuesday to cancel those tests," yelled Brazzos.

"I know, boss. Don't worry, they didn't do anything, and I've had it all packed up this morning."

"Good. That's good." Brazzos momentarily relaxed. He still needed to pull O'Donoghue aside.

Stuart then added, "I was back late last night and I saw Liam go into the laboratory after 7:00pm. Just saying."

"Enough. No more theories, no more tests, no more commissioned reports. It all has to stop. Are we clear?" Brazzos glared angrily at everyone before singling out the production manager. "Jim, your man is out of control. Get him to bring his report to me immediately and we will discuss this. I'll set him straight."

"He's not here, Tony," Jim hesitated. "He rang in this morning saying he was planning to work from home for a few hours and would be in after lunch."

—

As soon as the meeting finished, Brazzos called De Zaale to update him on the emerging problem, the new mixing report, and his suspicion that O'Donoghue was conducting lab tests and rewriting his summary report again, even after clear instructions to stop. De Zaale did his best to calm Brazzos down. "Change tracks, Antonio. How about you kid this O'Donoghue along, get the report, tell him you're interested in the detail. We need answers for the redesign anyway. Use your charm man, not a heavy hand."

"You have to be joking, Paul. O'Donoghue is a walking disaster. I'm going to get the Rodriguez boys to send him a message. I'll sort him."

"I didn't hear any of that, Antonio. I'm just telling you to not inflame him, get the report first before you do anything. Squash it or quarantine it. It's all protected, so just control the circulation."

—

Liam received the Mixing Masters report in his email and was finalising his report at home. He told Statler that he wasn't coming in until after lunch and he even thought about tossing it in altogether. Statler didn't seem too fussed anyway and only mildly asked for an excuse. Liam thought Statler would shit bricks if he told him he was drafting his report; a report that revisited the cause of the fatal accident.

First, he needed to finish the report, add the CCTV footage, reference the Mixing Master's opinion, and now add the laboratory trial.

The testing last night was an overwhelming success. He had the molten tech from Aussie's preparation in the glass flask, along with a small amount of bicarbonate. As he added the hydrochloric acid without using the stirrer, there was slight fuming on the surface and a mist of gas fogging the flask. Then with the proportion of acid completed, he switched on the stirrer and *poof*, an instant flash blew the stopper out of the flask. He repeated it three times with similar results and observed frothing and rising liquid ahead of a violent eruption each time. He finished the last trial by videoing it on his phone and then he tidied up as best he could, leaving a note for Aussie to finish the cleanup.

Once he finished his report, he copied it from his hard drive onto the USB stick, the one from Jeff Ogden, and then also copied it onto his private Seagate drive, to which he regularly performed a backup of his personal files, statistics, records, expenses, travel plans, and a multitude of other quirky things that was part of his obsessive nature. He pocketed the USB stick and placed the Seagate drive back into his hidey hole. He went into the kitchen to make a sandwich and a cup of tea, relieved his investigation was over. He was deep in thought while he ate his lunch.

Good job, Liam. Now to hand it in, when and where, the last step to contemplate for maximum effect. I must copy Sandy and Sue, maybe tomorrow.

The silence was broken when his phone rang. He stared at the number, the Agro Alliance switchboard. *How odd.* He answered the call, introduced himself and soon recognised the voice of Tony Brazzos on the line.

Brazzos had given Liam no time for small talk and quickly cut to the heart of the matter. "Liam, Jim told me you were working from home. I'm ringing to ask if you could drop in and see me this afternoon." He continued before Liam had a chance to respond, "I think we were a bit hasty in asking you to move into the synthesis plant. I've been giving it a lot of thought since we last met and would like to reconsider my decision. We really need you on the T-plant redesign and it would be wrong to ask someone new to come up to speed. So can we talk about that this afternoon?"

Liam couldn't believe what he was hearing, totally un-Brazzos like. "Of course. What time do you want to meet?"

"Give me a minute while I check my diary." The line went quiet for a minute before Brazzos returned. "Actually, it's a bit tight. Best I could do is around 5:00pm, otherwise tomorrow morning."

"Five o'clock is alright with me."

"Very good. Thank you, Liam. Also, could you bring a copy of the latest mixing report that you have. Stuart Jennison had a copy at today's meeting and his summary was technically confusing. I would appreciate if you could walk me through it, help me understand the issues."

Liam's mouth dropped again, hardly believing what he was hearing. "Certainly, I think it's the key to the accident. Do you want a hard copy, or I have it on a USB stick as well?"

"That's excellent, either hard copy or USB. Maybe both. I assume it will help in the redesign, but I remind you that it's still protected under legal privilege." Brazzos remained as calm as he could, priding himself on his acting performances.

"Of course," reassured Liam.

"Okay then, see you at five o'clock. One last thing though. We may have gotten off on the wrong foot this week, and I apologise. I want you to pack a bag and head over to Adelaide after our meeting. We need to follow up this mixing design stuff and you can meet the Mixing Masters people. You should get a review of the best current options and even look at designs for larger vessels. Besides, you deserve some time off – we cut your leave short after that accident."

"Thanks Tony, but that won't be necessary. I could do most of that by telephone or email." Liam appreciated that the offer was made but he wasn't sure if he could just drop everything, even if he wanted to.

"I insist. We need to make it up to you, and it's the least we can do." Brazzos nearly gagged on his own words. "You often drive and stop halfway, I hear. We will pick up the bill for the stop. What is halfway on that trip?"

"Dimboola is technically halfway, although Horsham is close ..." Liam was about to explain that the Golden Grain in Horsham was his preferred stopping place but was cut off by Brazos.

"All good, I have to run. See you at five. We'll cover the stop over." And before Liam could say anything else, the call had ended.

As he packed his bag, he couldn't come to grips with the turnaround. It was a complete about face, all inside forty-eight hours. Pleasant as well, considerate, a bonus week's holiday and a chance to reconnect with Zoe. His mind was racing. On the drive into the plant, he called Sarah and relayed the Brazzos conversation. He made a quick call to Zoe, leaving a message, and finally he rang the Golden Grain to book his room. He assumed he would pay for the stay and get it reimbursed upon his return. He smiled at the thought that he would add the return stay as well, and a steak dinner each way to boot.

—

Brazzos picked up the internal phone and told Suzi he needed Ernesto pronto. He then asked her to clear his diary for the afternoon and to schedule a time for Liam O'Donoghue for 5:00pm.

"I'll see Ernesto, then I have an important matter to attend and won't be back until 4:30pm," he said.

His last request was for Suzi to book a night stay, for Liam at a motel in Dimboola, explaining that he was doing a work trip back to Adelaide tonight and to get them to charge the stay directly to the company.

37

THE RODRIGUEZ BROTHERS SAT quietly in Miguel's car at the back of the Agro Alliance employee car park. Miguel and Gilberto Rodriguez had immigrated to Australia after their cousin Paul De Zaale had settled in Melbourne. Miguel was the older and wiser brother, with the nose and a sense for financial opportunities. Gilberto was not as bright and was always happy for Miguel to take the lead. He provided the muscle and did most of the heavy lifting or the dirty work. Together, they thought they were a powerful team, and they were often called upon amongst the Colombian network for their willingness to go where many wouldn't, and above all else for their discretion.

Cousin Paul had put them in contact with his colleague, Antonio Brazzos, and the boys were often hired for various activities at the West Footscray plant. Otherwise, they worked for themselves performing maintenance work, and security at times. They traded hot merchandise, laundered money, and stole cars on order. Miguel's speciality was in the lucrative market of Holden Commodore SS sedans.

However, this was the first time in Australia that they were hired to deal with a 'people problem' and they were promised a handsome remuneration if all went well: a bonus payday in cold hard cash.

Gilberto wasn't used to sitting still; he was a doer, not a thinker. "Why are we so early, Miguel? And isn't this a bit risky in the middle of the day?"

Miguel was keeping a close eye on the time, admiring his Rolex which was his prized possession. "Let me worry about all that. Antonio wanted us to be in position and ready in case things change. Mi amigo, we will be moving soon."

But the younger brother remained anxious, his hands jittering. "How are we going to know this O'Donoghue man?"

"Again, don't worry. You forget too easily." Miguel handed him a photo that Brazzos had provided in their meeting earlier that day. "Do you remember him? When we did that furniture shuffle, this was the fellow that sat on the desk in front of the offices we were moving. And, before you ask, that's his Mazda just over there."

"If you're sure, then I trust you. It's still daylight, and won't there be people all around this car park soon?"

"Most of the day shift knock off between three and four, and shift workers not until six. Besides, I told Antonio that any daylight request would cost him more. He was happy to pay, and he said he has a distraction planned. Now just wait. Another ten minutes. You have all the stuff, right?"

—

Liam was tidying his desk, thirty minutes ahead of his meeting with Brazzos when he received a call from the switchboard. It was Lauren re-patching a call from Brazzos and as soon as Liam answered, Brazzos apologised. "Sorry

Liam, I've been held up off site and looks like I won't be back until well after 5:00pm. Let's catch up after you get back from Adelaide."

"Okay, can do," Liam agreed, but was surprised that he found himself a bit disappointed.

"Do me a favour, though. Can you leave a copy of your mixing report and your summary findings in an envelope at the gatehouse, and I'll collect it later tonight?"

"You sure? I could just email it to you now if you'd like?"

Shit, didn't think about that. Brazzos quickly regrouped, clearing his throat. "Yes maybe, but I'd prefer a hard copy. I like to scribble notes, and it works for me better. That's if it isn't too much trouble."

"No trouble at all. I'll do it now."

"Thanks, Liam. That will work well. Have a good trip." Then Brazzos promptly hung up.

Liam grabbed an internal mail envelope and deposited the Brazzos hard copy before he headed off to the gatehouse. *This actually works better for me as well,* he thought. *I can get on the road a bit earlier and might still be in time for a steak at the Victoria Hotel. Also, I have a week to think through my strategy for our discussion.*

He dropped into the gatehouse and saw Willo was still on duty. "Hi there, Paul. The Bullyboy has asked me to leave this envelope for him here. He said he'll come by later tonight to collect it. Where shall I leave it?"

Paul smiled back at his friend. "Well, that'll be a first. He wouldn't know where we live. Pity I'll be gone by then. You can put it in that tray on the side, and I'll tell the night shift to be on the lookout for him."

"Thanks, mate. I can't stay and chat. I'm heading back to

Adelaide again and need to get going. If I get on the road now, I'll get to Horsham in time to have one of those steaks I've told you about."

Brazzos was sitting in his car on the opposite side of the street, parked in the empty space behind the dumpster next to the Sons of the West cafe. He spotted Liam entering the gatehouse and called Miguel. "Get in position now." He immediately hung up and called Ernesto. "Are you ready? Countdown minus five minutes. I'll text you again and then you need to hit the alarm straight away."

The Rodriguez boys moved their car across and set up in front of Liam's Mazda. They opened the bonnet and extracted a set of jumper leads from the boot, leaving it open as well. Gilberto put gloves on and grabbed his items from a box in the boot. He positioned himself leaning against the rear of Miguel's car.

Brazzos had his car running. He saw Liam exit the gatehouse and walk along in front of the administration block towards the employee car park, talking into his phone. Once he passed reception, Brazzos eased out and drove into the spaces near the gatehouse. He parked, turned the car off and walked into the gatehouse.

He knocked and entered, and before Willo had a chance to speak, he announced, "Hello, I'm Tony Brazzos, and I was hoping to catch Liam O'Donoghue before he left. He was going to leave me an envelope in the gatehouse for me."

"You just missed him, not but a couple of minutes ago. He was heading to the car park. You can probably catch him if you hurry." Paul turned his head to scan the video to see if he was in sight. "Yes, see there he is just at the front of the car park."

Brazzos, sensing a potential disaster, urgently distracted the guard. "Okay, good, I'll call him now and swing over there. Did he leave an envelope for me?" Brazzos then enticed the guard away from the screen in a pretence of looking for the envelope.

Paul walked across the small office space to collect the envelope while Brazzos was monitoring the screens over Willo's head. Paul offered it to Brazzos, while the boss was pretending to talk on the phone: "Yes, yes, I will see you in a minute." As soon as Brazzos saw that the Rodriguez boys had completed their work, he sent the preloaded text to his nephew. Then as he took the envelope from the gate guard, the site emergency alarm activated.

"Shit, what is that?" Brazzos yelled.

"I don't know, hopefully just a false alarm." Paul picked up his radio and called the shift supervisor as he ran out of the gatehouse past Brazzos towards the front of the property to close the gates. Brazzos was left alone watching the security vision.

Liam approached the Rodriguez brothers who were standing beside their car with the bonnet up, apparently broken down. Miguel was seeking his help. Liam acknowledged the men and opened his car remotely. Gilberto lent in and pulled the bonnet latch, then moved to the front to prize up the bonnet. Liam seemed to put his bag in the back seat and pass his car keys to Gilbert, who walked towards the driver's door. From the gate house security vision, Brazzos couldn't quite make out what happened next, but while Miguel was under the bonnet connecting the jumper leads, he seemed to ask Liam for something and pointed towards the trunk. As Liam walked around to the rear, Gilberto appeared at his side and in an instant, Liam collapsed and was bundled into the trunk. Even if there was a crowd nearby, they probably wouldn't have seen anything.

Seconds later, the bonnets were closed and both cars were seen heading out with the site emergency alarm ringing, Miguel driving their V8 Holden Commodore SS and Gilberto following in Liam's Mazda.

38

ZOE CALLED SHAW AND Smith on Friday morning and requested the day off. Her previous leave plans were cancelled when Liam returned to Melbourne for the plant accident. She ended up working the days instead and keeping the planned leave for a later date. Now that Liam had called and was returning for another week, she negotiated to take up her days in lieu. She had the morning to herself to potter around the house, clean and get everything ready for Liam's arrival, which she expected would be mid-afternoon. Her spirits were high and she looked forward to the week ahead with her brother.

There was a knock on her front door at 10:00am. It was at that moment her world would come crashing down. She opened the door to find two police officers waiting and she felt a sudden surge of anxiety. One of the police officers introduced themselves as Senior Constable Judith Barnes and Constable Luke Murphy. They asked if she was Zoe O'Donoghue. Zoe froze, speechless.

"Zoe, do you mind if we come in?" continued the police officer.

"Of course ... please ... come in." Zoe stepped back to

let them enter and ushered them down into the kitchen. “Would you like a tea or coffee?”

The police officers accepted a cup of tea, while Zoe opted for water. The young police officer offered to make the tea and gestured for Zoe to sit at the table alongside his senior. Zoe felt sick. She was shaking and feared the worst. *This can’t be good. Police officers at the door equals bad news. Stay calm.*

“Zoe,” SC Barnes started, “I’m so sorry to bring bad news, but your brother Liam has been involved in a car accident in Victoria last night and he was unfortunately killed.”

Zoe knew it. She’d had that sick feeling in her gut. She collapsed into the arms of the officer, sobbing uncontrollably. The officers, skilled in their role, let the news sink in. Constable Murphy brought over the cups of tea and a box of tissues from the counter. SC Barnes put a comforting arm around Zoe and held her until she settled.

“It’s such terrible news, and we are deeply sorry for your loss. Is there anyone we can call to support you?”

“N-no, there’s no one,” Zoey stuttered. We’re all that’s left of our family.” She paused and took a handful of tissues. “What happened?”

SC Barnes had the right tone and the right words. She waited until Zoe had regained her composure and explained that they didn’t have much to go on at that the moment. They had been contacted by the Victorian police in Horsham who found the car this morning. The car had apparently hit a tree not far out of Horsham. They checked the driver’s licence and the car registration to confirm that the car belonged to Liam O’Donoghue. They found a business card in the front console which led them to contact Agro Alliance in Melbourne who confirmed Zoe as the next of kin. SC Barnes advised that the preliminary findings suggested that car, a white Mazda, had failed to take a turn and ran into a large gum tree about forty metres off the road. A contact at Agro Alliance advised that Liam had left Melbourne sometime after 5:00pm and was heading to Adelaide, with a plan to stop halfway overnight.

"Yes, that's right," Zoe whispered. "He rang me yesterday to tell me he was coming back for a week. He had some meeting with an engineering firm and was also taking some leave. This is unbelievable. He is such a careful person, I can't believe he ran off the road."

"I understand, this news is hard to hear," SC Barnes said with empathy. She looked to her partner. "I can get Constable Murphy to stay with you for a while. We will also leave you some information to read when you're ready."

Zoe took the paper and just stared at it blankly, not reading it, not reacting to the police officer's words. SC Barnes stood and asked Murphy to stay for an hour or so, and to assist where he could. She would return or get a squad car to pick him up at some point. She turned to Zoe and said softly, "Look after yourself. Get some help or some support if you need. We can offer a counsellor, if you'd like." As she made to leave, she added, "When you feel up to it, Zoe, we need someone to make a formal identification in Horsham. Can you think about that and let Luke know?" With that, she gave Zoe another hug and then left.

—

The next few hours were a blur. Constable Murphy rang the Horsham police station and arranged for Zoe to meet with

Inspector Michael Wood the next day. The Inspector didn't have anything more to offer at that stage but mentioned that he would update Zoe in regard to the investigation in the morning.

Zoe operated in a daze. Everything was surreal. She vacillated between periods of inaction and bursts of energy. The packing of her bags for this dreaded trip took forever, interrupted by the calls she felt obliged to make. She made the calls to those near and dear, dreading each one.

She called her aunt and uncle, catching them on their latest grey nomad adventure somewhere on the Nullarbor. Zoe insisted they continue their trip and that there was no sense returning. She didn't have any details, nor an understanding of what was to come.

Next on her list of calls was Sarah in Melbourne. Sarah hadn't heard and was equally devastated, her world imploding the same as Zoe's. Sarah told Zoe she had tried to call Liam a few times yesterday evening but each call rang out unanswered, totally out of character.

Sarah also offered to come to Horsham, but Zoe again insisted it wasn't necessary. Zoe needed time for herself to work things out, not play host to others, to anyone, no matter who. Sarah told Zoe to stay at the Hatfield's when she came to Melbourne but Zoe tentatively accepted the offer. She didn't know how long she was staying in Horsham and possibly needed her own space. Sarah agreed to contact the flatmates and Liam's football friends.

Each call was a repeat of the last. The same message as if it were on some bizarre cyclic retake. The calls fell into a routine, the introduction, then a breakdown as she fumbled through an explanation of the accident, with the details as she knew them. An exchange of how and why, and endless repeating of 'I don't believe this'. Offers of help and revisiting the misfortune over and over again was soul destroying. Each call ended with an obligatory promise to keep in touch.

She called CJ in Sydney and then her girlfriends, and was exhausted by the time she finished packing and talking. She had a week of leave from the winery but called them to advise that she might be away for an indefinite period and was happy to take leave without pay if necessary. They were very understanding and offered her all the time she needed.

As she drove off, she called Ben at the Golden Grain and booked a few nights for her stay in Horsham. Ben had heard the local news, and he was pretty worried when Liam hadn't arrived last night. Now he knew for certain that it was Liam in the accident, he and Cora began to grieve the loss of a true friend.

39

BEN BETTESS HAD LIVED in Horsham for most of his life and had contacts everywhere in town. When Zoe had told him about Liam's accident, he made it his business to drop into the Horsham Police Station to chat with Woody. Ben and Mick were well retired from their football days but remained friends. As past premiership players, they had an unbreakable bond. The Inspector couldn't tell his mate all that much as they were still gathering information and awaiting feedback on the blood test results.

Ben asked about the accident site and was confused when Mick told him that it was a few kilometres out of town on the road to Nhill, just short of the Dimboola turn off. There's a curve in the road out there and it looks like your friend just drove straight-on, missing the curve altogether and hit a solid tree about forty to fifty metres off the side. It was in a direct line and there was no skid marks or deviations. It was too early to say definitively, but Mick's guess was that the driver probably nodded off at the wheel.

Ben was shaking his head. "Woody, something doesn't add up. Liam stays at our motel every time he travels to and from Adelaide, probably four times a year. He had a booking to stay last night and when I spoke with him, he was keen to have dinner at the Victoria. So, what was he doing on the road out to Nhill?"

"Sorry mate, I can't answer that. All we know is that we found the car this morning as daylight broke. A truck driver phoned it in. We haven't worked out when it actually happened. When we contacted the driver's place of work, they told us he left Melbourne around 5:00pm, so our guess is any time from 9:00pm. We might know a bit more once we get the blood results."

"Something's not right, that's all I'm saying." Ben left the station still confused.

—

Zoe arrived at the Golden Grain late in the afternoon and was greeted by Ben and Cora. They ushered her into their living room and sat together with a pot of tea and shared the nightmare.

Zoe was still in a state of shock and could hardly remember anything about the long drive from Adelaide. "I still can't believe it," she repeated for the umpteenth dozen time. "What am I going to do?"

Cora was trying to comfort her. "Zoe, love. You stay here as long as you need. It's free, no charge."

Zoe smiled and nodded but couldn't find the words to answer. Ben offered, "You can stay in our spare room if you'd like?"

Zoe shook her head. "Oh no. I can't do that. I'm happy to pay. If you don't mind, I would like to stay in Liam's usual room – I think it's on the corner."

"Are you sure?" asked Ben. "Number 11. If that's what you want, no problem and still no charge."

"Thank you, thank you both. I need to follow his routine, soak something of him in. It's silly but I'm still trying to work it out. Maybe by following in his tracks, something will talk to me." Zoe broke down in tears and was immediately comforted by Cora.

They spent the next hour together, eating and reminiscing, switching between laughing at Liam's quirkiness and crying in grief. It felt good for Zoe to be able to release her emotions in such a safe space. These good people were the support the Adelaide police were suggesting. Ben walked with her to her room after dinner and offered to go with her to the meeting with Inspector Wood and to identify Liam's body if she didn't feel ready. Zoe thanked him, gave him a hug and a kiss on the cheek. "You're so nice, Ben. You know Liam loved you guys. He always spoke about you, and he told everyone about the man with the big heart and the flashy shoes." They both laughed.

"Ben, I need to do the identification. Something I must do. But if you don't mind, I would appreciate if you could come with me."

"Of course." Ben hugged Zoe again. "Come up and have breakfast with us in the morning, say around 8:00am, and we'll go see Mick after that."

—

Ben elected to drive to the police station, although it was barely a kilometre from the motel, located in the centre of town on Roberts Avenue. Inspector Wood met Zoe and Ben in the reception and ushered them through to the visitors' room. Offers of tea and coffee were declined when Ben explained they'd just finished breakfast. Inspector Wood introduced himself as Woody and explained to Zoe that he was a long-standing friend of Ben's.

"I've brought you in here for a few minutes to outline the steps. First, I will take you around to the funeral parlour on Pynsent Street to conduct the formal identification. I know it might be stressful, but it will be good to get it done."

"That's okay," replied Zoe with a glum expression. "It's all bad, and I'm resigned to the worst."

"Then we'll come back here to discuss the investigation to date, and the next steps. But we can stop at any point."

Zoe and Ben followed Woody as they walked around the block to the funeral parlour. They were received by a parlour attendant, dressed immaculately in a sombre grey suit. The attendant was softly spoken and invited them through to the rear of the property and into the morgue. Zoe began to shake and felt slightly giddy, so Ben stepped up and put his arm around her shoulders to support her. They waited while preparations were completed inside. Zoe felt like time was standing still, her feet and heart were heavy. The rest was a blur. She entered the cold, stark room and when the attendant pulled back the sheet on the centre table she couldn't breathe. Liam, her dear brother, his lifeless body in front of her on the table. How long she stood there, she couldn't remember, only her sad uncontrolled sobbing and the draining of her own spirit. Before she fully realised, she was back at the police station, a return journey erased from her memory.

Woody guided Zoe and Ben back into the visitor's

room and made Zoe a cup of tea – English Breakfast, her preference – and coffees for himself and Ben. He offered them some biscuits. “This is all the police budget will allow. We have a choice between a teddy bear biscuit or a malt-o-milk. We should be grateful, I suppose. If the budget gets cut further as they suggest, then our tea and bikkies may be delisted altogether.”

He smiled to try and break the tension in the room. In his experience, any form of shock led to a mini-shutdown, and he was hoping that tea and biscuits would cut through. He would prefer to have gone through all the discussions before the viewing, but that was counter to protocol. It would be a disaster for the viewer if in fact the deceased was not the person the police had believed. He probably could have reversed the order in this case because the driver’s licence and the car registration alongside the known facts all pointed to Liam O’Donoughue. Police protocol was still the winner.

Waiting for the right moment – his experience, judging that it wouldn’t be before at least half a cup was consumed – the Inspector put on his official voice and proceeded cautiously. “Zoe … once again, I am sorry for your loss … Liam’s car was found about fifteen kilometres out of Horsham yesterday morning … just prior to the Dimboola turn-off.”

Zoe and Ben were both shaking their heads as Woody continued. “There was no evidence of braking and there were no skid marks. The blood tests have come back this morning and they were all clear … No traces of any alcohol or drugs.” He paused to let this news register. “The car unfortunately ran straight into a big gum. It looks like it veered at the last minute with the impact directly on the front panel and front driver’s door. Liam was wearing his seat belt, and the car’s air bags had been deployed. As a result of the impact on the right side of the car, Liam appears to have received a catastrophic head impact. The only good news is that we don't think he suffered and he was almost certainly killed instantly."

Woody stopped once more to let all news, some of which they already knew, sink in. The room fell silent for a few minutes until Zoe spoke. "None of this makes sense. He was such a careful driver, and he always stopped at Ben's motel. Why was he so far out of town?"

"As I told you yesterday, Liam even called me and made the booking," Ben added. "I spoke with him myself and he was intending to go to the Victoria Hotel for dinner."

"That's right," Zoe confirmed. "He told me the exact same thing. He was so fussy, bordering on anal-retentive. It was a routine he never broke. He stayed at Ben and Cora's motel every trip, same room every time. He had a steak at the hotel every time. Always the same."

"Room number 11." Ben laughed as he recalled his friend's insistence. "We would always relocate other customers to accommodate him whenever he needed a booking."

Woody nodded and began to take some notes. Zoe smiled. "You would have thought that Liam was on a commission for the amount of times he spoke about the Golden Grain, or that bloody steak at the Victoria Hotel. So, Inspector Wood, Woody ... it makes no sense that he was on the road to Nhill or Dimboola."

"I understand what you're telling me, and I'm equally puzzled. However, the facts are still the facts, and he was on the road to Dimboola. We found his driver's side window partly wound down, which is fairly typical of what driver's do when they're fatigued. We've also spoken to his workplace and although he is reported to have left around 5:00pm, he may have had a stop and may not have arrived into Horsham until late. It might have been too late for dinner … but that's pure speculation."

"Maybe …" Ben hummed. "Even so, he would still have stopped at our place. Often he gets his key from our lock box if he's going to be late."

Woody took another note and looked directly at Ben. "And if he was going to be late, would he call ahead, or would you just leave the key in the box regardless?"

Ben nodded understanding where that question was headed. "He would always call."

"Did he make that call on Thursday night?"

Ben dropped his gaze and feeling defeated, he flatly answered, "No. I'm afraid he didn't."

Woody had known the answer and had sympathy for Ben. "When we followed up with his employers, they mentioned that they had made a booking for him at the Dimboola Motel. They also said that the company was paying … Could it be possible that on this trip he felt duty bound to stay in Dimboola and drove on through?"

Another pause as these facts were absorbed, all still a puzzle.

Woody leant forward and clasped his hand on the table. "We think he was headed to Dimboola but it was later than he expected. He was tired, missed the curve in the road and it was a horrible mistake. Unfortunately, it's a bad bend in the road, and this is not the first time someone has driven off into that same tree."

"No, no, no!" Zoe shouted, with her head in her hands. "I don't believe it. My intuition says otherwise."

"I'm sorry. The news is terrible. We only have the facts that are in front of us. We've been in consultation with the coroner's office this morning, and they have indicated that they are considering fatigue as the probable cause of death. At this stage, there's not much more we can do. Again, I'm sorry."

Zoe couldn't speak and seeing that Woody had no more information, silence prevailed. Ben finally asked, "What next, Mick?"

Woody looked at Zoe and asked if she needed more time, to maybe come back later. There were a few decisions to make. Zoe felt lost and was just shaking her head. Her stomach stirred and an ache began pounding in her head. "No, let's do it now. Let's get it over with."

The next fifteen minutes were spent outlining the logistics. Woody asked her intentions for a funeral and in the absence of a clear plan, he suggested that Liam could stay at the funeral parlour's morgue. Zoe could take a day or two to decide and advise them of her instructions, but they would need directions within a week. Then Woody spoke about Liam's belongings and his car. Ben offered to arrange the car to be taken to his motel and stored behind the units, pending insurance or disposal to the wreckers. Zoe agreed to collect Liam's work items, his travel bag, and his other personal belongings. Woody rang a number and arranged for them to be available at reception on the way out.

Woody stood and went to the door. "I'll leave you now. Take your time and check out at reception and collect Liam's things." He shook hands with them both and made to leave.

As Woody opened the door, Zoe asked, "One last thing. If there is any other evidence, if something new comes to light, can we revisit this?"

Woody felt like this was a last hope against hope, clutching at straws, but accepted that grief had many dimensions. "Certainly. Don't get your hopes up, but we can if that helps."

Zoe half smiled and gave Woody a hug. "Thank you. That's something."

—

Back in Ben's car, Zoe thanked him for coming with her. "I appreciate your help. I don't know how I could've done that by myself. You are so kind and I am so grateful."

Ben smiled. "Zoe, you're like family. It's the very least I could do. What do you want to do now?"

"If you don't mind, could we go out and look at the accident site?"

40

THE RODRIGUEZ BOYS HAD many 'favourite' drinking places, but one of the best was The Railway Hotel in Port Melbourne. Despite becoming trendy in recent years, it still had that feel of its working class heritage. Miguel had made a reservation for three under the name Rodriguez and requested his preferred table – the one in the corner with the brick walls near the framed football jumper from Melbourne Victory. Even though the pub was often busy on a Sunday, this particular table offered the right amount of privacy to discuss their clandestine operation. They would hold their payment exchange and any debrief in Spanish, to further remain undiscovered to other patrons.

Brazzos turned up early with his backpack, anxious for the Rodriguez feedback. The meal and a few beers would be an added bonus. He sat on his own looking at the sporting memorabilia on the adjoining walls while nursing his cerveza, a Corona without lemon. The police had contacted Agro Alliance and Michelle Buchanan fielded the initial call. She already had the next of kin details and had called Brazzos to determine the purpose of Liam's trip to Adelaide. He was pleased to report it was a company trip to follow up on an engineering design and that Liam was booked to stay in Dimboola on the trip over. He thought he displayed an adequate amount of shock and sympathy when Michelle told him that Liam had been killed in a car accident outside of Horsham.

The Rodriguez brothers arrived together and joined Brazzos at the table. Another round of beers and then they placed their lunch order. Brazzos lifted his glass to a toast. "Saludos mis amigos, por el buen trabajo." *Cheers, my friends, for a job well done.* He placed his backpack on the vacant chair next to Miguel and smiled a big toothy grin.

"Tell me, it went smoothly, I assume? Are there any issues to worry about?" Brazzos asked, jumping straight into the debrief.

Gilberto was not a talker and sat enjoying his beer, thinking about counting the money. It was his biggest payday since arriving in Australia, all for a day's work, a drive in the countryside and all. He let Miguel do all the talking. "No problems at all, Antonio," Miguel continued with a grin. "Pretty easy, a simple job really. It wasn't our first rodeo, you know."

"Of course, but give me the rundown, please. The detail, just to close the deal," he sneered while patting his backpack.

"Well, we started in your car park, as you know. The distraction was perfect, and Gilberto had him knocked out and in the boot within seconds. Even if you were a few cars away, you would never have noticed. That was the hardest part, and from there it was a piece of cake."

"What did you use to knock him out?" Brazzos interrupted.

Miguel smiled and tapped his forehead with his finger. "Don't you worry about the detail. Tools of the trade. Just be happy that it was quick and easy. It was only temporary, maybe fifty or sixty minutes and doesn't show up in a routine blood test."

Brazzos suspected it was chloroform or something similar and didn't question how the boys got hold of it. "And then ..." He gestured for Miguel to continue.

"We had to stop for fuel. Paid in cash, no traces. Stopped in Ararat for food and checked the cargo. Gave him another top up to sleep some more. Stopped again on roadside after Stawell to check on passenger. Injection in between fingers for goodnight, lights out permanently."

"No one saw you, did they?"

"Of course not." Miguel shook his head. "Who do you think we are? Off road, dark, no traffic, quick and easy."

Gilberto sniggered. "Muy facil."

Miguel asked Antonio, "Why did we need to go all the way out to this Dimboola place? We could have done it just as easy anywhere."

"It had to fit the storyline. He was going back to Adelaide. Long trip, tired and drift off the road. How did you work that part?"

Miguel laughed and slapped Antonio on the shoulder. "Again, you don't need to worry. It's part of our service. We've done it many times, very easy." He looked at his brother and they smiled at each other knowingly. "Actually, this time it was excellent. I drove ahead and found the perfect bend in the road, no safety barrier, and big trees just back a bit. Fitted the bill perfecto. One hundred percent, it looked like he had missed the turn."

The food arrived and they took a break, eating and drinking. During the meal, Miguel explained that he called his brother to stop on roadside behind his car, which he had parked a few hundred meters short of the identified curve. They waited for over half an hour assessing traffic. Then they drove to a point opposite the tree, waited some more before they quickly pulled Liam out of the Commodore and sat him behind the driver's wheel of the Mazda. They stopped and waited a bit more while they set up the gearstick with a rope attachment, positioned the steering lock on the steering wheel and secured a weight in position to engage the accelerator. They lowered the driver's window to access the rope, and then with no traffic around, they turned the car on and pulled it into drive.

Gilberto laughed and gloated excitedly, "Worked perfecto. Car took off straight across the road and into the tree. *Bang!*"

Miguel added, "The best bit was just before it hit the tree, it swerved and veered to the left, hitting the tree on the right side of the car near the driver. Air bags popped but he was still knocked about. We retrieved the rope, weight, and steering lock. Finished. No traffic and then we left the area for someone to discover later."

"Sounds good." Brazzos nodded with raised brows. "Did you get the files and the USB stick?"

Miguel screwed up his face. "When we moved Liam into his car, we took his bag and left his laptop and phone in his car." Miguel handed Brazzos the recovered work bag; a nice leather satchel. "We checked through the bag but didn't find any USB stick. Only several reports, pens, and notebooks."

"Bloody hell, I need to get that USB stick. How am I going to lay my hands on that fucking thing?" Brazzos was huffing now, anxiety surging through him.

"Maybe he had it at work or at home, but it wasn't in the

car. Why does it matter? He could have told others about that 'theory' or whatever. It's not like he was going to keep it a secret."

"It's just untidy. Without a document, everything is just speculation. I'll check his office at work and I'll get you to do another job for me and check his home."

Miguel smiled and looked at his brother, nodding. "New job, new pay. Yes?"

Gilberto laughed and they haggled over the price. Miguel needed the address and agreed with Brazzos that they would get it done in the morning.

41

ZOE HAD ALL LIAM'S stuff packed into her car and left Horsham mid-morning on Sunday. She tried to pay for her stay but both Ben and Cora were adamant that it was on them on the proviso that she called if she needed any additional help. Zoe laughed as she asked, "How does that work? You give me a gift provided I promise to ask you for more help?" She was still smiling an hour later on the road. *Such a sad week and they make me feel good. What special people.*

For the next four hours, she drove absent mindedly, heading east to Melbourne, not knowing where to start. All she really knew was that there was something wrong. Liam would not drive beyond Horsham without contacting Ben.

She tried changing radio stations, playing music. Nothing took her mind away from the nightmare that she was now living. *Make a plan, Zoe,* she repeated to herself over and over. Nothing was obvious, so by default she decided she would immerse herself in Liam's life in Melbourne. From there, a lead would become obvious, surely! She only had a week to work it out, to find something that might make the police reconsider. Otherwise the world would move on and Liam would be listed as just another road toll victim.

As she approached Melbourne's West Gate Bridge, she called Sarah, maybe just to share her grief or tease out a starting point.

Sarah answered immediately. "Are you here yet and are you coming to stay with us?"

"Just coming through the tunnel heading towards Chadstone now. Thanks for the offer, I really appreciate it. But I feel that I need to be alone. I need some space to sort out my thoughts." Zoe didn't tell Sarah that she had already booked into the motel adjoining the Chadstone retail complex. It was only a few kilometres from the Hatfield's and close to Liam's residence in Oakleigh. This would be her base.

"Okay," Sarah sighed, "but don't hesitate to call if you need anything."

"Thank you. I think I'll go out to Liam's workplace in the morning and get a sense of the place. Maybe we could meet up later and I'd also like to visit his home in Oakleigh."

"I'll call Adrian and arrange for us to join them for their regular Monday night pizza dinner," Sarah suggested eagerly. "Let me know where you are staying and I will pick you up and take you."

"While we have a chance, can you tell me anything about Liam's last day at his workplace?"

"He called me as he was leaving the plant and he sounded very excited about going back to Adelaide." Sarah paused as she recalled the conversation. "Then he abruptly cut me off and he had to go. He said he would call back later, he was needing to help someone jump-start their car."

"Did he call back?"

"No, he didn't. I didn't hear from him again. That was the strange thing, because he would normally ring back straight away. I waited twenty or thirty minutes and called him. He didn't answer and I left several messages. Maybe the phone went flat, but I didn't speak with him again."

Zoe thought that it was so like Liam to lend a helping hand, but it was uncharacteristic for him not to have called Sarah back. She decided on her plan. First, she would check Liam's phones, then in the morning she would visit his workplace in West Footscray on the premise of collecting his belongings. She would immerse herself in the place, the start of her brother's fateful trip.

"Sarah, I'm coming up to the hotel-motel now. Let me call you back tomorrow after I finish at his workplace. Dinner with flatmates will be another step. It's not much of a plan but it's a start."

—

It was mid-afternoon when Zoe arrived at the motel, and she needed food. She recovered Liam's two phones from the stuff in the boot, took her bag from the back seat and checked in. *Now let's see what all the fuss was about. Liam constantly promoted this Chadstone as an epic retail centre – the largest in the southern hemisphere, supposedly.*

First thing was to find food, and she was blown away with the options. Food courts with glamour and many cafes or lunch spots as well as the chain type restaurants. She walked aimlessly, impressed with both the size and grandeur. *Okay Liam, you're right. I might need to do some retail therapy later.*

She settled on the chicken burger and a Coke Zero from one of the outlet chains. Nestled in a booth in the back, she took out Liam's phones. The password would be the first roadblock, but if she knew her brother, it shouldn't be a problem. He was so anal it was almost too easy. The choices were a variation of his birthday or a reference to the Port Adelaide football club. She was unsuccessful using the birthday options but smiled to herself as the burger arrived when 'power01' opened both phones.

There wasn't a lot of activity on Liam's work phone. There were several calls that Zoe presumed were work colleagues, names she vaguely recalled: Statler *(that's the Muppet Man, that much I remember)*, Jennison, Sandy, and Mario. There were also recent calls to contacts listed as 'Lab', 'Albert Cohen – WorkSafe', 'Cameron Oxley – Workcover', 'Michael Rosenbloom – Mixing Masters' and 'Sue Carpenter – RK Legal'. She wrote these names and contact details on a pad she had taken from the motel room.

The last call was from a mobile number not listed in his contacts at 4:25pm on the previous Thursday, which would have been just before he left for Adelaide. Zoe added the number to her list, thinking that she needed a notebook, which she decided would be her next purchase after lunch while she was in the shops. Scrolling back through the phone over the previous few days, it seemed like a lot of calls to the 'Shift Supervisor' and a few from the Agro Alliance switchboard. Then she opened up his photos and found numerous images of chemical plant parts. The latest pictures included various equipment items all covered with an orange stain, obviously from the accident site. The last was a video inside a laboratory. She watched the video which had Liam's voice overlayed in describing the experiment and ended with his excitement as the contents from a flask spraying up and out of the bottle.

Zoe assumed that this was the basis of Liam's investigation. Maybe it held the link to the plant accident that cut short his previous trip to Adelaide for her birthday. Tears welled in her eyes as she realised that there would never be another celebration with her brother, ever.

She opened Liam's private phone. There was plenty of activity with a list of many names. Adrian, Rick, Ross, Tom, David, Tony, and on and on, and CJ of course. Mostly football mates, she presumed. Most of the recent calls were to Sarah, some others to herself and a few to Sandy – a name she had heard Liam mention and which she presumed was the Sandy also on his work phone.

She found a call to the Golden Grain at 10:30am on the Thursday he travelled – obviously his booking of the hotel for the trip. Nothing about a Dimboola motel, so this confirmed to Zoe that he was always intending to stop in Horsham, never intending to go onto to Dimboola. Then she opened his work phone again and noticed a call from the Agro Alliance switchboard at 10:15am. Playing amateur detective, she presumed this was a call that initiated the decision for the trip. Liam would have immediately made the contact to Ben at the Golden Grain once the trip was arranged. She took out her own phone and searched for the Dimboola Motel.

"Hello, Dimboola Motel," the cheery voice answered. "How can I help you?"

Zoe wasn't prepared for a cheery voice and took a second to gather herself. "I'm not sure if you can help me. My brother was booked to stay with you last week but didn't arrive." She took a big breath to calm herself further. "Unfortunately he had a car accident outside Horsham."

"Yes, I remember. I'm so sorry for your loss, dear. I remember because we thought we had a no-show. The next day we found out that he was involved in that car accident just before the Dimboola turn-off."

Zoe thanked the lady, not wishing to revisit details about the accident. "Do you recall who made the booking in the first place and when would that have been?"

"Give me a minute, love." Zoe heard papers flicking in the background as the lady searched through her records. "Yes. I have it here. It was a lady from Agro Alliance, a Suzi Murray. The booking was made at 11:15am and they arranged pre-payment for the night."

"Thank you," replied Zoe, "that's helpful. One last thing. Has Agro Alliance used your hotel previously?"

"Sorry, I can't say definitively. They don't have an account with us, but to the best of my knowledge they haven't, and I've been here for over ten years." Zoe thanked the lady for her help and ended the call, but not before making another mental note to follow up with Suzi Murray at Agro Alliance.

Returning to Liam's phone, it revealed no other calls after the Golden Grain until late in the afternoon, with a call to Sarah at 4:55pm, which matched what Sarah had said this afternoon. Then there were a few missed calls from Sarah, about twenty minutes apart, with no message. There were two more calls from Sarah with messages. The first was at 7:00pm with a voice message: *"Loddy, you said you were going to call. That was a couple of hours ago. I've tried you several times. Please call. Maybe your phone has gone flat. Call me as soon as you can. Love you, Loddy."* The last call was at 7:02pm with another message: *"Drive safe, sweety. I'm off to tennis for a few hours. Talk to you when you get to Horsham. Charge your phone, you dummy!"*

Sarah had told Zoe that she didn't hear back from Liam that night and it was totally unlike him. Zoe agreed completely; he always called back. She checked his phone and it still had 40% charge, and it wasn't on silent, so a flat phone made no sense. Zoe always knew this was never an issue. Liam would have had it on charge and his private phone was paired with his car so he would normally have picked up. This added to the mystery because it was totally out of character for Liam.

—

With a new notebook in hand, Zoe set up in the motel room and began writing notes and a plan. A list of things to follow up, another list of contact names from Liam's phones and a list of questions. The latter included the booking of the Golden Grain, telling Ben, Sarah and Zoe that he was intending to eat at the Victoria Hotel, no contact with Ben of any change of plan, failure to call Sarah after leaving work, unanswered calls from Sarah and that afternoon, the observation that Liam's satchel was not among the possessions recovered from his car.

Zoe doodled on a separate page: why, what, where. She knew her brother was a creature of habit and something was amiss. The facts didn't add up.

42

PALMER STREET SEEMED TO be half asleep when the Rodriguez brothers arrived as the sun was rising over the Dandenongs, casting long shadows down the street. They pulled up a few houses back from their mark and waited, enjoying the remnants of their McDonalds breakfast and coffee. Miguel left Gilberto in the car to observe the neighbours while he walked along the street, returning on the opposite side. He paused outside Liam's house and saw some lights signal the start of a morning routine. There was an abundance of cars parked in the street and two cars parked in Liam's driveway.

The stakeout might last several hours as Brazzos had no real knowledge of the living arrangements, only the address. They presumed Liam was renting with mates. Miguel had stopped at the local McDonalds when he ordered their breakfast, and he had arranged for another breakfast for two to be delivered to the Palmer street address at 8:30am. He paid in cash. He was on his second reconnaissance mission as the order arrived. Miguel conveniently stopped at the letter box pretending to do his shoelace up as the delivery driver knocked on the door. He overheard the confusion as they asked around inside who had made the order; Miguel counted three voices. The driver apologised for the mistake, obviously the wrong address, and he left to return to McDonalds.

Ninety minutes passed before they counted three people depart the house. Then they drove up and parked outside. Gilberto, dressed as a delivery man, got out and took a parcel to the front door. He knocked and there was no answer, so he returned to the car with the parcel in hand. The boys drove off and parked further down towards the end of the street, still with a view of Liam's house. They waited another thirty minutes watching the house before they drove back and parked a few houses back, alighted, donned their gloves, and walked into the boys' front yard, straight down the side without stopping and around to the back.

How easy was it, the boys had left the back door unlocked. Not that it would have been an issue – locks were never a problem for the Rodriguez boys; they'd been picking locks since they were kids. Once inside, they quickly identified which was Liam's room; there was a cap and jacket in the cupboard with Agro Alliance logos and a folder on the desk marked 'T-plant Accident'. Gilberto went outside and took cover in the shadows of the side of the house on lookout, while Miguel went to work.

Miguel had already earmarked the folder for collection but focused on finding this USB stick. He meticulously turned everything over, looked under the bed, in all the cupboards, careful to return everything as it was. There was a record collection, a small desk, and a few books. The only paperwork he found were licence receipts, insurance papers and other documents neatly filed in one of the desk drawers.

Miguel knew that there was no computer. *We left that in his car. If this kid worked from home, it was on the work computer from his briefcase. Otherwise he was a nerd and super neat freak.*

Miguel searched the kitchen and the living room, including all the drawers, cupboards, and shelves. Lots of footy stuff, more records, and tapes. No USB stick. Two hours later, with the search complete, he grabbed the folder and joined Gilberto. They walked briskly out of the yard, discretely, and were back in the car calling Brazzos as they drove out of the street.

Brazzos answered the call without any greeting, simply telling Miguel he didn't have much time and was in a hurry.

"All good, my friend. I'll be quick," Miguel answered. "The job is finished, checked everywhere. There is no USB stick. If it were here, we would have found it. The bloke was a neat freak ..."

Before he could continue, Brazzos cut him off, telling him it wasn't an issue anymore. He had retrieved the USB stick from the sister.

"Well, that solves that then. Let's catch up for lunch at the Railway tomorrow for payday."

With his temper rising, Brazzos spat, "What pay day? You didn't find the USB stick! It was in his bloody pocket, you fool. You should have found it on the job last time."

Miguel's attitude quickly changed as he countered, "Now you listen to me. We did the job last week and all was well, no hitches, solved your little problem. Then you commissioned us for another job. I am reporting that the second job is done, and we expect to be paid."

"I haven't time for this. I have the USB stick, so thanks anyway."

Miguel looked at his brother with a glare that could have cut through steel, and responded again, "That's not how it works. If you have the USB stick then you should have called and cancelled the job before we took the risk."

"I only just received it now."

"Not our problem. We did as you asked and now you pay. Besides, we did recover a nice thick folder about your accident. I suppose you'll want that?"

Brazzos sensed he was being backed into a corner. "Maybe, depends on the content. I can't do the Railway tomorrow."

"Let's make it the Plough Hotel in Footscray instead, at 12:00 noon. Bring the cash and we'll give you the folder."

"Okay 12:00 noon at the Plough, but I'll only be bringing half of the money."

"I've already told you that's not how it works!" Miguel yelled. "Are you for real? All for a few lousy thousand dollars and you want to bargain. We agreed on a job, we took all the risk, and no one welches on the Rodriguez boys. We are not called Calica for nothing, if you get what I mean. Here's the deal: you can bring half the cash tomorrow and the other half ... you can bring that tomorrow as well."

43

ZOE CALLED THE HR department of Agro Alliance on Monday morning and was passed through to Michelle Buchanan. Michelle passed on her deepest sympathies and offered to be of assistance. While Zoe appreciated the wishes, she had come to accept that this was going to be the new 'norm'. Everyone would say how sorry they were, such a loss, how they could help, etc, etc.

"I'm in Melbourne and just wanted to connect with Liam's work. I can't believe this, so I just want to get a sense of where he was before he left last Thursday."

"Of course," said Michelle in a comforting yet controlling manner. "That should be okay, but we are located in the St Kilda Road offices, and you will need to go out to the plant in West Footscray."

"Thanks. I have his work stuff to return, and I wanted to collect any of his personal belongings from his desk and maybe his locker, if that's all right?"

"That should be fine, just ask for Tony Brazzos at the site. I'll give him a call now and tell him you're on the way ..." Michelle paused, trying to think of a way to finish up. "If Tony isn't available when you arrive, make contact with

Suzi Murray. I'm sure she'll be more than happy to look after you ... Take care and don't hesitate to call if we can be of any further help."

—

On arrival at the plant, Zoe parked in one of the front visitor's parking spaces outside reception. She pulled in beside another driver who had just arrived, who was hesitating with the driver's door partly ajar as he let Zoe finish parking.

They both locked their cars at the same time and acknowledged each other as they walked towards reception. Zoe left Liam's belongings in the car to retrieve after she talked with Mr Brazzos. The other visitor, Cameron Oxley, stopped at the sliding door to allow Zoe to proceed ahead of him. Zoe smiled and thanked him as she headed across to the reception desk.

"Good morning," offered the receptionist.

Oxley stood back to allow Zoe to go first, which received another smile and a thank you. "Hello, I'm Zoe O'Donoughue, Liam's sister. I'm here to see a Mr Brazzos, I think."

The two receptionists looked at each other and nearly lost it. Lauren spoke first. "Oh my dear. We are so sorry. Your brother was such a great guy." Elise was already out from behind her desk and giving Zoe a hug. Lauren followed and the group hug continued for several seconds, leaving Oxley stunned. He felt awkward and out of place and surprised.

Lauren added, "Come and sit down." She took Zoe by the hand and ushered her to one of the reception waiting chairs on the other side of the entrance way. "Elise, can you ring Suzi and get Brazzos or someone to come down?"

Cameron Oxley was virtually abandoned while the full attention was focused on Zoe, who he'd heard was Liam O'Donoghue's sister. He tried to decipher what was happening. The receptionist had mentioned that Liam was such a great guy. Now tears. Something must have happened.

"Excuse me, ladies," Cameron interrupted. "I'm here to meet with Liam myself, but is there something wrong?"

Zoe sobbed while Lauren looked at him before lowering her head. She whispered, "I'm sorry to tell you, but unfortunately Liam was killed in a car accident last week."

Cameron's face dropped. "No. I'm so sorry. I wasn't aware. I was just talking with him last week. How horrible …" Not knowing what to do or say, he sat down in the other visitor's chair next to Zoe, speechless.

Elise broke the silence, telling the group that Mr Brazzos was on his way down. Cameron turned to Zoe. "I don't know what to say. I'm so sorry to hear about Liam."

Zoe nodded, slowly recovering her composure by taking a number of deep breaths.

Brazzos strode into the inner reception and introduced himself. Zoe stood to greet him and shook his hand, while Cameron stayed seated in the background.

Brazzos announced with as much sincerity that he could muster, "We are so sorry for your loss. It has come as a complete shock to everyone here. Your brother was a valued employee."

Zoe was so incredibly numb and could do nothing more than nod. Cameron sensed the consoling words had a hollow ring and noticed the receptionists looking at each other rolling their eyes as if to say, 'What the …?'

Brazzos continued, "I believe you have Liam's work

things. I know this is a difficult time, but I appreciate you bringing them in."

Zoe mustered her strength. "Yes, they're in the car. I'll get them in a moment. Firstly, I was hoping to visit his workplace and collect his personal belongings."

"That won't be necessary. I'll get someone to pack them up for you and you can collect them later. If you could bring in the other stuff though. He should have keys, a mobile phone, a laptop and USB sticks."

Zoe was taken aback with the brush off. "I wanted to just get a sense of where he worked, you know. This is all so sudden, and I'm still trying to understand everything. It would help me to start with his desk, his home—"

"Yes, I appreciate your loss," Brazzos interrupted. "As this is a chemical plant, we have restricted access. I'll get his items boxed up for you. Now can I come with you to get Liam's company things?"

Cameron Oxley stood up. "Don't worry, mate. I'll help her. You seem to be busy so we'll drop them off in an hour, back here at reception." Without hesitating, he took Zoe's hand and walked her out the door, leaving Brazzos aghast.

Lauren looked at Elise and they shared a smile and a gentle nod of affirmation. *Nice one.*

Cameron dropped her hand after they exited the sliding doors. As they walked back together to their cars, Cameron apologised for Brazzos. "I'm sorry about that, he was plainly rude. You didn't deserve to be treated like that. Let me buy you a coffee. Take some time and we can revisit this again. I might be able to help."

Zoe followed the stranger as they crossed the road to the nearby cafe. They sat at a corner table and Cameron went and ordered a cup of tea for Zoe, a large coffee for himself and a couple of muffins to share. He waited for the drinks and carried them to the table.

"Here you go. Let me introduce myself. I'm Cameron Oxley from Workcover, and I was here today to serve some papers on Agro Alliance."

Zoe recognised the name from Liam's phone. "Thanks Cameron, I appreciate what you did back there. I know it shouldn't matter, but he was a bit rude."

"Sure was. Certainly poor form and totally lacking any class." Cameron passed across a muffin. "He could easily have granted you access to the production office, escorted by someone. A few minutes, what's the harm?"

"That's what I thought. I still can't believe Liam's gone. It makes no sense. I was thinking maybe if I started here and at his house, I might be able to make some sense of it all, maybe find a reason for ..." She stumbled and didn't finish her thoughts.

"Don't worry, Zoe. I'm going to make a couple of calls and I'll arrange to come back tomorrow, and if necessary you can be my assistant."

Zoe was more than a bit confused but managed to smile at his offer. They sat for a few minutes and enjoyed their muffin and drink. Cameron explained about the plant fatality and his role with Workcover. Liam was his contact for the follow-up and for arranging documents and the interviews. He was excellent, fastidious – in fact, better than most – and was genuinely trying to find the root cause of the accident. Zoe revealed that she had heard snippets from her brother and mentioned to Cameron that she thought Liam was doing tests and had some sort of theory.

The discussion switched to Liam's accident and Zoe allowed herself some extra grieving by outpouring her feelings. She had so many unanswered questions. It was completely out of character for Liam to drive past Horsham; this was the centre of her problem. She relayed the uncharacteristic failure to answer his phone and the missing satchel.

An hour later, after wide ranging discussions, Zoe accepted Cameron's offer to go with her while she returned Liam's belongings. Zoe went to the bathroom while Cameron made a couple of calls to rearrange his plans to serve the notice on Agro Alliance.

Zoe carried Liam's keys and phone while Cameron had the laptop. They were welcomed back by the reception ladies. Lauren suggested they go through into the training room. It was empty, and you could be in private. "I'll call Suzi and get her to come down. We don't need any more help from the Bullyboy."

Zoe and Cameron were ushered into the training room and they politely declined the offer of tea or coffee. They waited patiently for Suzi to arrive. Zoe was looking at her new friend while he paced around the training room, thinking, *Nice man. I know Liam would have liked him.*

The laptop, keys and phone were on the desk in front of her when she had an epiphany. "Where's the charger for this laptop?"

Cameron turned towards her. "What do you mean?"

"Another thing that puzzles me. Where was Liam's

satchel? He had this beautiful leather satchel that I bought for him when he graduated, and it wasn't in his car."

"Okay, maybe he left it at home or here at work," suggested Cameron.

"Maybe. Unlikely though. He took it everywhere. He used it to carry the laptop, and he always had the charger. There was no charger in the items the police found. Why would you travel all the way to Adelaide with a laptop and not bring your charger?"

"Good thinking, Zoe. Add it to your list of questions. Eventually something will speak to you."

Suzi Murray knocked on the door, interrupting this line of thinking. "Hello Zoe, I'm Suzi. The reception girls asked me to come down and collect a few things." She sat next to Zoe and put an arm around her shoulder. "I can't imagine how you're coping. I loved Liam like a brother myself."

Zoe had to regroup again and gave Suzi a return hug. "These are the work things we're returning. Mr Brazzos is expecting them and I also want to collect Liam's things."

Suzi waved at her, shaking her hand to dismiss the issue. "Don't worry about my boss. He can be a bit brash. He told me he was arranging to collect Liam's stuff. I'll make sure it happens."

Cameron introduced himself to Suzi. "I'll be coming back with Zoe tomorrow. I have some business to follow up with Jim Statler, and we can collect everything tomorrow. Mr Statler was Liam's boss, wasn't he?"

"Yes, that's right. Call me tomorrow when you arrive, if you'd like?"

Cameron nodded. "We will. Thank you for your help.

Can you also keep an eye out for Liam's work bag, a leather satchel. Apparently it's missing. Maybe he left it at work."

Suzi turned her eyes up and squinted them. "Of course. I know that bag. It was a beauty and the envy of many. It rarely left Liam's side."

"That's right," Zoe said. "That's right," she repeated. "It makes no sense that it wasn't with him in the car!" She shook her head. "Suzi, can I ask you another question?"

"Of course. Anything. Anything at all. Your brother was one of the best."

Zoe explained her dilemma about the Horsham or Dimboola stopover, reinforcing that Liam had always without fail chosen the Golden Grain at Horsham. He would have stopped there almost twenty times in the last few years. She still couldn't understand why he had driven past Horsham and headed to Dimboola.

Zoe asked, "Why did you book the Dimboola hotel and not the Golden Grain?"

Suzi agreed. "I know. Brazzos asked me to make the booking, saying that he had spoken with Liam and that Dimboola was halfway. I know Liam stays in Horsham and when I suggested it, Brazzos wasn't listening. He just waved his hand, was on his way out of the office and basically ordered me to make the booking at Dimboola." Suzi paused, her eyes flicking from Cameron, and then to Zoe. "It wasn't my place to question him, so I made the booking. It didn't make any sense to me, and Brazzos wasn't up for any discussion. Liam told me many times about the Golden Grain and the bloody steaks at the Victoria Hotel." Zoe and Suzi both laughed spontaneously.

Suzi gathered up the items and noted the absence of the USB stick. “Zoe,” she asked, “Brazzos mentioned something about a USB stick as well.”

“Yes, sorry. I must have forgot. There was only one though, apparently it was in his pocket. I must have left it in the car.”

Suzi put the remaining items back on the table and together they all walked back out to the car. After retrieving the USB stick, she hugged Zoe again. “Thanks and so sorry for your loss, *our* loss. Leave your number with the reception and I’ll call you once we pack up his things, otherwise just call me tomorrow when you get here.”

Suzi left them and returned to pick up the other items from the training room, while Zoe and Cameron made plans to meet tomorrow.

—

Sarah met Zoe for the first time in the lobby of her Chadstone hotel. They recognised each other from photos that Liam had shared, but greeted each other as if they were long lost sisters. They retired into the small adjacent bar. Zoe ordered a couple of wines, and they sat quietly at a side table not knowing where to start. Sarah broke the ice and before they knew it, their emotions overflowed and they chatted endlessly for an hour. Small talk about their day, travel and work was quickly brushed aside so that they could focus on the loss of the jointly loved Liam.

Zoe pulled out her notebook and they reviewed and debated the contents and Zoe’s ‘list of questions’. Zoe added the extra item of the missing laptop charger. Sarah bought the next round of drinks and suggested they work up different scenarios that could explain the facts. The one thing they both were sure about was that Liam didn't drive past the Golden Grain without calling someone.

Finally, without any established theory, they shut the book and headed to Sarah's car. It was Monday night, and the flatmates would be home for their pizza committee meeting. It was time for Zoe to meet the boys and get a bearing on Liam from his homelife. Sarah had called Adrian earlier in the day and arranged to bring Zoe and to get the clearance for extra pizza from Roscoe. Adrian had snorted with laughter and told her it was all good – Ross was as upset as anyone and would welcome meeting Liam's sister.

Sarah somehow found a vacant spot out the front of the boy's house in Palmer Street and joked to Zoe that it was a lucky dip to find a park in the afternoon along the street. Zoe steeled herself and followed Sarah into the domain of the football flatmates. As expected, it was a boys' house with nothing fancy and just the simple necessities. The boys were empathetic and made Zoe welcome.

Rick brought the pizza with him when he arrived, and they all settled around the scant furniture which consisted of Liam's couch and a few chairs. Zoe was reserved and let Sarah steer the conversations. As they finished their pizzas, Sarah mentioned Zoe was wanting to look over Liam's stuff and asked if that was okay. Of course they all answered in unison. Adrian added, "Take your time. Can we help with anything?"

Zoe liked these boys and saw her brother fitting in nicely. "No, not really. I'm just getting a sense of everything at the moment. I suppose I'll have to put my mind to what to do with his stuff eventually, but it's a bit early. Still all raw, if you know what I mean."

The boys mumbled their agreements. Sarah noted, "Actually, we're looking for his work satchel – you know that leather bag he had. It was a graduation gift from Zoe, so it's very sentimental."

"I know it well," Adrian said. "I thought it was attached to his body the amount of times he had it with him."

Rick added, "Last time I saw it was on Thursday morning when he was working from home. He had it on the kitchen table over there and he was on his computer working on some report. He told me he was finishing up some theory about that accident they had. He seemed excited."

Zoe smiled, knowing how much he loved that gift. "Yes, he did love it. The weird thing is that it wasn't found in the car after the accident."

"That's not right," Rick replied. "Someone must have knicked it."

Zoe had her doubts. "Maybe ... but the computer and his phones were in the car. Why take the bag and leave the computer?"

"Mmm ..." was all Rick could muster. "You stumped me there." The room fell silent, reflecting on the satchel puzzle.

Rick recalled separately, "I remember coming home that night and Liam had left a folder of his work on the kitchen table. Quite thick it was, with photos on top. It wasn't like the neat freak that your brother is to leave it lying around. Probably too big to fit in his bag. So I put it together and chucked it into his room on top of his desk."

"Thanks, I might take a look," Zoe said.

They packed up the pizza boxes and the boys did their

thing: Roscoe retired to his room and the other two returned to watch *Survivor*, before heading out later. Zoe and Sarah went to check Liam's room. They looked through his cupboards, everything neat and orderly as expected. It was a pretty sparse existence of clothes, records, books.

"What are you going to do with all this stuff, his bed, his couch?" asked Sarah.

"Good question. I have no real idea. I don't think I really want anything. I'll check through it again when I can think straight."

Sarah put her head out of the door and yelled to Rick, "Hey Rick, where did you say you put that work folder of Liam's?"

Rick trundled down the hallway and approached the room. "Right there, his desk ..." He paused as he entered the doorway and saw no folder. He shrugged. "It was right there." He pointed to the spot. "He must have come back and grabbed it."

"No, that can't be right," noted Sarah. "He spoke to me on the phone as he was leaving home. He was going to work to meet his boss. He said he was already packed and was heading off to Adelaide that afternoon. He then spoke to me again as he was walking out to his car. His meeting had been postponed for some reason."

Zoe continued the thought process. "So Rick, if you found it on Thursday night, he was already on the road to Adelaide and couldn't have come back to get it. Where is it now?"

They located Ross and Adrian and quizzed them, both declaring they'd never noticed the folder. Rick was adamant. "I am telling you, I left it in his room, right where I showed you. One hundred percent I did."

"Think back again," Sarah suggested. "Not on his bed, not in the lounge?"

"No. Right here on the desk, like I said. It was late in the afternoon, and I remember looking out his window and saw old Eddie on his front balcony."

"Okay. So, did you close the curtains then?" asked Zoe, then looking at the other boys. "Why are the curtains closed, if Rick could see Eddie?"

The three boys all pleaded their innocence. Adrian explained, "We never go into Liam's room. Rick putting that folder away would be a rarity."

Sarah shrugged, looking at Zoe. "Another thing for your list of questions file."

"I don't like this," Zoe muttered. "That folder means something. Have you boys had any break-ins or other things gone missing, anything unusual?"

Adrian told the girls they had a strange visitor this morning, a delivery from Uber Eats or DoorDash or one of those types of services. "Strange thing was no one had ordered anything. It was a couple of breakfast meals from Maccas."

"What happened? Did you take the food?" asked Sarah.

"Nah, just told the dude he had the wrong address."

Ross laughed. "You should have taken it, mate. A free breakfast."

"You would have, wouldn't you, Roscoe?" quipped Rick.

"That's interesting, a random wrong delivery and a missing folder," Zoe noted. "What if that was a scouting mission? What if they were after that folder? What if there's something important in Liam's theory? Why were the curtains closed?"

Ross was shaking his head. “That’s a bit farfetched, don’t you think? Wouldn’t they ransack the place?”

Zoe didn’t answer, but she felt like this was telling her something. The boys left the girls to continue on with their thoughts. Zoe gave Sarah an enquiring glance. “Something’s not right here as well.”

Sarah nodded. “Let’s go and have a chat with Eddie.”

“Who’s Eddie?”

44

IT WAS BUSY AT the Plough Hotel for a Tuesday lunch hour, which meant that the meeting with the Rodriguez brothers and Brazzos would be in semi-public. Speaking in Spanish would provide some level of cover, but not as much as Miguel would have liked. He decided it would be best to make it quick: a beer and an exchange and then vamos.

Miguel and Gilberto were positioned on a back table. They were each on their second drink when Brazzos finally arrived, twenty minutes after the agreed time. Miguel glared. "You're late. I thought we might have to hunt you down."

Electing to speak in Spanish, Brazzos explained that he was a busy man. "Let's get this done. Have you got the folder?"

Miguel pointed to Gilberto who was grinning back at his brother, patting the folder on the table.

"Very good, let me have it!" ordered Brazzos.

"All in good time, my friend. First, show me the money."

Brazzos moved closer and leaned into Miguel. He handed him an envelope at the same time, and whispered, "Let's get it done. It's too busy here for my liking." He nervously looked around before taking a seat at the table.

Miguel handed the envelope to his brother, who then passed him the folder. As Gilberto counted the notes below the table, Miguel was quick to say, "I trust it's all there as we agreed."

Gilberto was shaking his head in concern as Brazzos answered, "Half, as I told you. You guys messed up with the USB in the first place and I got it back myself. Half is all you get."

It was Miguel's turn to shake his head. "No. We have already talked about this, and the deal is the deal." He shuffled his chair closer to Brazzos and handed the folder back to his brother. "You dirty, no good bastard. You want to penny pinch your country men all over a thousand dollars?"

Miguel moved even closer and got right into Brazzos's face. His turn to whisper, "Well listen here, mother fucker. If you're not careful, the deal is about to change again. Because of the respect we have for our cousin, you have forty-eight hours, until Thursday, to produce the rest of the cash, otherwise the price escalates. You might be the 'Bullyboy' back at the factory, but that doesn't cut it with us Columbians, and you know it."

Brazzos went to stand, but Miguel wasn't quite done and shoved him back in his chair. "We've had a little read of your folder, and it seems to us that you have a lot more at stake than we do. If it weren't for cousin Paul, we would be going for a ride together right now."

Brazzos glared back and went to stand again. "Now we are done!"

Miguel and Gilberto followed suit and moved in. Miguel shoved Brazzos firmly in the chest again while Gilberto kicked his shin. Miguel grinned. "Last chance, mi amigo.

Cash by Thursday, same place, same time. Otherwise we talk to our cousin and then the price will be twenty thousand. After that, we send this O'Donoghue theory to that Work Safe place."

Miguel gestured to Gilberto and they walked out with the folder and the envelope, leaving Brazzos sitting alone nursing a sore leg.

45

ALTHOUGH ZOE INITIALLY EXTENDED the invitation, Cameron insisted on paying. He liked this girl; she was organised and had a steely focus. She had fished out Cameron's phone number from Liam's list and called him late last night to arrange an earlier meeting. Cameron was impressed with her organisational skills and the forethinking to extract such detail.

She was excited and had a theory to discuss and she wanted to bounce her ideas off someone she could trust. She also thought that she may have needed his help.

Cameron ordered a plate of eggs and bacon, while Zoe chose a toasted focaccia. As the food arrived, Cameron looked at his new friend. "Tell me this theory of yours."

"Let me start with my list of questions, items that I'm struggling with. They make no sense. Sarah and I added the missing charger to the list yesterday. Last night I caught up with Liam's girlfriend and we went around to his place to meet his flatmates. They told me Liam had left a large folder with notes on the plant accident on the kitchen table. One of his flatmates put it into his room last Thursday night, and now it's missing."

Cameron was listening, but still not getting the relevance. "Maybe they were mistaken, or Liam collected it or it is misplaced."

"That's the thing," Zoe explained as she got a bit excited, "it was definitely there. One of his flatmates is adamant that he put it in his room. He even recalled seeing his neighbour through the window at the same time."

"Okay, what else?"

"The curtains were closed when we went into his room. So, on my list I have also added: where is the folder on the accident, and why were the curtains closed?"

"Who knows …" Cameron said, thinking this was still only circumstantial at best.

Zoe went on to explain that she went with Sarah to talk to the boys' neighbour. Old Eddie, a retired ex-factory worker who spent his days sitting on his front balcony drinking beer. He hardly moved from the spot and the boys joked that he had become part of the background. The boys had made friends with him and often had a beer with him on a Sunday afternoon.

The story continued. They took a couple of beers over and joined Eddie on his balcony. He was sorry to learn that Liam was killed in a car accident. He hadn't seen him for a few days and assumed he might have gone back to Adelaide. *Nice lad, that Liam.*

We told Eddie that the boys had a weird visitor early in the morning, a McDonald's food delivery that was apparently sent to the wrong address. Zoe explained the story relayed by Adrian. Then on that same day they had lost some possessions in the house. The girls were asking Eddie if he happened to see anything.

"Jackpot," Zoe laughed. "Not only did Eddie see the follow-ups, but he jotted down the driver's number plate and took photos."

"Wow." Cameron was impressed, enjoying the bright eyes that were beaming at him. "What happened?"

Zoe repeated the Eddie story. Apparently the 'so called food delivery' was before Eddie had taken up his regular post, in his office as the boys said. But shortly after a car pulled up in front of the boys' place and a delivery man got out of the passenger side and went and knocked on the door. The boys must have left for work because no one answered. The delivery man didn't leave the parcel, but just got back into the car and they drove off.

"Nothing unusual about that, though. That could happen any time. Parcels are not always left behind. Often they get redirected back to the post office."

Zoe continued smiling at Cameron. "Yes, you might be right. But Eddie thought it was odd on several accounts. What delivery service has a driver and a delivery man? What delivery service uses a Commodore SS? Why didn't they leave a note to collect the parcel? Why were they looking around everywhere as if to check on people watching?"

"Good work, detective Zoe. I'm impressed. But still, so what?"

"Well back to my list of questions. Is it a coincidence that on the same day we have a potentially fake food delivery, a random delivery not received and a missing folder with potentially important information? I think not."

Cameron was now smiling at her exuberance and wondered what she was going to come up with next.

Zoe explained that the boys reckoned they'd never seen

Eddie move, that his beers miraculously appeared and that he faded into the background. Well, a little while later, apparently this Commodore had returned and parked a couple of houses down the street. Eddie sensed that something was fishy. He watched two guys get out and put on gloves, walk into Liam's place and disappear around the back. That was when curtains were closed. Eddie had just watched, monitoring the new visitors. One of them came out and lurked at the rear of the property, like a watch-out. There was no sound in the place and the watch-out stayed in position for over an hour. He vacated his place to take a leak against the side fence. That was when Eddie had walked to his letterbox and down the street a few houses. He took a photo of the Commodore and the number plate before strolling back to his place. This time he went inside and camped in his front lounge room.

He sat and waited with his phone camera ready, with a clear view of Liam's house and the side driveway. After another forty or fifty minutes or so, the two men came out, one carrying what he thought was a bundle of papers. They stopped to look around before returning to their car. Eddie took another few photos.

"That's fantastic. How are the photos?"

Zoe opened up her phone and handed it to Cameron to flick through the images. She continued, "So another couple of questions: why the cloak and dagger to get a folder of notes? Why is this folder so important? The place was left undisturbed and if we hadn't questioned a couple of things no one would have been the wiser. Rick moved the document, otherwise we wouldn't have even known it existed.

They re-opened the curtains in the lounge room but forgot about the curtains in Liam's room."

Cameron raised his eyes, very impressed. "We should talk another time. I've been thinking of going into private practice as an investigator and maybe you might want to be my partner."

They laughed but it was short lived as they reflected on Eddie's facts. Cameron went and ordered some more drinks, another coffee for himself and water for Zoe. On his return, Zoe said, "I've been thinking about something Sarah said. She suggested we should create a scenario that considers the facts as we understand them. That might answer my list of questions."

"Good idea," agreed Cameron. "And I assume you've already started."

"Yes I have." Zoe nodded, pleased by her work. "How about this for a theory?"

She outlined her theory; the draft she had worked on last night, slept on and was still thinking about on the drive to Footscray this morning. Everything was a hypothetical theory without any concrete evidence. But it fitted the facts. She still had leads to follow-up and was waiting on answers to a couple of calls. She knew she could do this with Cameron's help.

46

BRAZZOS RETURNED FROM THE Plough in a foul mood. He barked at Suzi when she commented that he was back early and told her to mind her own business. The afternoon didn't get any better and he snapped at anyone who crossed his path. Statler was under fire because that Workcover man hadn't given them his final report yesterday. Brazzos recognised the man when he went to deal with the O'Donoghue girl. Oxfam, or whatever his name was, butting his sorry head in and then he took that girl away just as he was about to get that stupid USB stick back. Fortunately, the USB stick was delivered shortly afterwards. Then Workcover man hadn't delivered the final report. Brazzos thought maybe he was thrown when O'Donoghue wasn't here, but then he should have given it to Statler or Billings. Brazzos was worried there was some problem, but was later relieved when the Workcover man rescheduled for this afternoon.

Brazzos stuck his head out of his office and snapped at Suzi, "When did that Workcover fellow say he was coming back?"

"He said he was meeting with Statler today," Suzi answered bluntly, still annoyed at Brazzos for his rude behaviour.

"Yes, I know that, but what time?"

"I don't know. He said he would call me when they arrive."

"Why call you? What have you got to do with it?"

Suzi gulped as his eyes bore straight through her. "He was also bringing Liam's sister back to help her collect his belongings. They were going to check with me if the stuff was ready."

"Bloody ..." was all Suzi heard as he slammed his door, mumbling under his breath as he returned to his desk. He called Suzi on his internal phone. "Tell Statler I want to see him immediately and get Ernesto up here as well."

Cameron and Zoe left their cars at the cafe and walked across the road to the reception, where they were greeted by Lauren and Elise as if they were long lost friends. Cameron advised that they had an appointment with Jim Statler and that they were also hoping to collect Liam's personal belongings. Lauren tried calling Statler, but the two calls went straight through to message bank. She tried the supervisor's desk and Jake answered, informing her that Statler had been called up the front apparently. He suggested he would send Mario up to escort the visitors and asked if they would like to wait for Statler in the production office.

Zoe was still chatting with the reception ladies when Mario arrived. He conveyed his condolences to Zoe and then escorted them to the production office. Jake was at his desk but stood up as soon as he saw Mario. He approached them. "You must be Zoe. I'm so sorry about your brother. He was a decent bloke."

Cameron was set up on the spare desk to wait for Statler's return while Mario directed Zoe to Liam's desk. He had received instructions this morning from Suzi Murray to start packing up Liam's personal belongings, but he had only just made a start.

Zoe thanked Mario. "So this is his work base. A desk and a single three door filing cabinet? Not much really."

Jake came over and said, "Most of his work was either on his computer or in his head. He was a really talented engineer. More than that, he could really relate to the blokes, not like the management now. He was sharp as a tack, unflustered by drama and super efficient."

Zoe smiled at the kind words. It reflected her love for her brother and her own thoughts and feelings. She helped Mario sort through the sparse belongings and before they knew it, Liam's life work was placed into a single archive box. There was nothing really significant. The box ended up containing a couple of photo frames (one of Zoe at a recent Christmas in Victor Harbour and the other of this year's Port Adelaide football club team photo), a calculator from his uni days, some pens, a pair of scissors, a pocketknife, a notebook, and a dish with unknown origin. They left the stapler, paperclips, and Post-It notes on the desk.

"It doesn't amount to much. I'm not sure what I expected." She looked at Jake. "I suppose you're right. A computer and a smart mind is enough nowadays."

Mario opened the filing cabinet and was surprised to find that it was essentially empty. He flicked through each drawer and was dumbfounded. "What's this?" He gestured at the cabinet. "It's all empty."

Jake peeked over Mario's shoulder. "I'm not surprised.

Ernesto was down here yesterday. He said he was getting some files. I thought it was just something routine. Not all of them."

Zoe overheard the conversation and looked over to Cameron, who was sitting patiently at the spare desk. Cameron raised his eyes in reply and nodded slightly, acknowledging that he was thinking the same thing. *Strange, that doesn't feel right!*

Zoe sat in Liam's chair trying desperately to reconnect with her brother, get some spiritual sense. Mario joked that she was moving into the chair and Jake countered with, "And that would be the best looking engineer we ever had." Zoe blushed and the light-hearted banter and laughs continued until Jim Statler entered. Statler looked at his visitors and watched Mario pick up the box from Liam's desk.

Cameron stood to greet Jim, but Statler was too distracted to notice. He approached Mario. "What have you got in that box? Let me check it before we send it off."

"Not that much, boss," Mario said dismissively. "Just a few of Liam's things."

Statler snatched the box from Mario and placed it back on the desk. He filed through the contents and was pensive as he took out the notebook. "I think we'll keep this, may have company information."

Zoe shrugged as Statler put the notebook under his arm and walked away, releasing the box back to Mario. "Were there any USB sticks?"

Mario stared back at him. "If it isn't in the box or on the desk, it wasn't here. Why are you asking about USB sticks anyway? That's totally random."

"Don't worry then," countered Statler. "Just checking for company property."

Jake couldn't resist adding a barb. "Is that why his filing cabinet has been cleared out as well?"

"Don't know what you're talking about," Statler snapped. "Take this lady back up the front while I talk to Mr Oxley."

Mario picked up the box and smiled at Jake. Statler gestured to Oxley to follow him into his office. Zoe winked at Cameron and walked over to the supervisor's desk. "Jake, before we go, can you call Suzi Murray for me?"

Jake placed the call and waited with Mario for Zoe to finish. The call was quick, and Zoe handed the phone back to Mario. "Suzi wants you to arrange access to Liam's locker."

Zoe asked Jake if he knew whether Liam had some report on the accident. Jake said he was working on something but he had never seen the written report. He told her that Liam had a theory about the mixer and was planning some tests in the laboratory.

"Are you ready?" Mario interrupted. "We need to go to the gatehouse to get the locker keys."

"Hang on, Mario." Jake held out a hand, insisting he had more to say. "There was a strange incident. Liam apparently had some notes he was making on the accident and one day he was called up the front for some meeting. When he came back, he had lost all his notes. It was bizarre. It was his notes, files, emails, everything on his computer about his 'theory' – all gone. I was here and he was stumped. He gave me the summary as I have just said, mixer and lack of MOCs. We reckon that Ernesto, the production assistant up the front, had got into his system and wiped the detail."

"I hadn't heard any of this. You've to be joking!" Mario exclaimed.

Jake replied, "Nothing could be proven. Liam said Ernesto had asked to access the MOC database on his laptop for some reason, around the time when Liam left for the meeting. So, it's just speculation."

—

At the gatehouse, Mario introduced Zoe to Paul Wilson the security guard, who she soon discovered was another good friend of Liam's. Willo grabbed the master key for the lockers and took Zoe across to the change room, checking first that no one was inside having a shower. They opened up and checked Liam's locker. Zoe was disappointed that there was nothing substantive inside. Just his work boots on the bottom, spare uniforms, his helmet, a torch, and a jar of coins.

Zoe took the coins and thanked Willo. "Is that all there is? I was kind of hoping to find his work bag – a leather satchel."

"He wouldn't have left that behind," Paul insisted. "He took that everywhere. I was on deck in the gatehouse last Thursday and he came in to give me some report. He certainly had the work bag with him then. I remember seeing him on the CCTV walking down to the car park. He had it then, slung over his shoulder."

"You saw him last Thursday? Please tell me more."

47

ZOE WAITED IN HER car and made a few calls while waiting for Cameron to finish up with Statler and return to his car. The cafe was closed and she was sitting making notes. She had new facts to share with Cameron, a new ally in her quest for the truth. While her theory was still just a theory, things were starting to piece together.

She extracted Liam's travel diary from the boot and was fully focused on making some calculations when Cameron's knock on her window made her jump. Startled, she yelled at him, "You scared the shit out of me!"

"Sorry, I tried to knock quietly. How did you go with the locker?"

"Nothing of any note there, just uniforms and boots." She opened the car door to talk. "But I got some extra information and made some calls, and a few things to add to my theory. Have you got a minute, or an hour for that matter?"

Cameron explained that he needed to get away quickly but still wanted a summary. He had some follow-ups himself. Zoe wanted to hear how his meeting went with Statler and was slightly disheartened that the detective duo was breaking up. Cameron saw the spark in her eyes fade and her exuberance drain; he didn't want this project to end. He was fully engaged in it and he also felt that there was more to be uncovered. Detail that might even impact his Workcover case. Secretly, he wanted to spend more time with this girl.

Cameron looked at her thoughtfully. "Can we catch up a bit later, maybe do dinner? I can debrief on the Statler meeting, nothing big, just interesting. I also want to hear your new theory additions but I have to get somewhere this afternoon."

Zoe sighed, yet was partly relieved. "Well, I've arranged to meet Sandy Hudson tonight at the Hobson Bay Hotel. Do you want to join us? We could brainstorm our findings with Sandy."

"Done, it's a deal." With his spirits lifted, he leant over and gave Zoe a kiss on the cheek. "What time?"

"6:30," Zoe replied, staring at him as he bounced around to his car. She put her hand on her cheek. *Nice boy, great ally, not a boyfriend.*

—

Sandy and Zoe were seated on the rooftop bar at the Hobson Bay Hotel, having met in person for the first time, but seemingly well known to each other through many exchanges via Liam. Sandy was explaining that this was a favourite catch-up venue for herself and several old Agro Alliance mentors, and in fact she was having dinner with Liam in this exact place the week before Liam's car accident. Sandy explained that Liam was still checking out detail on the accident and she had invited him to meet the old production and engineering managers. Liam mentioned that the plant had changed some aspect, a new agitator in the vessel that erupted. The old guard had given him some ideas; they wanted him to check CCTV vision from a different part of the plant and talk to an expert on mixing.

Zoe had been taking notes and flicked back a few pages. "Michael Rosenbloom from Mixing Masters?"

"That's right, that's him. Where did you get that?" Sandy laughed.

"It was one of the contacts I copied from Liam's work phone."

At that moment, Cameron found his way to the top deck and approached the ladies. He was smiling as he caught Zoe's eye. "Nice meeting room, ladies."

Sandy stood and introduced herself. "Sandy Hudson, you must be Cameron."

They shook hands and sat down to consult the menu and order some drinks. Cameron explained that in his work on the Agro Alliance case, many of the interviews had mentioned her role in process safety. They were all very complementary. Sandy questioned whether this was another interview.

Cameron laughed. "Hardly, just a note that many respected your work. Now I believe Work Safe have snapped you up. How's that going?"

Sandy relaxed. "Starting in a few weeks." Then with a serious tone, she added, "You two should know that I'm probably bound by confidentiality clauses about anything to do with Agro Alliance. Even at Work Safe, I won't be able to disclose existing stuff."

"Absolutely, totally understandable," Cameron reassured her. "I'm only here to assist Zoe with her theory on Liam's accident. Agro Alliance is a separate issue, a random coincidence."

Zoe wasn't sure and said, "I hear you, Sandy. I know there are legal boundaries. I disagree with Cameron though – there is no coincidence in my mind. Liam didn't have an accident. I genuinely believe he was killed and something about Agro Alliance is central to the matter."

Cameron and Sandy stared at Zoe. She was adamant. Drinks arrived and they toasted to each other's health. Cameron looked at Zoe and suggested, "While we wait for the dinner, why don't you tell us your theory? We can unpack your 'list of questions' and we won't comment nor compromise our disclosure obligations."

"Good idea," agreed Sandy. "But we can add some 'neutral' comments or observations where relevant."

Zoe took a large sip of her wine and started:

"The plant accident was a bad mistake, unfortunate accident, person in the wrong place at the wrong time. Things go wrong. Liam wasn't so sure and he was working out the fundamental cause. He was planning tests – Jake told me that today. He drafted a report and had it on his computer and on a USB stick. The bloody USB stick. I should have kept it and checked it out.

"He was coming back to South Australia to talk with this Michael Rosenbloom, my guess. He told me he was meeting an engineer to talk about mixers. I think that his report was bad news for Agro Alliance, maybe even for some people. I don't like that Mr Brazzos. Can I say that? He seems shady. He might be just a bully, but he had some unhealthy obsession with the USB stick.

"So I think that this report of Liam's had to be silenced. Liam's home is raided and the files go missing. Today in Liam's office, all his files are gone. Jake tells me that previously some emails on this work also went missing. He reckons Ernesto was involved, whoever Ernesto is—"

"Ernesto is a new recruit," Sandy interrupted. "He's actually Tony Brazzos's nephew."

"My theory is that Liam came to grief in an attempt to extract the report and silence him. Maybe things went wrong and they had to make it look like an accident. They, whoever they are, knew he was going to South Australia and they faked this car accident just before he got to his hotel in Dimboola.

"But that's the whole problem. Liam would never stay in Dimboola"—(Sandy is nodding furiously)—*"He always stayed at the Golden Grain in Horsham and has a steak at the Victoria Hotel. Last Thursday, he told me, he told Sarah and he told Willo the gate guard that he was going to Horsham. The only reference to Dimboola is that Agro Alliance booked it. When I asked Suzi why she made this booking, she said that Brazzos insisted – it is halfway. She tried to tell him otherwise; she knew Liam stayed in Horsham, but Brazzos was insistent.*

"My theory is that Liam didn't even know about the Dimboola booking. So he's mugged and driven to Dimboola. The accident is staged, I don't know how. Everyone thinks it's an accident, bad bend in the road, booking in Dimboola, tired. Inspector Wood in Horsham basically has it as a closed case. We can't prove that Liam didn't know about the booking. Maybe he did drive on?

"But ... Liam's work bag, the leather satchel is missing. He had it on him when he left. Willo saw it on his security CCTV. It wasn't in the car after the accident and we haven't found it anywhere. So the muggers fake an accident and take the bag, with files, photos or whatever. They leave the phone and laptop to make it look like an accident and not a robbery/murder. But it looks strange and they forgot to leave the laptop charger. Why does someone take a laptop without a charger. If I weren't asking questions then no one would question it and Liam would have died in a car accident."

Zoe was on a roll but paused as the meals arrived. Then she resumed.

"Willo also told me that on that Thursday afternoon, Liam came to the gatehouse to leave a package – a report, apparently – for Mr Brazzos. Willo reckons that Brazzos has never ever been to the gatehouse. So isn't that another strange coincidence? Liam told Willo that he was supposed to meet Brazzos that afternoon, but Brazzos had called him to say he was running late and suggested he leave the report at the gatehouse and he would pick it up later that night. More questions: Why not email it to him? Why not leave it at his office with Suzi? Just strange.

"Liam leaves the report behind and goes off to the car park. Guess what? Brazzos turns up a couple minutes later saying he was hoping to catch up with Liam. Another coincidence – too many coincidences for my liking. Willo gives him the envelope with the report and tells him that Liam is on the way to the car park and he shows him on the CCTV vision. Supposedly, Brazzos gives him a call.

"We have Liam leaving the site around 5:00pm and that's the last contact with him. His girlfriend Sarah tries to call him several times over the next few hours, all calls going to message bank. My theory is if he has been kidnapped, he can't answer the calls.

"Today I thought to check Liam's travel diary and I called Ben Bettess in Horsham to ask him if he could get me the mileage and fuel tank levels from Liam's car. Ben got back to me this afternoon and this presents another set of unanswered questions. Liam was obsessive about filling out his fuel log, which he kept in his car. He still does today – just a few weeks ago he was doing it when I went with him to visit my relatives in Victor Harbour. He won't leave the petrol station until he has it all recorded."

Zoe showed them the diary, flicking through pages and pages of data.

"I studied the diary, and his last recording showed me that he may have been low on fuel last Thursday. He hates going too low in fuel, so he most assuredly would have filled up sometime early on the trip to Horsham. Ben told me that the mileage on the car after the accident is 106,544km, and the fuel gauge was roughly half full.

"Looking at his history, his tank is about 45 litres and he gets around 500 km on a tank. If the car is half full now then he would have filled up somewhere between here and Ballarat, and if there are errors in my figures, at least before Ararat. Look here – he last filled up in Oakleigh and he recorded the mileage at 105,752km. By my calculations, he didn't drive nearly 800km without filling up and still have a half full tank. It's certain he wouldn't have filled up without completing his diary, so I suggest he was either not driving or he was kidnapped."

Zoe sat back, excited but exhausted. Her theory had a lot of circumstantial facts, but both Cameron and Sandy couldn't deny her logic.

"Zoe, I told you I had to leave this afternoon," Cameron said. "I couldn't talk then."

"Yes, and I was hoping to hear how you went with your meeting with Statler," Zoe said, eager to get more information. Sandy observed the two bouncing off each other and thought that there was something developing between them.

Cameron gave a debrief of the Statler meeting. He had been prepared to issue the Workcover charges, which he explained were about poor systems and poor supervision, an open finding which would still attach a large fine. He told the ladies that he held that back and told Statler that he needed to make a few extra enquiries. Zoe and Cameron had agreed to hold it back and test the Agro Alliance managers a bit more, based on the hearsay that Liam had some extra new information.

"What did Statler say about that?" asked Sandy.

"He wasn't happy. I suspect Brazzos had wound him up to press for closure." A smile grew on his face. "He didn't give anything away and he was strong to counter any suggestion of new information. So I suggested that I wanted him to check if Liam had any information and also requested I have another interview with a couple of staff."

Sandy looked at Zoe and saw her face glow with pride. "A fishing expedition, I assume."

Cameron nodded. "The bait is pretty weak, but it's just a last cast to see if I can catch anything. I've had it cleared by my seniors and the worst case scenario is there's nothing and I'll deliver the charges as prepared later this week. Zoe has turned over a lot of ideas and there may be something in what she's saying."

They ordered another round of drinks and Cameron was eager to share his other news. "When I left Zoe this afternoon, I caught up with some mates in the police force and had them look at the photos Zoe received from Eddie at Liam's place in Oakleigh."

Zoe explained the amateur surveillance that Eddie the neighbour had taken to identify the paperwork thieves.

Cameron resumed, "The car is registered to a Miguel Rodriguez from Braybrook. The owner is not known to police, but the interesting thing was that he had only recently emigrated to Australia. Guess where he's from?"

Zoe and Sandy shrugged while Cameron waited with

a silly grin. Then it hit Sandy. "Don't tell me he's from Columbia ..."

"Bingo." Cameron held his hand up to give Sandy a high-five.

Zoe wanted to hug him. "More coincidences. Brazzos is under pressure and the mysterious files go missing, stolen by a compatriot."

Sandy could hardly believe what was unfolding. "We've had a couple of handy men work at Agro Alliance in recent times, odd jobs. Mark Rodriguez and his brother Gary."

Cameron raised his glass. "Could be the same person. My mates tell me he emigrated along with his brother Gilberto, and they were sponsored by Paul De Zaale."

"No way," exclaimed Sandy, and said to Zoe, "He's the big boss at Agro Alliance, at St Kilda Road. He hired Brazzos."

Silence fell over them as the facts were piling up. There had to be something more. It was starting to smell like a conspiracy.

—

Sandy indicated that Liam had a theory about the plant accident and had discussed some aspects with her. It was pure speculation, but from what they were discussing it may have been close to the mark. She told Cameron what she had already told Zoe about the earlier meeting at this Hotel when Liam was asking her old mentors about mixing systems and MOCs, both areas that she hinted could be worth pursuing.

Sandy raised her hands. "Unfortunately I don't think I can tell you anything else – legally, I mean."

Cameron understood and indicated that he would have

to discover any extra details alone. Zoe frowned. "Maybe you can't disclose stuff in response to the plant accident, but what about if it assists in solving the murder of my brother?"

"I'm not sure I can make the distinction, Zoe," Sandy offered. "If only we had another copy of Liam's report that you could offer up separately."

Cameron agreed. "If you had that and gave it to the homicide squad as potential evidence, we could get it from them because it might be of separate public interest."

"That's it!" Zoe sprang to her feet and walked up and down to the edge of the roof tap bar. "That's it!"

She returned and hugged both Sandy and Cameron separately, leaving them bemused and grinning.

"Here's the plan."

48

BRAZZOS HAD HIS MONTHLY catch-up with De Zaale in the afternoon, but was still on edge and majorly distracted after his meeting with the Rodriguez brothers. De Zaale knew he was anxious about the Workcover case but could see that his site manager seemed extraordinarily worried. "Are you okay, Antonio?" he asked after they had gone over the monthly figures.

"Yeah ... all good," Brazzos stumbled in reply, trying hard to keep his nerves in check. "The Workcover guy was at work today and I was expecting him to bring the final report, the charges, or their findings. Statler was meeting him after lunch. I'm waiting to hear, maybe a bit on edge, you know."

De Zaale knew all too well. He was convinced that some shortcuts had been taken and Brazzos was in the middle of it all. Last time they spoke about it, Brazzos was fuming about the O'Donoghue kid and threatening to get his cousins involved. He thought he had cooled him off, but all the same Brazzos was a hothead at the best of times. De Zaale worried what his subordinate was capable of.

De Zaale offered him a whiskey and slapped him on the back. "Here, have a drink, take your mind off all that. It will all work itself out. Tambakis and RK Legal are quite sure it will end with an open finding."

"Thanks, Paul." Brazzos sat back with his glass. "You're probably right. I thought Statler would have called by now. I'll leave him a message and chase him up in the morning."

Statler was summoned to the office first thing in the morning, and Brazzos was not happy. "What happened with that Workcover man yesterday? Why didn't you call me?"

"Sorry, boss," Statler replied sheepishly. "I was waiting for him to call back in the afternoon and make a follow-up plan. I was waiting to know that stuff before I called."

"What stuff? What the hell are you talking about?"

Statler tried to explain that the Workcover report was not yet finished and that Oxley had visited to tie up some loose ends. Oxley indicated that he would make formal requests on extra detail. "That was what I was waiting on."

Brazzos wasn't satisfied and told Statler that he should have still called, that it was a bad decision and he needed to step up. Statler apologised but was annoyed by Brazzos's words. "His request only came through this morning."

"Okay, so what's all the big drama that still needs attention after all this time?"

Statler handed over a copy of the email he'd received. Brazzos quickly reviewed the document and threw it back at Statler.

There was a list of items, longer than he'd expected. Oxley had requested to review CCTV vision from all sources that may show the T-plant. A second round of interviews were requested which included Stuart Jennison and Dean Rodgers from maintenance, Mario De Silva the permit writer, Jake the shift supervisor, and the laboratory technicians that tested T-plant products. Furthermore, the Oxley list included new interviews with Ernesto Gonzales the MOC coordinator and with Brazzos himself. Finally, there was a request for data on the reaction vessel design and the agitator specifications and any findings that the Agro Alliance investigation had uncovered.

"Shit," exclaimed Brazzos. "What are they wanting all this for? Are they restarting the whole fucking thing again?"

"I don't know, Tony. We were under the impression that the report was almost finished and this second round of requests was just to tidy up the loose ends."

"Don't be stupid, man!" Brazzos roared. "Tidy up the loose ends, I'll be buggered. They're digging for something. What have you told him?"

Statler was immediately on the defence. "I haven't told him anything. He's coming out again this morning to set up a schedule."

"Okay, I want you to piss off and work from home, take the day off. I don't care. Tell Suzi, tell the gatehouse and tell the reception girls that you're not well and that you're going home. That will give us some time to re-group. I'm going to speak with Tambakis and De Zaale."

—

Brazzos called his nephew Ernesto and arranged to meet in the open courtyard space in front of the canteen, making it out as a chance meeting. He needed to be careful with whom he spoke and what he said. Ernesto was intimidated by his uncle and always felt inferior. He never wanted to disappoint him and he tried hard to make his mother proud, even if that meant he had to do his uncle's dirty work.

They shook hands when Ernesto arrived, Brazzos squeezing harder than necessary. "How are you, my boy? Did you get that job finished yesterday?"

"Yes, Uncle. All finished," Ernesto said, keeping his eyes down to avoid any eye contact.

"Good. Files all shredded? Anyone ask what you were doing?"

"No, the supervisor was there, but I told him I was working on some files. He left to go into the plant and no one else came by. It took me a couple of trips, but it was all done."

"Excellent, Ernesto. Your mother would be proud of you. What about the laptop I gave you and the backup files?"

Ernesto wasn't so sure that his mother would actually be proud, but kept that to himself. "Yeah, that's done as well. The laptop was easy and I stripped everything and took it back to IT yesterday afternoon."

Everything seemed to be falling into place. "And what about the backup files?" Brazzos insisted.

"That was a bit harder, Uncle. I had to get access to the backup disc and the IT boys were hesitant. I told them we had lost some of the work for planning the plant rebuild and that I wanted to check back on details about the vessel, from the last download."

Brazzos waited impatiently for Ernesto to continue. He gestured as if to say 'and ...'

"They asked Ogen and he said it was okay. Once I had

access, I looked through all the work on T-plant and anything with Liam O'Donoghue referenced. I didn't have time to pick and choose, so I just wiped the lot."

"That's the man. Very good." Brazzos slapped him on the back. "Now, one last thing. Workcover may ask to interview you. If they do, you are not to agree to any interview. Do you understand? No interview! Don't agree to anything, don't say anything, don't give them anything. Nothing, understood?"

Ernesto was worried but relieved. "Why would they want to talk to me?"

"Don't you worry about it," Brazzos said. "Something about MOCs. You don't have to agree and I will make it sounds like you're too inexperienced to make a comment."

—

Having sorted Ernesto, Brazzos's next step was to get RK Legal on board. He returned to his office and made the call to Angelo Tambakis. After an hour of discussion with the lawyer, he felt relieved. Time to have a drink. While he was on the phone to Tambakis, Suzi got a call that Oxley had arrived. Brazzos excused himself from the lawyer for a minute and had Suzi convey back to the Workcover man that he was busy, Statler had gone home and to reschedule for another day.

Brazzos sat back and reflected on the drama that was unfolding. Everything had been on track up until this point, but what were these new Workcover requests about? Fortunately, Tambakis was confident that nothing was disclosable, not the recent work, nor any hypothetical theory from Liam O'Donoghue. Tambakis was almost certain that the recent request for follow-up interviews was a fishing expedition. "Play a straight bat," he said. "It will go away. Don't offer anyone for any more interviews."

Tambakis was going to prepare a defence and would argue that the extra interviews were bordering on harassment. "We have been more than cooperative," he said, "and we now all need to move on."

Brazzos looked at his whiskey. *Cheers – right on.*

49

ZOE'S PLAN WAS IN full swing on Wednesday. It all dawned on her when Sandy had suggested, "If only we had another copy of Liam's report that you could offer up separately." Of course there was another copy. On what planet did Liam only have one backup of anything? Something as important as this report would have been on his laptop, on the backup USB stick and also on his portable storage unit at the bare minimum. Zoe had seen it before; a red 1Tb Seagate unit. Liam used it to store hundreds of his mindless statistics, fuel records, expenditure trends, footy stats, and graphs. She even had a good idea where Liam would keep it – hidden in plain sight, another quirky yet predictable habit of her brother.

Instantaneously, she knew what to do. They sat at the rooftop at the Hobson Bay Hotel late into Tuesday crafting the plan. Cameron was going to go back to Agro Alliance and stall with a long list of requests. Most importantly, Zoe wanted Cameron to check for the vision of Liam leaving the car park on the fateful night. Sandy was limited in what she could do because of her confidentiality obligations. However, Zoe wanted her to talk to Michael Rosenbloom in South Australia. His initial report on the design features of the T-plant, if it existed would be disclosable, something that Cameron could use as leverage. Zoe would ring Sarah in the morning and ask her to check Liam's house again, but she was confident that the missing drive and the report would be there.

Zoe was going on a road trip back to Horsham. She had already called Inspector Wood and briefed him on her theory. She had a meeting with him at 2:00pm and she hoped to get Liam's case changed to a murder inquiry, maybe even get authorisation for an autopsy. Woody was receptive without committing. The circumstantial evidence was too big to ignore, but inevitably he would require something more. She also called Ben at the Golden Grain and in addition to booking the night in room 11, Ben agreed to attend her meeting with Woody. Cameron questioned why Zoe didn't make the meeting by phone instead of driving all that way back to Horsham. Zoe laughed and explained that she was going to stop at every petrol station from Footscray to Ararat, timing the trip. She had formal authority, received from Woody, for any footage of the petrol pumps at the approximate time that Liam's car was coming through, based on a 5:00pm departure from Footscray.

"Bloody marvellous," Cameron declared. "We have to talk about this private detective collaboration."

Zoe was up early on Wednesday morning and arrived at the Agro Alliance site at 7:00am. This was the start of the hunting mission. It was an early start as she needed the time to stop and arrange CCTV viewing at the petrol stations, but late enough to be able to talk with supervisors and not just night attendants. She started out with so much promise in her heart, but secretly afraid that the station owners would not be cooperative or that vision did not exist. It was a chance, and fortune favours the brave – her father would've said. Stay positive, be optimistic.

She was prepared to stop at every petrol station enroute, but her calculations from Liam's diary had the stretch from Bacchus Marsh before Ballarat through to Ararat as her most probable options. She had stayed up late into the night and listed forty potential stops but she discounted the early large stops on the western ring road. *Too soon, too early*. She decided to cull several other options which she could revisit on her return on Thursday and had narrowed the list down to five for her initial focus. Her first stop was at an outbound BP truck stop near Rockbank, on the Western Highway. It was off the road and large enough for cars to mix without standing out.

Zoe filled her own car with $10 of fuel and wandered into the shop. She bought an iced coffee and paid for the fuel. She made small talk with the attendant and asked if she could talk with the manager. Unfortunately, the manager was not available.

The attendant looked at his watch and informed her, "Too early, love. 7:30am is not on his radar. Try again after 9:00am."

She took his phone number and made a note to call back later. *Maybe this isn't going to work. Too early for management. I'll stop for breakfast at the next one.*

She drove on to the next stop on her list, the Ampol at

Bacchus Marsh arriving at 8:00am. It was still too early to see any supervisor, so she grabbed a chicken breakfast meal at Oporto and took a seat. The supervisor wasn't expected until 8:30am, so she sat quietly checking her notes and referencing her calculations for when Liam's car may have come through this point. With almost an hour to kill, she called Sarah to check on her progress.

Sarah answered immediately. "I was just about to call you, what timing. You were right, we found it. How did you know it would be there?" Sarah had woken Adrian, who helped her lift the couch up, unzip the cavity underneath and out popped the portable Seagate drive.

"I know my brother." Zoe was chuffed and really did understand the way Liam operated. "A few years ago we were looking in a surf shop in Henley Beach. It was early spring and I fancied a long winter full-length coat that was on sale. It was great, my colours and all, but still too pricey and winter was over. Anyway, Liam went back a few days later and bought it for my birthday, even though it was six months away. He hid it from everyone by putting it in the couch cavity. We all laughed and I remember him telling me that the best place to hide something is in plain sight. We obviously couldn't see it, but we'd sat on that couch for the next six months."

"Well, you were right. We have it. What do you want me to do with it now?"

"I want to get it to Cameron or Sandy as soon as possible. They need to check to see if Liam's accident report is saved on that drive. It will be, I'm sure. If I text you their numbers, can you arrange something with them? That would be awesome."

"I'll do it now. This is the breakthrough you needed. Love you, Zoe."

Zoe was buzzing. She forwarded the numbers to Sarah and then texted both Cameron and Sandy with the news and the plan. She was still excited and in a daze when the station attendant tapped her on the shoulder. "Our morning manager has arrived, if you would like to have a chat?"

"Of course, thank you." Zoe jumped up and followed the attendant to the counter, where an officious lady with long red hair was checking what looked to be a logbook. Zoe waited for the lady to finish and then introduced herself.

Karen, the red-haired lady, was an older woman with lots of rings on her fingers. She listened while Zoe explained her request to view CCTV vision of the bowsers from last Thursday, looking for a car that was involved in a crime. That was Zoe's storyline, and she included a white lie that she was a private detective working with the Horsham police. Karen said she was rather busy and didn't really have time this morning and suggested that Zoe leave the details of the time period and she would look at it in the afternoon if she had a chance.

Zoe was disheartened but understood her position. "We appreciate whatever you can, but it is a matter of urgency. By the way, how long are your tapes recorded? Our timeframe is six days ago and we don't want to let anything slip."

Karen wasn't convinced and began mumbling about some other work issues.

Zoe lifted her chin. "There are two options as I see it. I can look over it myself, right away, if you set me up, or otherwise I can get the police to come and serve a warrant and we can take the tapes to the station and view them there." Zoe paused, hoping she had sounded convincing enough, before adding, "I'm sorry to be pushy, but at the end of the day, it is part of a major crime investigation."

"All right, let's be quick." Karen gestured for Zoe to follow her into the office area. It only took fifteen minutes to scan back to last Thursday and Zoe sat with Karen while she fast forwarded to the time period, an hour each side of 6:00pm. Random cars pulled in and out, but none were Liam's Mazda.

Zoe thanked the supervisor and left. Karen grumbled under her breath that it was a waste of her time. Maybe proprietors like CCTV for when it serves their purpose but feign interest otherwise. Zoe smiled at her own story: private detective, police warrant, major crime scene. There were many stops to check and the tapes may not all have seven days of recording. *Press on, Zoe.*

—

Cameron Oxley arrived at Agro Alliance at 10:30am as he had arranged with Statler the day before, but was surprised to learn that Statler had gone home early. He asked at reception if he could speak with Mr Brazzos but was stumped when the message relayed back from Suzi was that Brazzos was unavailable. Cameron excused himself and walked up to the gatehouse. *I know what's going on here; we've spooked them. They're probably lawyering up and will decline any interviews.*

He knocked at the gatehouse and introduced himself. Willo was on duty and offered his visitor a tea or coffee. Cameron gratefully accepted and chatted with the guard about weather and football. With a coffee in hand, he switched his focus. "I was initially scheduled to meet

Mr Statler and Mr Brazzos, but they're both unavailable at the moment. I'm following up on a list of items we discussed yesterday, one of which was to look at the CCTV vision of the plant from security. Are you able to help me?"

"Definitely, I think I saw Statler leave earlier and we hardly ever see Brazzos over here. Where do you want to start?"

"Firstly, how far back do your tapes record? I'm guessing that the T-plant accident is too far?"

Willo shrugged. "We keep it for forty-eight hours, then it transfers over to a backup drive that keeps one week of data. We change the backup tapes every Sunday and keep five weeks copied." Willo opened a cupboard with the tapes lined up on a shelf. "It doesn't seem that we have the accident on file, but I'm sure the plant has a copy."

Cameron sat on the stool and felt his shoulders slump, knowing it was a slim chance. "We had requested the main vision some time back, and we got something that looked straight down the centre road. It showed the orange plume, but not much else. We were looking to see if you had other vision from a different angle."

"Fair enough," said Willo. "Again, our tapes don't go back that far. You could check with the IT department. They sometimes take a copy. Maybe because of the accident they have other copies and other angles."

"Good idea, thanks. Can you show me what the other vision options look like?"

Willo set Cameron up at the front desk and scrolled through all the options, stopping and explaining each angle and the focus for that shot. Cameron leaned forward to study the vision, captivated by what he was seeing. "Can you show me the car park vision again?"

The car park vision came up and clearly showed the walkway from reception across the front garden into the employee car park. Cameron could see four rows of cars as clear as day and a fifth row partially obscured.

"That's very interesting," noted Cameron. "I'm also interested in any vision of Liam O'Donoghue when he left last Thursday. Were you on that day?"

Willo nodded and relayed his story about the report, Brazzos's unexpected arrival minutes after Liam had left and the coincidence of the emergency alarm that sounded moments later. Willo went to the cupboard and pulled out last week's tape, which covered that day. "It should be on this one. I remember seeing Liam at the top of that walkway. I pointed him out to Brazzos when the alarm went off."

—

Zoe continued on her mission from petrol station to petrol station. Her next stop at the Mobil station westbound at Ballan hadn't revealed anything. The tall skinny supervisor was only too pleased to flirt with Zoe while rolling back through their tapes. He even offered to check other times so as to extend his time with her. She had to use her 'warrant' argument when she stopped at the BP roadhouse at Ballarat but was unsuccessful. Unfortunately, she left with just a manager's number and a doubtful answer whether the tapes even went back that far. She added it to her notes. It was the obvious stop on the highway and if necessary, she would look at others on the exit roads. She counted twenty in the Ballarat area, which was a disappointment, as she had earmarked Ballarat as her sweet spot.

She left Ballarat and saw a text from Cameron. It was approaching lunchtime and she had two more stations to check on her focus list: Beaufort and Ararat. She called Cameron and let him know that Sarah had located the hard drive in Liam's couch and told him that she had asked Sarah to get it to him or Sandy.

"Don't worry, Zoe. She has already called me and I'm on my way to get it now. We've struck gold here this morning."

Cameron recounted his news from his meeting with Willo and summarised the story from Liam's last day. "Brazzos was dodgy and apparently arrived minutes after Liam left the gatehouse. It smells like a set-up to me," Cameron claimed. "Then shortly after Willo saw Liam on the CCTV footage enter the car park, the site emergency alarm went off, sending Willo into action. Maybe a coincidence."

"Too many bloody coincidences for my likin'," countered Zoe.

Cameron went on to explain about the backup tapes and how Willo found some footage of Liam leaving on that Thursday night. "Liam certainly had his work satchel with him, you can see it clearly. The vision has him on the phone as he walks to his car and stops to assist another car that seems to have a flat battery." Cameron was jubilant as he relayed the rest of the story. "The vision is partly restricted as it's on the edge of the CCTV coverage but I saw Liam put his bag in the back seat of his car. He hands his keys to one of the two blokes while the other connects up some jumper leads. Liam can be seen walking behind the other car and the vision is not good. A few minutes later, the other car starts up and the bonnets are closed. The other car moves out and then a few minutes later is followed by Liam's car."

"Do you actually see Liam driving his car?" asked Zoe.

"No, I didn't see who was driving which car. I have the tape and will drop it into my mate in homicide and see if they can enhance the vision in some way."

"That's great, another coincidence with jumper leads when Liam goes missing. I'll ask Sarah again about when she was talking with Liam."

"But Zoe, that's not all. You'll never guess what the make of the other car was and who was the other driver was." Cameron's voice squeaked with excitement.

"No," she gasped, "don't tell me it was a Commodore SS and our Miguel was at the wheel."

"Exactly. Yes, same number plate and all. Zoe, I think homicide will be extremely interested in this."

—

By the time she'd finished talking with Cameron, Zoe had arrived at the next station on her list: the United Roadhouse in Beaufort. It was on the other side of the road, probably too small for them to use and stay inconspicuous, plus it was on the side back to Melbourne. She hesitated and was about to skip it altogether. She elected to pull up and give it a try anyway. She could stop, take a toilet break, and call ahead to Inspector Wood. Things were coming together. Once inside, she ordered a coffee and grabbed a pre-packed sandwich with egg and lettuce, before sitting at a table near the food servery. The manager was off-site in town somewhere and would be back in thirty minutes.

Flicking through her phone, she wanted to tell everyone she was onto it. Her brother didn't have an accident; she'd always known that was wrong. She called Sarah to check on her plans, learning that she was on the way to meet Sandy and Cameron at the Hobson Bay Hotel. *Our new head office.*

She called Sandy to advise her that a portable Seagate drive had been recovered. Sandy told her that she was taking her laptop and that they would check the files on the drive and she hoped to find Liam's report. Zoe gave her the password that she had deciphered in case that might be needed. Next on the call list was Agro Alliance and the gate house. Willo repeated the story of the emergency alarm and confirmed that he saw Liam put his satchel into his car. Zoe asked Willo to transfer her to Suzi Murray and updated her about the missing satchel.

With adrenaline running, Zoe called CJ in Sydney and gave him a twenty-minute summary, then Ben at the Golden Grain was next. All this recapping brought clarity to her thoughts. Her theory was piecing together nicely, and she considered that her story was coherent and plausible. Finally, she called Inspector Wood to confirm their meeting. She indicated that the petrol station exercise was still ongoing and that she had a few more to check. She gave him the recent detail about the recovery of a hard drive, the vision of the Commodore SS and potentially some vision of her brother leaving his work. Woody was impressed and felt there was sufficient merit to reopen the case.

The United Roadhouse manager returned and was directed to Zoe's table by the counter staff. "Hello, ma'am. I believe you've been waiting for a while. How can I help you?" he asked as he sat down next to her. He seemed very friendly and was calm and engaging – a bit like her Uncle Joe, she thought.

Zoe outlined her request, complete with the story about being a private detective working with the Horsham police. She explained that she had checked several stops already and their analysis felt that the stretch between Ballarat and Ararat was when the car was refuelled. She laid all her cards on the table, getting the sense from the previous encounters that this may get the right attention and assistance. She left the heavy-handed warrant for another time if needed.

Geoff the manager was most understanding and eager to help. Either the demands of the Beaufort Roadhouse were not challenging enough or he was one of nature's gentlemen, maybe even a little bit of both. "Let me get my computer and log into our security system. Can I get you another drink?" Not waiting for Zoe to answer, he whistled at the counter. "Another coffee for the lady and I'll have a hot chocolate please, Jen."

Geoff returned at the same time as Jen delivered the drinks. He sat next to Zoe, opened his laptop, and flexed his knuckles. "Now then, Zoe, let's have a look. What time are we looking at, and what sort of car were they driving?"

Zoe felt as though something promising was about to happen. "Thanks for the coffee." She raised her cup in a salute to Jen. Refocusing, Zoe explained that the cars were last sighted leaving Melbourne – Footscray, to be exact – at about 5:00pm last Thursday. "I'm mainly looking for a white Mazda 6 but also interested in a white Holden Commodore SS, and we have the registration numbers."

"Okay then. It takes about two hours to get here from Melbourne, so that would be around 7:00pm last Thursday. If you're sure about that departure time, we can start around 6:30pm and scroll forward at double speed."

They agreed and Geoff set up the unit to log back to 6:30pm on the Thursday. They sat back studying the screen roll forward, with their eyes glued on the petrol bowsers. It seemed a quiet night as only a few customers were being recorded in their first few minutes of viewing. The time stamp flicked on to 7:00pm and there seemed to be a surge of customers. Geoff adjusted back to real-time viewing as they continued to monitor the activity.

Then it happened. At precisely 7:12pm, Zoe saw a white Mazda pull up behind another car. She jumped up out of her seat. “There it is! That’s the Mazda.”

Geoff paused the screen so they could review the vision. They inched it forward frame by frame until the Mazda was pulled up at the bowser. Zoe was beside herself. “That’s the car, that’s Liam’s number plate.” She made notes about the time and the location while the camera rolled on. The driver didn’t get out of the car and seemed to be waiting. From the CCTV vision, it was too hard to identify the driver. Despite the lights at the petrol pump, only the exterior was clear. The car interior was too dim to distinguish the driver.

Zoe looked at Geoff. “Why is he just sitting there?”

“I don’t know. Let’s watch on.”

The petrol cap was on the passenger side and it suddenly popped open, but still the driver remained inside the car. Then another car, a Commodore, pulled up at the same bowser but in the adjacent isle. This time the driver immediately got out.

“That’s the other car, for sure, same number plate. And that’s our suspect.” Zoe excitedly pointed directly at the driver, who she now knew to be Miguel Rodriguez. Miguel walked over to the bowser next to the Mazda and filled the

Mazda, then using the same pump filled the Commodore. He then entered the service station and made a payment. Both cars pulled out at the same time, hooked out of the station across the road and sped off in the direction of Horsham. At 7:24pm on the time stamp, the cars were gone and all was quiet again at the Beaufort Roadhouse.

"I can't believe it," exclaimed Zoe. "That's them. We've got them." She could have kissed Geoff. "Can we look over that again? And I need a copy emailed to the Horsham police."

Geoff was pleased with himself and was almost as excited as Zoe. They relooked at the vision to try and identify the Mazda driver, but it wasn't clear enough. However, they were able to ascertain that there was only one driver and that the cars were obviously travelling together. In the replay, they could see Miguel talking with the unknown driver, nodding, and giving him the thumbs up. Geoff made a copy onto a USB stick and emailed the clip to Zoe and to Inspector Wood at Horsham.

Zoe was so relieved and broke her 'detective cover' to give Geoff a hug on leaving. *Mental note to self. I must always stop and refuel here at Beaufort's Roadhouse, for ever more.*

50

THE MEETING AT THE Hobson Bay Hotel was well underway at the same time that Zoe and Ben arrived at the Horsham police station. Sandy had arrived first and was established at the rooftop bar looking out over the bay at the Melbourne skyline. Sarah was next to arrive and introduced herself to Liam's work colleague; a lady Liam had admired and spoke of glowingly. Sarah explained in detail about the recovery of the portable Seagate device from beneath the lounge room couch. She handed it across to Sandy to connect to her laptop, as Cameron arrived.

Cameron gave the girls a light peck on the cheek, then headed to the bar, returning with a bottle of wine in an ice bucket and three glasses. Sandy was loading the drive while Cameron gave a summary of his visit to Agro Alliance, highlighting the vision that showed the Rodriguez brothers meeting Liam in the car park.

Sarah commented, "So now we have vision of these Columbians at Liam's home nicking his papers and at Liam's work potentially intercepting Liam last Thursday."

"That's right," agreed Cameron. "And Zoe has texted me

that she found more vision of Rodriguez fuelling Liam's car at a regional petrol station halfway to Horsham."

Sandy's head whipped up. "Say that again."

"Zoe the private detective has found vision of Liam's car at Beaufort. There was no sign of Liam. She suspects Inspector Wood has enough to open the case, maybe hand it over to the homicide squad." Cameron could see the relief in Sarah's eyes. "And the Rodriguez brothers have links with Brazzos and the Agro Alliance CEO."

Sarah was nearly in tears. "I'm speechless. In just a few days, this horrible accident that had so many unanswered questions has completely flipped. I can't tell you how I feel – I'm bordering on anger and elation. Mad that the love of my life is gone, but unbelievably happy that we, us girls and you, Cameron, have solved a case that was all but dismissed."

Sandy lent over and took Sarah's hand. "Maybe Liam's bloody karma bus has finally arrived."

Sarah laughed while Cameron sat there confused, not understanding the reference. "We can explain that later. It was one of Liam's sayings," Sandy said, then pointing at her laptop, added, "I've found Liam's report. It is quite lengthy but it has a number of images, references to attached documents and a video."

Sandy clicked on the video and they watched what looked like a simulation in a laboratory fume hood, with Liam providing summary commentary. The contents erupted on the screen and Liam's voice was jubilant. Sandy looked at Cameron. "This might make a good read but I'm worried that it may not be admissible. What do you think, Cameron?"

—

Inspector Wood was waiting for Zoe and Ben to arrive at the station. He invited them to the small visitor's room and served them tea and coffee and a few police ration biscuits. Woody stood and put his hand onto his friend Ben's shoulder. Looking across at Zoe, he told her, "We have good news."

Zoe perked up. "Yes sir, I hope so. The vision from Beaufort's roadhouse should have been sent to you earlier. Did you get it? It shows Liam's car without Liam."

Woody moved across to a seat opposite Zoe. "I know, I've seen it already and it's a great start."

Zoe's jaw almost dropped. *A great start?*

Woody didn't let her dwell on his words for too long and quickly continued, "No, sorry, Zoe. Don't get me wrong, everything you told me this morning has been enough to re-open Liam's case. We are actively working on it as we speak. I've already spoken with the homicide boys in Melbourne."

Zoe relaxed slightly and took a deep breath as Woody explained Cameron's vision from the Agro Alliance car park had been analysed by the Melbourne boys. They believed Liam was mugged and thrust into the boot of the Commodore SS. Zoe had her head in her hands. *I knew it, just knew it all along.*

"But the best news is that a bright young constable here at Horsham followed up on your CCTV idea and has made another breakthrough," Woody added. Zoe and Ben looked up and waited on his words with eager anticipation. "It's the icing on the cake. Zoe, you have been absolutely fantastic. I think we have them."

Ben couldn't handle the suspense any longer and pushed for understanding. "What are you talking about, Woody? What's this icing on the cake?"

Woody was all smiles. "Well, our very own Constable Drummond figured out that something might be gained if he contacted all the transport companies that operate between Melbourne and Adelaide. His good policework has made the breakthrough."

Woody explained that several trucking firms make the trek, east and west between the two cities every day, and most have webcam vision and truck tracking systems as part of the modern transport management process. "Well, with the timing from Agro Alliance car park and then your time stamp from the Beaufort Roadhouse," he continued, "we were able to narrow down the timeline that would have taken Liam's car to the Dimboola accident site. Constable Drummond contacted the truckers and had them scour for web cam vision on trucks that were in the area east of the accident site for up to an hour before our calculated accident timeframe.

"After a lot of persevering and hard policework, we found it. Let me show you Drummond's reward." He flicked on the monitor in the room, which was connected to a pre-loaded computer, and pressed play.

The gathering at the Hobsons Bay Hotel continued well into the evening. They each read Liam's report: Sandy and Cameron read it twice over, and Sarah could only bring herself to read it once, but she had loads of questions. Cameron called his superiors and was confident that the report would be admissible. He had already started some work on his laptop at adjusting the charges. The attachment from Mixing Masters was fundamental information that was part of the plant history and the other plant vision was in their requests. Both were automatically admissible. The rest of Liam's report could be argued by the lawyers as private and confidential, but Cameron's superiors felt confident that it was still good, especially as they would receive it formally from Zoe and the police department.

Sandy knew she could not discuss this report with her new colleague Albert Cohen, but was rather happy it would become available in the expected exchange between Workcover and Work Safe. The matter was not directly discussed but Cameron could understand Sandy's quandary. Sensing her unease, he tried to make it easier. "Sandy, what are you thinking? Are you worried about a breach of confidentiality?"

Sandy was a bit startled and turned to view the city skyline as she considered her response. "Not really. I can't directly get involved. Off the record, this report underlines many issues that have arisen at Agro Alliance recently."

Sarah was struggling to follow the discussion and offered to get another round of drinks and some food to share. Cameron waited for Sarah to leave and revisited the discussion with Sandy. "I understand, and you need not say anything. Trust me, Workcover and I have many concerns and I'll be sending this report across to Albert as soon as possible. I know how awkward this is for you."

"Thank you." Sandy exhaled a relieved sigh as they exchanged a knowing look.

"Sandy, if you don't mind my asking, why exactly did you leave Agro Alliance?"

The built-up emotions that Sandy had been harbouring

were about to be released. Sandy was shaking as she privately recalled the Brazzos and Billings nightmare. Sarah took a large breath to forestall any tears. As Sandy regained her composure, she relayed the story of her 'Jekyll and Hyde' supervisor and the total management breakdown. Her departure, she said, was just one in a string of changes, the loss of experience all in the quest for buying compliance and 'yes' men.

As they explored the complete overhaul of the site's leadership, it dawned on Cameron that so many capable people were effectively paid out. He pondered aloud, "How do you have so many rounds of redundancies, yet retain the same staffing structures? Wouldn't the tax office ask questions?"

Sandy sighed. "I'm so glad someone else can see that. The redundancies were not real redundancies. Just their way of removing obstacles." She paused in reflection and scoffed. "At one stage, the quote from management was: 'If you have been here more than ten years then you're part of the problem'."

Cameron then realised the extent of the dictatorship in play. "Don't buck the system, toe the line. But that devalues experience altogether, doesn't it?"

"It sure does, and then when the new management knows nothing about process safety, all the major hazard facility requirements go to hell in a hand basket." Sandy had to change the subject as this was making her frustrated and angry. "There's a lot of work to be done at that place, and it's a pity that dozens have walked out with redundancies only to be replaced with 'yes men and women'."

—

Zoe called Sarah late in the afternoon as the Hobson Bay party had switched from detective work and phone calls to a celebration party. Cameron was shouting dinner for the ladies when Sarah took the call. Zoe and Sarah had grown incredibly close over the past week, akin to a sister band. They treasured their connection because it was helping them to keep their memories of Liam alive.

"How is it going in the bush?" asked Sarah. "Let me put you on speaker. Cameron and Sandy are here with me in the office and we're about to have dinner."

"In the office? What do you mean in the office?" asked Zoe.

"Keep your voice down, Zoe. We're on the roof top bar at the Hobson Bay Hotel. We've been here all afternoon and have claimed it as our new headquarters. We do have a few randoms from the public rolling in as well ... how rude, hey?"

"Okay. Sounds like I'm missing out. We've had a great day here and I'm taking Ben, Cora, Tina, Inspector Wood, and Constable Drummond out for steaks at the pub. In honour of Liam."

The Hobson Bay group toasted Zoe, raising their glasses. Cameron was eager for an update. "What's the news to celebrate down there?"

Zoe was so excited, so full of excitement that she didn't know where to start. She recapped her road trip and the CCTV success story from the Beaufort roadhouse, repeating what she thought she had already told Cameron earlier – she couldn't remember exactly what she had said to who. Then she explained that the Horsham police had upgraded the case to a homicide investigation alongside Cameron's contacts in Melbourne. They were arranging for a postmortem of Liam's body and the instructions were already being sent to the holding morgue.

She explained that Constable Drummond had picked up on the CCTV strategy and had contacted several trucking companies. They had a rough timeframe and apparently the trucking companies were more than eager to assist. Inspector Wood told Zoe that the Horsham community and the police worked closely with these truckers to keep the peace and encourage stopovers in Horsham.

Drummond was lucky to discover vision from a truck web cam of Liam's Mazda driving through Horsham at 9:20pm that Thursday. He then checked the vision of local business entities and captured the Mazda with enough clarity to confirm the driver was not Liam. They then captured the Commodore SS passing the same spot three minutes later.

This narrowed down the time frame further, and with the addition of footage from another truck they had struck the jackpot. The Mazda was observed parked on the side of the road just short of the accident site at 9:35pm. The driver was out of the car standing by the passenger seat having a smoke. The same truck captured the Commodore SS about 500 meters later, probably on rendezvous with the Mazda.

Zoe was so hyped up that she kept talking, while the others struggled to ask any questions. They just sat collectively in awe of her. Cameron couldn't resist. "What's next, Zoe?"

"Woody has forwarded everything to the homicide boys in Melbourne, and he believes that they will regroup in the morning and probably pick up the Rodriguez brothers. They'll arrest them on suspicion of murder."

Zoe added that the Horsham police had already started a forensic check on Liam's car. They agreed that the accident must have been staged and although the exact method was not clear, they had suspicions and apparently would check for some sort of fragments. Woody had told her that once a theory was clear, the forensics team were so well drilled that they could literally find a needle in a haystack. They were also making plans to triangulate the cell phones of the Rodriguez brothers and Liam's two phones.

"Inspector Wood is confident that they will find some evidence. He thinks that the Rodriguez driver would have worn gloves, but there would be other DNA from a four-hour drive. Also, once they arrest the brothers, they will conduct a search of the Commodore SS."

"Fantastic, well done, great news," relayed the Hobson Bay trio.

Zoe took a deep breath. "I forgot to tell you about the tape Cameron gave the homicide team from Agro Alliance. They were able to enhance it and it's near certain that Liam was knocked out with something, a rag over his face and bundled into the boot of the Commodore. So they will almost find some evidence there as well."

Cameron beamed, despite the situation. "Well done again, Zoe. You've really excelled yourself."

"I don't know about that. The police are doing all the work now. Constable Drummond is a legend and everyone has helped so much."

"Maybe," agreed Cameron, "but if you didn't question several things, like the Dimboola location, the missing bag, the phone calls, the hidden report in the couch and the bloody travel log ... the whole thing would have been dismissed and considered as an unfortunate accident."

Sarah added, "Don't forget about old Eddie and the curtains."

Zoe laughed. "Of course not. I'll leave you guys to your dinner. I've got a date with a steak next door."

Sarah signed off for the team. "Have a good night. Are you coming back tomorrow?"

"... I'm not sure what to do now. Woody says it's all in hand with the Melbourne team, so I might go back to Adelaide. I'm halfway there already. Not much left—"

"No Zoe, we have one more thing to finish," Cameron cut her off. "I – we will need your help on Friday."

"Okay ... what is it?"

51

SUZI MURRAY WAS SURPRISED that Brazzos wasn't in the office when she arrived on Thursday morning. She started later most mornings, around 9:00am after dropping her two kids to day care, and to sweeten her deal she stopped at a good coffee place and brought morning coffees for herself and Brazzos. He was fussy and insisted on the special blend from the shop he'd found in downtown Footscray, which suited Suzi because it was walking distance from the day care centre.

She left his coffee on his desk and returned to her morning duties, and on Thursdays this included having the meeting room coffee machine set up, ordering muffins from the canteen and making copies of any documents that Brazzos required. That was another reason she thought it strange that Brazzos wasn't there, as he was always making sure he had the weekly reports to study ahead of the meeting. Suzi would often have to chase detail from accounts or elsewhere. "Best be prepared," he would say. "I hate surprises."

She was settled back at her desk and still no sign of Brazzos when the phone call came.

A stranger with a Spanish accent abruptly asked, "Is Brazzos there?"

"No, I'm sorry. I haven't seen him this morning, but I expect he will be here at any moment. Can I tell him who's calling?" Suzi enquired.

"No need for that," the stranger snapped. "Just tell him not to be late for today's meeting."

"Yes, but what meeting, where and with whom?"

"Just tell him: same time, same place. He will know. Tell him not to be late." The call ended.

How strange, thought Suzi. She made a note of the time and the blunt message and went about her business.

Finally, Brazzos called Suzi to make some sort of apology for being late. "Sorry Suzi, I have another appointment today. Can you cancel the production meeting this week?"

She was surprised and felt duty bound to call the managers and cancel the meeting. She tried to tell her boss about the strange caller, but he dismissed her quickly. He claimed it was a lunch meeting about important matters that he had arranged ages ago, and apparently it had slipped his mind. He advised that it might be a lengthy meeting and he would work from home this afternoon.

Suzi sat back a bit stunned. *I'm calling bullshit on that, Bullyboy! You never forget about meetings and I think that stranger was not a work colleague.*

After making the calls to the site managers, she was still bemused and went to check his diary; a large 1-day to a page journal that lived on his desk. There was nothing for today other than the standard 11:00am production meeting. If he had pre-planned anything, he would have made some entry in his diary. Her 'bullshit radar' was flashing as she flicked back through his diary. She sat in his chair and read that for the previous Tuesday he had a pencilled in Plough Hotel lunch at

12:00 noon. She couldn't remember that booking – but then she didn't keep the diary – but she did remember him coming in on Tuesday afternoon in a foul mood and he had snapped her head off and got all bossy wanting her to chase up Statler and Ernesto. *That's right, he was in a right mood. And if it was lunch, it wasn't one of his long ones. Sounds fishy ...*

She put the diary back on its resting place, moved the chair back into position and checked the waste basket. That's when she noticed the closet on the side of the room was partially open. She went to close the door and caught a glimpse of a brown leather satchel.

—

Cameron received a call from Zoe at 10:00am and swung into action. He called Sandy Hudson and checked if she was free for a light lunch at the Plough Hotel and he explained the task. They met at 11:15am and took a seat in the back corner, positioning themselves with a view over most of the restaurant. They ordered a couple of drinks, coffee for Sandy and a milkshake for Cameron, and told the waitress they would take a bowl of wedges and onion rings for starters while they considered the menu.

"What's the scoop again with this undercover surveillance?" asked Sandy.

"Zoe had a call from Suzi at the plant and she thinks that she has found Liam's leather work satchel in Brazzos's office. Actually, she's certain. Zoe asked her to check for an engraved stitching on the inside: LOD. Bingo, it's the same."

"That will no doubt be of interest to the police. So why are we here?"

Cameron explained that Brazzos had received a strange call from a Spanish-sounding speaker this morning, and he had now cancelled his regular weekly meeting. Suzi thinks he's meeting up with the same people he had listed in his diary from last Tuesday. It still didn't make sense to Sandy until Cameron relayed the story of the grumpy boss returning prematurely.

"Zoe thinks that it might be some clandestine meeting, and she wanted us to base ourselves here in case anything goes down," Cameron said. "It might come to nothing, might not even be here. Worst case scenario is we have lunch. Maybe you can tell me about the role that you're undertaking at Work Safe."

The unlikely lunch date continued with phones out on the table ready to record anything. Their large menus sat unstudied but in position to raise as shields if necessary. The wedges and onion rings were early finished and the waiter was deferred another ten minutes when Cameron saw the Rodriguez brothers take a seat over on the side. He nudged Sandy and from behind the menu pointed at the new arrivals. "That's our men, so we're on. They're off to the side and not in direct line, but let's be cautious all the same."

—

Miguel and Gilberto were pleased that Brazzos had arrived on time. They had their doubts whether he would even show at all. That would have forced them into some strongarm tactics. It wouldn't have bothered them and in some sick way it might have provided some fun, but with respect to their cousin, they preferred a fast and simple resolution. The boys had a beer apiece and were seated at a table on the side wall looking across at everyone else. Patrons were filing in and the place was busy with waiters handing out menus and taking orders.

Brazzos approached their table and elected to stand rather than to take a seat. He looked around and with an air of frustration demanded, "Let's get this done. Where's the folder?"

Miguel stared back at him with a steely glare. "Of course, have a seat. Don't make a scene."

Begrudgingly, Brazzos sat down and held out his open hand. Miguel looked at his brother and then back at Brazzos. "Not so fast, mi amigo. First the cash." He was abrupt and held out his own hand.

Brazzos sighed deeply as he extracted an envelope from his pocket. "This is blackmail and I'm not happy."

Miguel took the envelope and handed it directly to his brother. "Listen, my friend, there is no blackmail involved. We've discussed this before. It's about honouring the contract, our agreement. Nothing more, nothing less!"

Brazzos wasn't really listening, eager to depart. He glared back at the elder Rodriguez brother. "Whatever!" Then he thrust his hand out demonstratively and demanded, "The package!"

Miguel gestured for him to settle. "Let Gilberto count the money and you will have the package. Chill for a minute. Can I get you a beer?"

"I'm in a hurry and you guys have stitched me up." Brazzos's face burned bright red, looking like he was about to explode. "Just hand it over."

Gilberto nodded to his brother, confirming that all was

in order. Miguel took the package from the spare chair and stood, which enticed Brazzos to stand as well. “Now that wasn’t too hard,” he said as he handed Brazzos the package. He leaned closer while still gripping his half of the package and whispered in Brazzos’s ear, “I’m telling you again. There is no stitch up. You ordered the contract and we are all in it together.”

Brazzos yanked the package clear and made to walk off, but bumped into Gilberto who had moved around the table. Miguel smiled at Brazzos. “Don’t ever ask us for any favours again.”

52

PAUL DE ZAALE RECEIVED a call from the Work Safe. The CEO was requesting his attendance at a review meeting, which had been arranged to coincide with the Workcover final report. De Zaale tried to illicit the detail and was angling an apology, but the Work Safe boss made it clear that it was in his interest to attend.

De Zaale tried calling Brazzos throughout Thursday afternoon, leaving several messages. His secretary had contacted Suzi in Footscray and was told that Brazzos had cancelled his weekly meeting and that Tony was apparently working from home for the afternoon. De Zaale knew something was wrong. He told Cynthia, his secretary, that he was leaving for the day and that he had a meeting at the plant in the morning at 10:00am. He left asking her to block out tomorrow, and he headed off to the Brazzos house.

Brazzos froze when he answered the door, shocked to see his boss standing in front of him. Before they could exchange any pleasantries, De Zaale pushed past Brazzos into the entry and demanded, "Where in the hell have you been all day?"

"Just stuff I had to sort out," Brazzos answered without conviction.

De Zaale took off his coat and threw it on a chair in the living room. He made his own way to the bar and grabbed a couple of glasses. "I'm all ears, so spill the beans. Something's up."

—

De Zaale held a pre-meeting in the executive meeting room at the Footscray plant the following morning. Brazzos was sullen and settled at the table and the RK Legal lawyer, Angelo Tambakis was seated on the other side, taking centre stage. "This is all standard practice. They will provide a summary of their findings and make their charges. We don't have to respond today. We should just take the report and advise that we will review and respond at a later date ..." Tambakis paused, pleased that he had their full attention. "We can appeal any charges and debate issues at another time. This is the time to be silent – don't argue or contest anything. We must remain calm and in control."

De Zaale relaxed, based on the confidence of his lawyer, but he was still puzzled. "Why is Work Safe attending when it's a Workcover finding?"

"That's a good observation and a good question," answered Tambakis, "but it's not unusual. Since our discussion late yesterday, we have reviewed this in our office. We think it is a direct result of your MHF status ..." He paused again. "You have had some bad feedback in recent times from the MHF annual inspections, so we think it's their positioning to further influence you to strengthen your controls."

"That's crap," Brazzos grumbled. "What do you mean?"

Tambakis took the outburst in his stride and looked at

Brazzos directly. "Well, to be absolutely frank, they have been critical about specific issues, MOC systems, leadership, and other matters. You seem to have quite the combative relationship with them. This is their opportunity to ram their position home."

De Zaale attempted to diffuse the rising tension. "So we don't argue and Work Safe are only invited as an interested party. Is that what you're saying?"

Tambakis stood up and started pacing, which was his customary distraction. "I wouldn't be presumptuous enough to say that it's as simplistic as that. But principle, yes. The result is almost certain to be an open finding and the charges will be around systems and supervision. That is where Work Safe will be looking to take leverage going forward." The room slumped into silence as the Agro Alliance bosses struggled with the storyline. Tambakis resumed his seat. "That is, unless they have new information or a different angle."

De Zaale nodded unconvincingly and looked at his site manager. "That can't be." Then addressing Tambakis directly, added, "We have recorded and copied everything that we have provided. Anything else would be undisclosable according to your guidance."

"That is correct," Tambakis said. "They had a recent second round of requests which indicates they had something else in mind. This may have arisen from subsequent reviews or detail from a past interview. But ostensibly nothing new factually, nothing that is disclosable."

Brazzos remained uncharacteristically quiet, slumping a bit when De Zaale introduced the O'Donoghue theory. "There have been whispers that our engineer Liam O'Donoghue had developed a theory on the accident and was proposing to conduct laboratory tests. Maybe this whisper has reached their ears?"

Tambakis stood again and began his pacing once more. "That is pure speculation. As far as I know, from what you have advised, the tests didn't happen and the theory is only speculation. Sadly, Liam is no longer available to offer any opinion, none of which would not be disclosable at any rate."

Brazzos chipped in, "That's right. We haven't seen any report, nothing concrete."

"So they might have been on a fishing expedition, but without facts, the charges will still rest broadly on supervision and systems. Whether you like it or not, that is the catch-all to give them something. They will want to make a stance and prove their own standing. Someone has to be held account for the loss of a life on your site."

De Zaale frowned. He was not convinced. "I hope you're right, Angelo, but I have a bad feeling. What about the mixing report that they requested. Is that significant?"

"Not really. It was a statement of what was built, but little bearing on the present. Besides, while they asked for it recently, that wasn't actioned and they're now finished. Again, we think it was a fishing expedition. Unfortunately, we won't know until they present their charges." He clapped his hands and closed, "But whatever they present, we don't respond. Receive it and we can appeal on speculation or non-disclosable matters."

—

Tambakis, Brazzos and De Zaale remained in their executive meeting room having instructed Suzi to assemble the visitors and hold them for five minutes before they joined the meeting, set up in the bottom level training room.

The Agro Alliance group entered the room, surprised to find just two visitors both conferring at the front. De Zaale took the lead, made the introductions, and offered the men to sit at the pre-set table at the front. Albert Cohen was representing Work Safe while Cameron Oxley from Workcover was the one who had requested the meeting. There was no small talk, no offers for tea, coffee, or water. Straight to business.

Oxley opened the exchange. "Thank you for your presence. We have a few issues to address this morning. So I will jump straight to it."

Under Tambakis's orders, De Zaale and Brazzos remained silent while Oxley outlined the findings. He explained that Workcover initially had intended an open finding with two significant charges for lack of supervision and lack of appropriate systems. Tambakis was internally in agreeance and the others were relaxing, until Oxley added, "But subsequent information has led us to reinforce the charges and to add extra charges."

Tambakis, acting as the agreed spokesperson, calmly enquired, "That seems unusual. We would be interested in understanding this subsequent information and obviously the changes in the charges."

"Of course, that will become clear as we progress," the Workcover investigator said. "The charges on systems remain broad to cover general oversight of your MHF processes but now have specific extra detail addressing poor management of change practices and inadequate integrity management governance on the T-plant vessel."

For Tambakis's clarification, the meeting switched to an expansion of the detail behind the extra charges. Tambakis was concerned that the detail seemed to infer additional knowledge of specific change issues. The asset integrity issues were something Tambakis knew would stick, given poor records of vessel inspection.

Oxley resumed, "The specific charges are of direct interest to Work Safe, and I will let Albert explain their position in a few minutes." He gathered his notes again and looked to Brazzos. "We are also laying a charge of 'Industrial Manslaughter' against Mr Antonio Brazzos and a charge pending of 'Misconduct' against Mr Jim Statler."

Brazzos rose from his seat and threw the chair backwards in a stand of annoyance. "What bullshit!"

Tambakis was on also his feet and grabbed Brazzos by his shoulder to calm him down, while responding, "Under what grounds can you make such an outrageous charge?"

De Zaale observed the grandstanding in front of him but was distracted as another visitor entered the room. Everyone turned to see a police officer walk towards them, accompanied by a man in a suit, followed by two additional police officers, neither as decorated as the man in front.

"Excuse me, gentlemen," voiced the man in the suit. "I am Gerard Williams from Victoria Police." He revealed his badge and introduced his sergeant and the attending constables. "I am a senior detective with the homicide squad and I am hereby arresting Mr Antonio Brazzos on the suspicion of conspiracy in the murder of Liam O'Donoghue."

Brazzos stormed towards the detective but was apprehended by the uniformed police and promptly constrained. They had Brazzos's arm up his back and he was duly handcuffed. Williams looked at his Sargeant and asked him to read Brazzos his rights.

Brazzos was silenced and sat in the back with a constable on each side, while Williams spoke with De Zaale and Tambakis. He explained that they had been following leads on the O'Donoghue case and had sufficient grounds for the arrest. Brazzos yelled from the back of the room, "Total bullshit. I was here in Melbourne. That lad O'Donoghue had a car accident on his way back to Adelaide. Absolutely nothing to do with me. Let me go." He squirmed as the police tightened their grip on each arm.

Williams didn't look back as he kept his focus on De Zaale. "We have enough information for the charges, rest assured."

De Zaale looked at his lawyer, who simply shrugged. Williams continued, "We have a couple of suspects – persons you may know – Miguel and Gilberto Rodrigeuz, in custody and they are assisting our enquires. We have sequestered their car which is now a key component of the ongoing investigation. There's plenty more but we have enough for the moment to take Brazzos into custody."

De Zaale looked back at Brazzos and squinted in concern. He let Williams continue. "We're also serving a warrant to inspect these premises and my team are currently securing items from Mr Brazzos's office, including his computer. Other officers are talking with your IT team and we have interviews in progress with Mr Jim Statler and Mr Ernesto Gonzales. They are also assisting us."

Brazzos remained defiant but had no comment. He slumped back into his chair feeling decidedly sick. Williams stepped back and allowed Cameron Oxley to resume. "We have worked closely with the police after discovering a report from Liam O'Donoghue, that we believe was the trigger that has led to his untimely murder."

Tambakis was cautious, tentatively skirting the issues around the criminal charges. "I'm not sure any report or speculations of issues is material to the Agro Alliance case. We will contest whether it is disclosable."

"Of course," countered Cameron. "However, it was provided by a member of the public independent to Agro Alliance and is now publicly available as part of this homicide case, which renders it admissible in a court of law. You can lodge an appeal in due course, but I suggest it is substantive and material."

Tambakis looked at De Zaale who was trying to stay calm while internally about to erupt. They looked at each other, disbelieving what was happening, and their eyes widened as if to say, 'Let's get out of here'.

"We know nothing of this."

Detective Williams stepped forward. "We believe that your Mr Brazzos knew everything about it. We have witnesses that confirm a break in by the Rodriguez brothers at O'Donoghue's house and the extraction of files. We have undercover operatives that witnessed an exchange yesterday at the Plough Hotel where we allege the same files were being handed to Mr Brazzos." He smiled back towards Brazzos. "And that is just the tip of the iceberg."

Albert Cohen cleared his throat and said to De Zaale, "Based on the findings from Workcover and the issues around your site leadership, Work Safe has taken the process safety issues seriously. We have written to you and Brazzos previously expressing our concerns."

De Zaale frowned, confused by the situation, while Tambakis remained expressionless and numb.

"Accordingly, we are serving you a notice today to suspend your licence to operate as a major hazard facility, effective immediately." Cohen let the statement settle before adding, "You have the right to appeal and can take legal advice on this matter. However, unless you invoke the appeal, you must cease to operate any processes with the chemicals listed in this notice from 7:00am next Monday morning. Furthermore, you will be required to divest your site of all inventories below the trigger levels by the subsequent Monday."

De Zaale looked at the lawyer, who was internally back-stepping from this avalanche of information. "I'll take that under advisement. What is the bottom line?"

"We have lost confidence in your ability to operate a major hazard facility and effectively you have to shut down that part of the plant."

De Zaale had a mess on his hands. This was going to take some unpicking. His site manager charged, his cousins involved, his business shut down, and his reputation in tatters. There was nothing left to say, just to get these people out of there and sort out what was next.

No one was moving, so he suggested, "Let's finish up and I'll talk with our people."

He looked at Tambakis who was re-evaluating the RK Legal position, when the training door opened again as Suzi entered to give De Zaale a message. De Zaale read the message about a raid on the St Kilda Road offices by the Federal Police, Cynthia having relayed it to Suzi with some explanation about redundancies and tax avoidance. He sat dejected as the whole world of Agro Alliance was falling apart.

The police officers had lifted the handcuffed Brazzos from his chair and were leading an exodus from the room. As Brazzos got to the open door, he saw Zoe O'Donoghue standing alongside Sandra Hudson and Sarah Hatfield. "What are these bitches doing here?" he spat.

He glared at the women until he noticed that Zoe and Sandra were wearing white gloves, Zoe holding a leather satchel and Sandy a bundle of files.

Cameron walked up behind him and whispered emphatically in his ear, "Apparently they're here for just one reason and one reason alone … to drive the karma bus."

ACKNOWLEDGEMENTS

The Karma Bus is my first novel and has scratched an itch that has been with me for over twenty years. I love reading and find that the settings in novels create a sense of time and history. I have several stories and countless characters bouncing around in my mind, so I enjoyed bringing some of them together.

My deepest thanks is to my wife Leanne for living the journey, the stories and the characters with me, and then being my first editor. Her insight and rewrites were inspiring, which led me to broaden the work to a group of friends, all avid readers that I trusted for honest feedback – Adrian and Paula Fernon, Stuart Herron, Jodie Hornsby, Ciro Iacovangelo, Sandy Sutherland and Tony Sheahan.

They provided the confidence for me to take the story further and seek publishing support. Green Hill Publishing have been inspiring and I am indebted to their support and feedback. Kaitlan Sharpe and her support from Sarah, Keely and Gabby brought my idea to realisation. They were able to blend the detail requirements with a sense of fun that made my journey all the better

The storyline in *The Karma Bus* is totally fictional but inspired by the technical expertise required behind improving process safety in high risk industrial chemical processes. In this part of chemical engineering, safety is more than trip and knock hazards. It requires multiple layers of controls and rigid adherence to managing changes and inspecting asset integrity. The work of process safety specialists (experts) the likes of men and women that live in the image of Sandra Hudson makes these chemical complexes all the safer for our community.

To tell the story and sell the message it was important to bring a villain into the mix. Managers never act as poorly as those in this story, but the message is that they need to be challenged to respect the process safety systems and ensure they are robustly sustained. Without leadership and experience the safety basis is lost.

If you have managed to get this far I hope you have enjoyed the read and the having survived the heavy technical components have a wider appreciation of how little things matter.

I had a lot of fun scratching my itch and my favourite characters were Sandy Hudson and Zoe O'Donoughue, the latter who I hope will reappear in future writing projects to help solve other mysteries. Of course a nod to old Eddie the neighbour, who is indeed based on a true life Eddie.

Leigh Gunn was born in country Victoria and grew up in suburban Melbourne. His working career consisted of over forty years was as a chemical engineer in the petrochemical and chemical industries, across several countries.

He has since retired to the Mornington Peninsula where he lives with his wife Leanne and spends his time reading, golfing, gardening and engaging with his grandchildren.

The Karma Bus is Leigh's first novel. The storyline and characters, while totally fictional, are loosely-based or exaggerated from his experiences across various work environments.

www.ingramcontent.com/pod-product-compliance
Ingram Content Group Australia Pty Ltd
76 Discovery Rd, Dandenong South VIC 3175, AU
AUHW010327190126
422249AU00001B/1

9 781923 589049